Dreamweaver CS5

Mastering the Basics

Grant Gamble

Dreamweaver CS5 Mastering the Basics
Copyright © 2010 by Grant Gamble
TrainingCompany.Com

ISBN 978-1-906990-01-5

Notice of Rights

Notice of Liability

Trademarks

Source Code

The source code for this book is available for download at the following URL:

http://www.trainingcompany.com/downloads/dreamweaver.aspx

Contents

Try it for yourself!

Try it for yourself!

8. Tables 87

Try it for yourself!

Try it for yourself!

Try it for yourself!

13. Site Management and Checking **225**

Try it for yourself!

Try it for yourself!

11. JavaScript Behaviors and Spry 257

Try it for yourself!

Try it for yourself!

Try it for yourself!

1: Getting started

Due to the massive increase in the importance of the web over the past ten years, a staggering number of people have become involved in the development of websites in some shape or form. Adobe Dreamweaver has become a close friend to a high percentage of these people, enabling them to become productive very quickly and to build standards-compliant web pages without having to become experts in the technologies that drive the web.

This book is designed for those who are new to both Dreamweaver and to web development in general and who need to know enough about both of these topics to be able to build a basic website, test it and then make it live. Whether your role will be using Dreamweaver to edit web pages or whether you plan build your own website, we aim to help you master all the basic principles involved.

Not everyone who builds websites or edits web pages has aspirations to become a full-time web developer. The term web developer normally refers to someone who not only builds websites but also understands the main technologies that underly web pages: HTML, CSS, JavaScript, ASP, ASP.Net, PHP, etc.

In the early days, web developers favoured hand-coding over the use of visual tools such as Dreamweaver. Many dismissed them as being more trouble than they were worth—a messy clutter of floating palettes. They found the previews too slow and, in the early days, the code generated was often messy and needed cleaning up.

With each release of Dreamweaver, there was a steady stream of converts. The code generated by the program when working visually is standards-compliant; and working in code view or split screen view—where code is displayed alongside a preview of what the page will look like—has done a lot to win coders over to Dreamweaver.

Web designers tend to focus on the creative aspects of the web development process. Their primary role is to create attractive, appropriate web pages which function in a logical and user-friendly manner. Web designers need to concern themselves with many issues unique to the web, such as ease of navigation, the load time of each page and whether or not pages will be indexed by the search engines.

Dreamweaver's design tools offer assistance to web designers in all these areas. Naturally, it does not teach people how to design. However, its WYSIWYG (What you see is what you get) interface and the fact that it now previews so many aspects of a web page as you design it, make it a popular choice for web designers. Of course there is not always a clear cut line between web developer and web designer; they may be one and the same person.

In the same way as computers and information technology have become a part of most people's working life, more and more people are finding themselves being asked to provide content for their company's websites and intranets, often without any previous background in design or coding. Anyone in this situation obviously has many different skills to master. For such general users, Dreamweaver can play a pivotal role in the whole business of how websites are created and managed and will usually become a key tool in a newcomer's web arsenal.

Since web development is such a vast and complex subject and since Dreamweaver allows you to visually manipulate so many different underlying technologies, it will probably take several years before anyone completely new to web development can attain any degree of mastery of this complex sector of computing. However, as far as learning the core elements of Dreamweaver, three months should be adequate. The key thing is to practice by using Dreamweaver to build websites: there is simply no better way to learn. Each time you go through the cycle of planning, building, testing and deploying a website, you will gain more experience and confidence in using the program.

What is Adobe Dreamweaver CS5?

Adobe Dreamweaver is a multi-purpose web development tool aimed at inexperienced and experienced developers alike. It uses standards-compliant web technologies such as XHTML and CSS. Web content can be imported into a Dreamweaver site at any time without the danger of the program modifying your code in eccentric ways. In the same way, pages created in Dreamweaver can be taken out of the Dreamweaver environment and used elsewhere.

Although Dreamweaver is not necessarily the best environment for creating all types of website, it is not an environment which one easily outgrows. It can be used both for creating basic, static content consisting of client-side pages as well as more sophisticated dynamic content including server-side pages. In other words, it is suitable for developing the content found on the vast majority of websites.

Visual development versus coding

In the early days of the web, there were basically two types of software tool which could be used to create web pages. The first type allowed you to edit the code which produces each of your pages. The second type offered you a WYSIWYG interface in which you could work with the text, images and other objects as they would appear on your pages. As you did so, the program automatically generated the necessary code.

Dreamweaver originally fell into the second category. However, the fact that it quickly developed excellent features for editing code, site management and collaboration meant that it soon belonged to both categories. This may help to explain why it has become such an industry-standard tool for website development.

Dreamweaver contains all the tools you will need to create, manage and update a website. Sites can either be created from scratch or, if they already exist, pages, subdirectories and images can be converted into a Dreamweaver site. Even if you have no knowledge of the underlying web technologies, Dreamweaver allows you to quickly and easily become productive in the website creation process.

Interactivity

Dreamweaver boasts an impressive array of, easy-to-use commands for adding interactivity to your web pages. Dynamic effects like rollovers, pop-up windows and the showing and hiding of page content can be achieved without any programming. Dreamweaver automatically generates the necessary JavaScript code for you. Similarly, Adobe's Spry technology, based on CSS and JavaScript, provides easy access to complex, interactive functionality. Using Spry, you can easily create interactive, drop-down menus, advanced layout elements such as tabbed panels and add sophisticated form validation to prevent visitors to your site from submitting erroneous or inappropriate data.

Dynamic (server-side) content

Dreamweaver also allows the inclusion of dynamic, data-driven content into your websites. It has powerful code-generation facilities for connecting to databases and database servers, for creating search and results pages and for setting up user authentication.

Website management

Dreamweaver also includes sophisticated site management tools. Unless you are mainly concerned with creating email newsletters and similar promotional material, your web development activity will largely consist of building and editing all of the pages that work together to form a website. You may also need to work on several such sites simultaneously.

Dreamweaver offers powerful tools for maintaining consistency across your pages and for modifying and updating elements across the entire site. As your site progresses, the program allows you to preview and test your pages, to synchronize local and live versions of a site, to check links and browser compatibility and, naturally, it incorporates FTP client software for uploading and downloading files to and from a server.

Dreamweaver also allows teams of developers, designers and other website contributors to work together on the same files without treading on each others toes. When Dreamweaver's collaboration features are activated, opening a file causes it to become unavailable to other members of your team and flags the file as currently being modified by the person who opened it.

What is a website?

Adobe Dreamweaver CS5 is used for building and maintaining websites. A website is a collection of files which reside on a server and work in concert to present digestible content to your visitors' web browsers.

Most websites are hosted on web servers owned by specialist hosting companies. A large website will have a dedicated server or even servers, whereas most typical websites will share space on a server with other sites.

Visitors to a website are often referred to as clients; they gain access to the content on web servers using a variety of operating systems and a variety of browsers. They usually find this content either by clicking on links from search engines and other locations or by simply typing a URL into the address bar of their browser.

Client-side content

The content that clients access on websites can be divided into two main categories: client-side and server-side. The term client-side refers to web content which is compatible with the user's browser—material which the browser software can actually open, display or execute (in the case of scripts). This category includes HTML, the basic component or raw material of a web page. It also includes those technologies which enhance HTML: CSS, JavaScript, Flash, etc.

Client-side files can be recognized by their file extensions: .htm, .html, .css, .js, and so on. When a client requests a file with one of these file extensions, the server sends it to the client's browser and moves on to the next request, as shown in figure 1-1.

Server-side content

Server-side content refers to files which contain scripts to be executed on the server itself rather than being sent to the clients' browser. This requires that the server is running the appropriate scripting software. Dreamweaver offers fairly sophisticated functionality for developing server-side content using PHP, ASP or ColdFusion as the scripting environment.

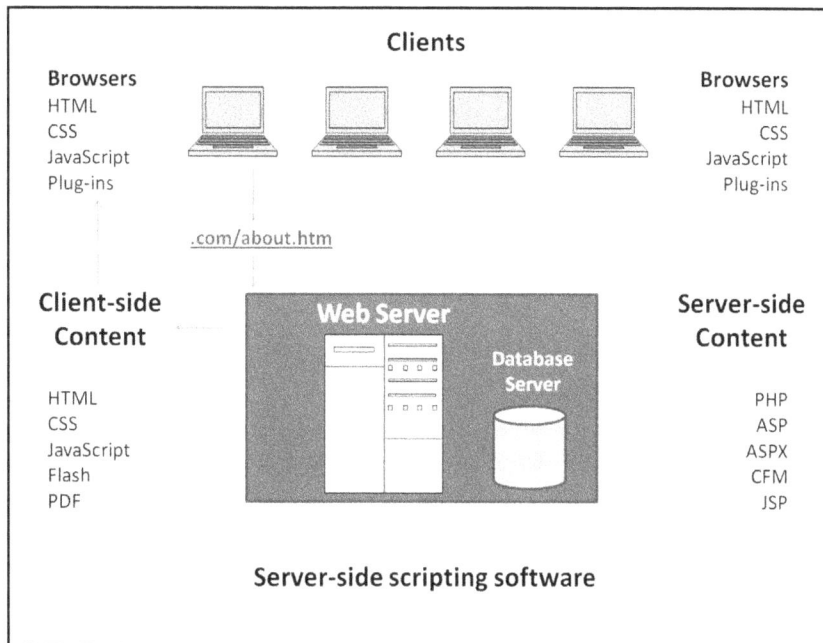

Figure 1-1: Client-side content is returned to the client upon request

When the client requests server-side content, the server launches the software necessary to run any scripts contained in the file requested. Server-side scripts frequently interact with databases, extracting information based on the client's request and sending it back to the client's browser as dynamic client-side content— dynamic because it does not exist in any static form on the server, but is created on the fly. (This process is illustrated in figure 1-2, below.)

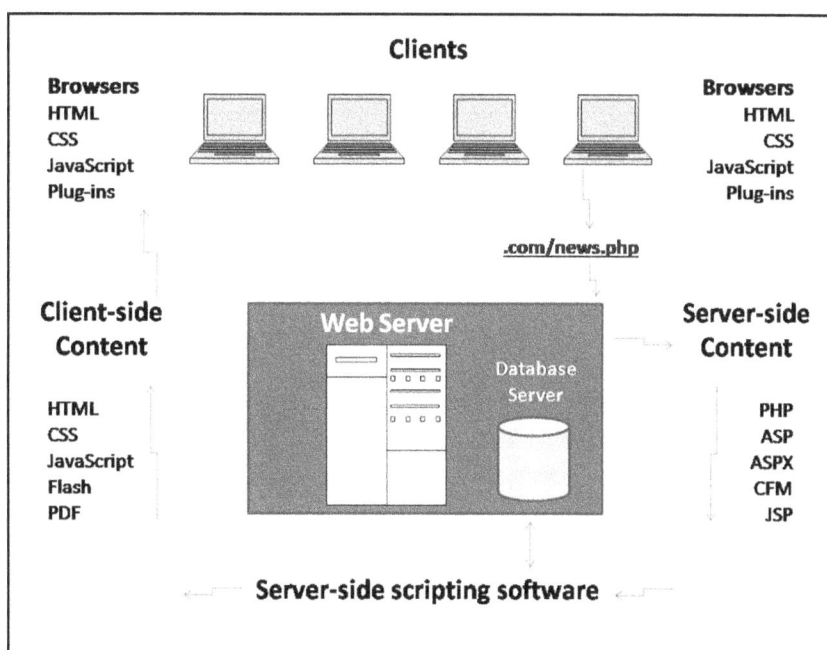

Figure 1-2: Server-side content contains scripts which run on the server itself

In this introductory title, we will be focusing on how to use Dreamweaver to create basic websites containing client-side content: XHTML, CSS and JavaScript.

XHTML

The cornerstone of client-side content is HyperText Markup Language (HTML)—or, as it is known in its current incarnation: XHTML; a stricter and more consistent version of the original HTML specification. HTML/XHTML is a simple markup language which is used to describe the content of web pages for the benefit of browsers such as Internet Explorer and Firefox.

Structurally, HTML pages consist of a hierarchy of elements, as shown in figure 1-3. When written, HTML code consists of tags representing these elements. (See figure 1-4.) Elements which contain other elements or text are represented by opening and closing tags.

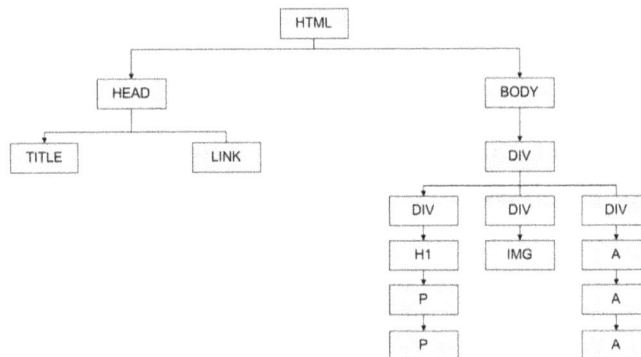

Figure 1-3: Hierarchical structure of an HTML page

```
<html>
    <head>
        <title>Contacting Us</title>
        <link href="css/screen.css" rel="stylesheet" type="text/css" />
    </head>

<body>
    <div id="wrapper">
        <div id="header">
            <img src="images/logo.gif" />
        </div>
        <div id="nav">
            <a href="about.htm">About</a>
            <a href="finance.htm">Finance</a>
            <a href="contact.htm">Contact</a>
        </div>
        <div id="main">
            <h1>Contacting us</h1>
            <p>Our contact details are as follows:
            Rechelof Venture Capital<br />
            Apex House<br />
            122 Hanley Road <br />
            London<br />
            EC5 3YN</p>
        </div>
    </div>
</body>
</html>
```

Figure 1-4: HTML tags reflect the hierarchical structure of elements

HTML is the main fabric from which web pages are made and, in learning to create websites, it is logical to begin by familiarizing yourself with the creation of sites containing mainly HTML content. Dreamweaver allows you to manipulate and create HTML content either by using intuitive visual tools or by editing code.

CSS

While HTML code is used to describe the content and structure of a web page, Cascading Style Sheets (CSS) is used to control the formatting and layout of web page content. HTML and CSS work together to enable the browser to display your content as you designed it.

JavaScript

JavaScript is a simple scripting language which can be used to add interactivity to web pages. For example, when you are filling out a form on a website and information entered into a field is incorrect, JavaScript can be used to notify you that the content must be changed.

Plug-ins

All modern web browsers are fully capable of digesting HTML, CSS and JavaScript. With the addition of extra software utilities known as plug-ins, other technologies can be included in websites. Two examples of popular plug-ins are Adobe Flash and Apple QuickTime. All of this content is completely compatible with the client's browser—once equipped with the plug-in; hence the term client-side content.

Planning and storyboarding your site

Before you can build a site, you need to have a firm idea of how it will function and what pages it will consist of. This usually involves storyboarding; sketching out the functionality of the site to ensure that nothing is left out and to get an idea of how large a project you are letting yourself in for. (A simple example of such a sketch is shown if figure 1-5 on page 8.)

If such sketches need to be shown to others for approval, they can be created in a drawing program such as Adobe Illustrator or any of the Microsoft Office programs—especially Visio. If all else fails, there is always pen and paper!

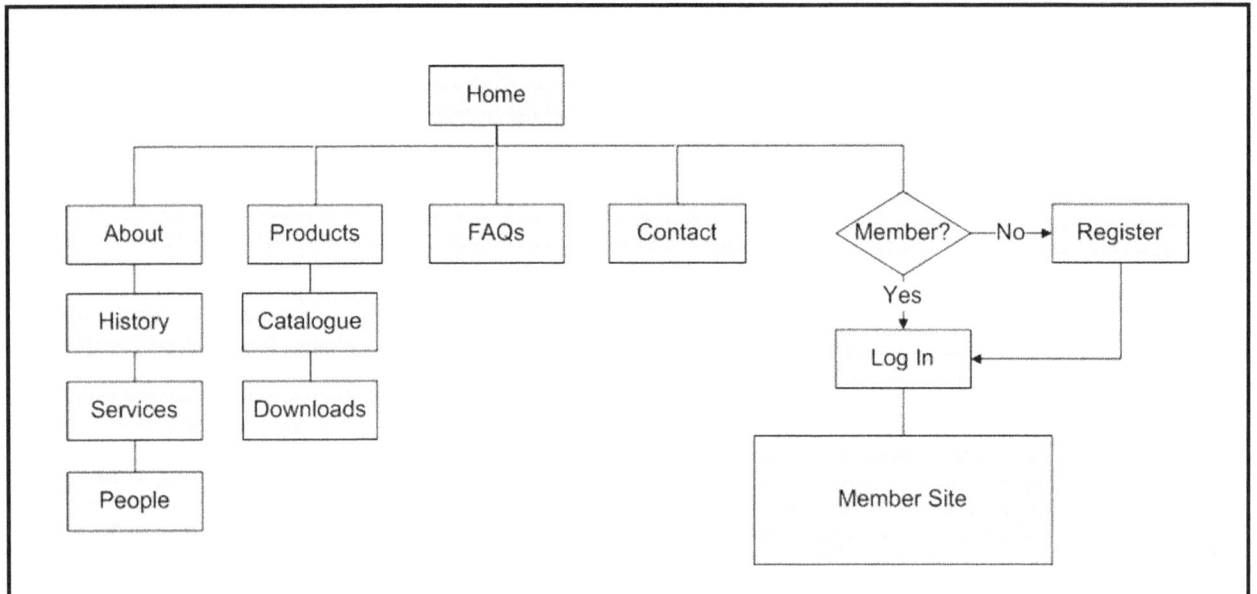

Figure 1-5: Storyboarding a site

Site design

Designing a site is another step that needs to be done outside of Dreamweaver, typically using programs such as Photoshop, Fireworks and Illustrator. These programs all contain a feature called slices which allows you to "chop up" your design into its functional units—such as buttons, banners, footers etc.

You can then apply useful options to the slices such as attaching a hyperlink. For example, figure 1-6, below, shows the **Slice Options** dialogue box from Adobe Photoshop. The name you enter for each slice will be used as the name of the image which Photoshop will generate for you; and a link will be created to the page specified in the URL box.

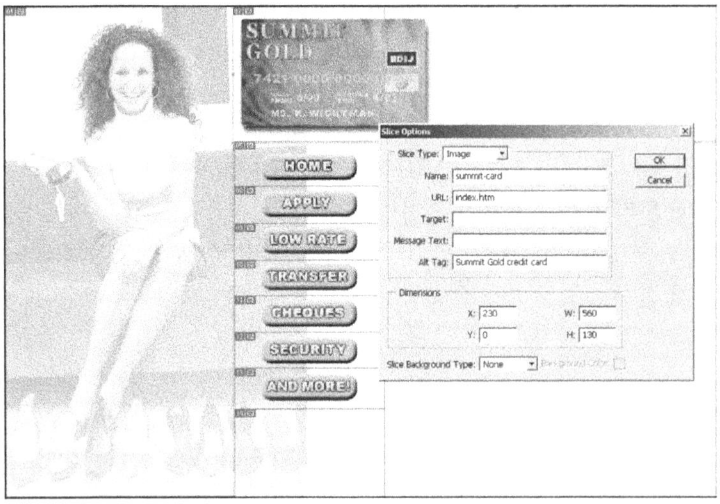

Figure 1-6: Setting slice options in Adobe Photoshop

Programs like Photoshop and Fireworks are ideal for quickly generating a working prototype of a site which can be used for demonstration purposes, since they allow you to export your design as an HTML page—admittedly, neither standards-compliant nor web-ready; but complete with images and links.

What if you simply do not have the resources to come up with a decent design? Well you can always follow the modern person's axiom: when in doubt, turn to the web. Sure enough, there are many sources of free web templates which you can download and adapt for your own purposes. One of the best is the **Open Source Web Design** website: http://www.oswd.org. Here you will find hundreds of fully working CSS designs which the creators have agreed can be used free of charge. There is usually a link to the author's website at the bottom of the page or some other slight acknowledgement of their generosity.

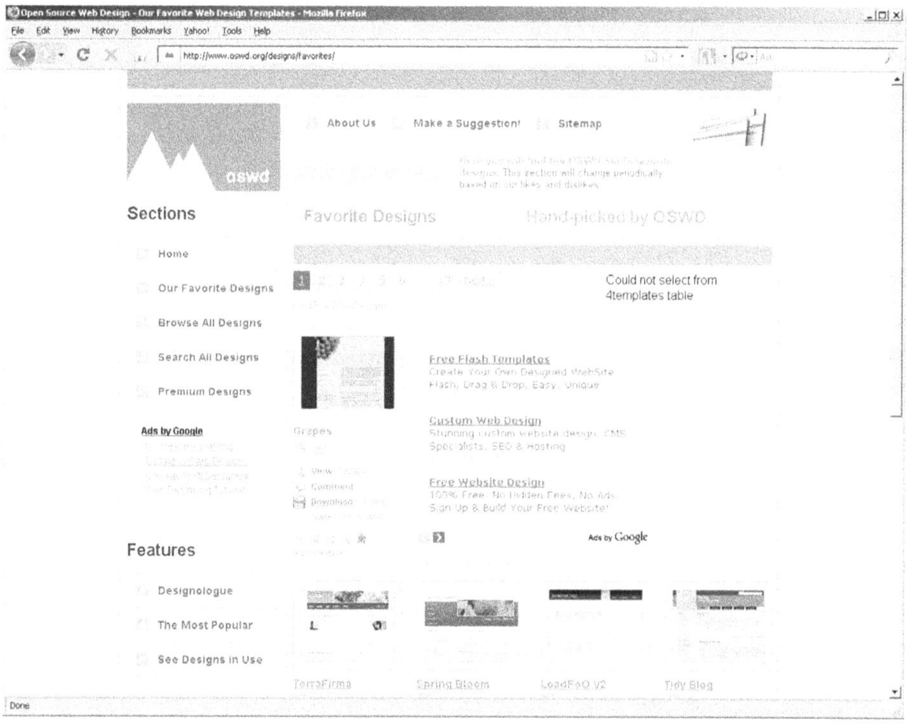

Figure 1-7: http://www.oswd.org offers hundreds of free designs

Creating a Dreamweaver site

When you build a website in Dreamweaver, you do not simply start creating web pages willy-nilly; you begin by defining a new site and then you create the various pages within it.

To create a new site in Dreamweaver, choose **Site > New Site**.

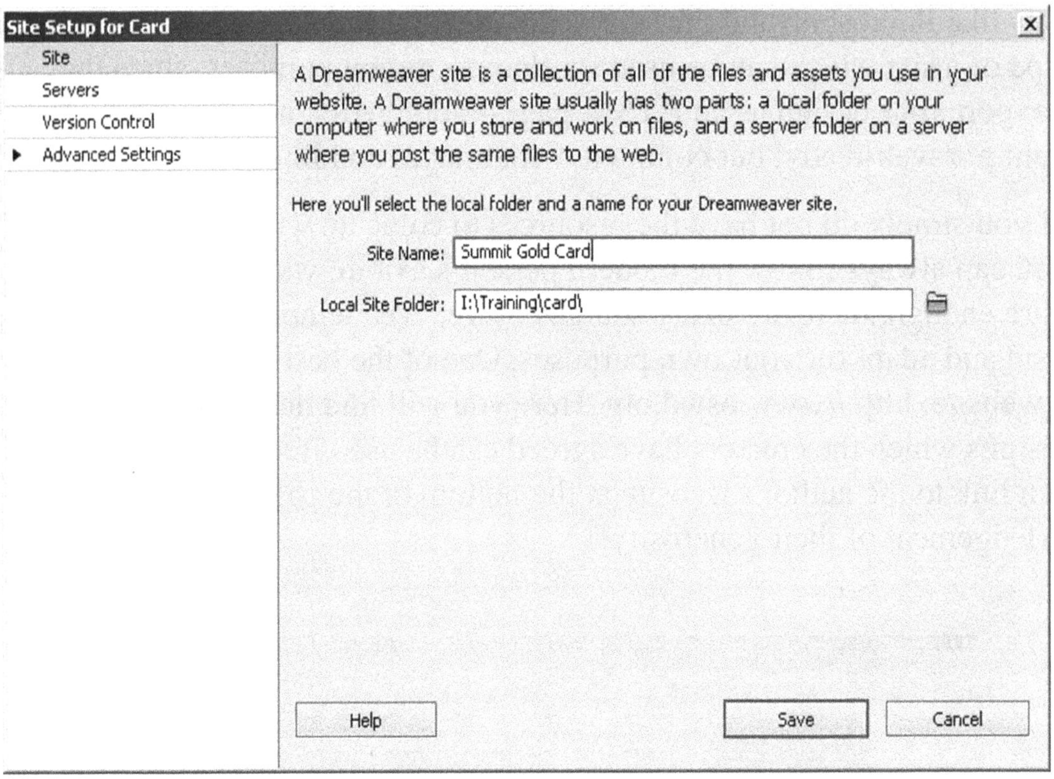

Figure 1-8: The Dreamweaver CS5 Site Setup dialog

The Site Setup dialog window which appears has four categories of information: Site, Servers, Version Control and Advanced Settings. This arrangement represents an improvement over previous versions. It is clearer and gives you rapid access to just those site settings that you need to change. This is particularly true if you do not yet have all of the necessary information and just want to plug in the bits that you do know and then move on to building the site.

The two key elements in defining a new Dreamweaver site are the **Site** and **Servers** categories. **Site** information applies to details of your personal, local version of the site—the version that only you can see; stored on your workstation or laptop. Information supplied in the **Servers** category tells Dreamweaver how to connect to the server hosting your site—and, if necessary, other servers that you may want to use for testing purposes. For a discussion of Site information, see Chapter 13: Site Management and Checking, page 239.

Site Information

Site Name

First you need to enter a name for the site. This will only be seen by you as you work on the site in Dreamweaver; so feel free to enter any descriptive name.

Local Site Folder

As we have seen, a website consists of many different files and several different file types. Before you begin to create any of these files, it is important to designate a location for them all. Dreamweaver refers to this folder as the Local Site Folder; "local" implying "for your eyes only"; in contrast to the live version on the server.

The Local Site Folder will contain your version of a given website, the version that you develop and test. When you are happy with a file that you have created and tested in the Local Site Folder, you upload it to the server to make it live.

There is nothing special about the folder itself; just create a folder in any convenient location. If this is a brand new site, the folder may be completely empty. If any resources are available, they can be placed inside the Local Site Folder. For example, the Local Site Folder in figure 1-9, below, shows sub folders for images, flash movies, PDF files and video clips.

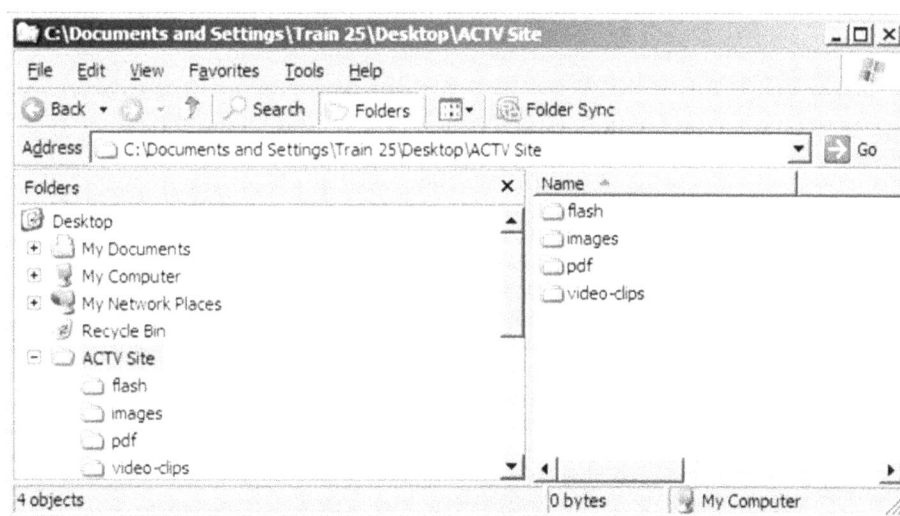

Figure 1-9: A Local Site Folder with its sub folders

If the site is an existing one which is already live (let's say for example; all of the files have been emailed to you or have been downloaded via FTP), the site files can be placed inside the Local Site Folder ready for editing in Dreamweaver.

To show Dreamweaver the location of the Local Site Folder, click on the **Browse for folder** button (the folder icon), navigate to the folder, open it then click the **Select** button, on a PC, or the **Choose** buton on a Mac.

Advanced Settings

That's it for the **Site** information and that is—initially at least, all the information you need to supply before you can start work on your site. You can enter the server information later, when the site is near to completion. There is, however, one other piece of information—located in the **Advanced Settings** category—which you should get into the habit of supplying: the default location for images.

Default Images Folder

The Default Images Folder is a sub-directory you create inside the Local Site Folder and which you designate as the default location for images. To access this feature, click on **Advanced Settings** then **Local Info** on the left of the Site Setup dialog. Next, click on the **Browse for folder** button next to **Default Images Folder** and locate the folder that you wish to use.

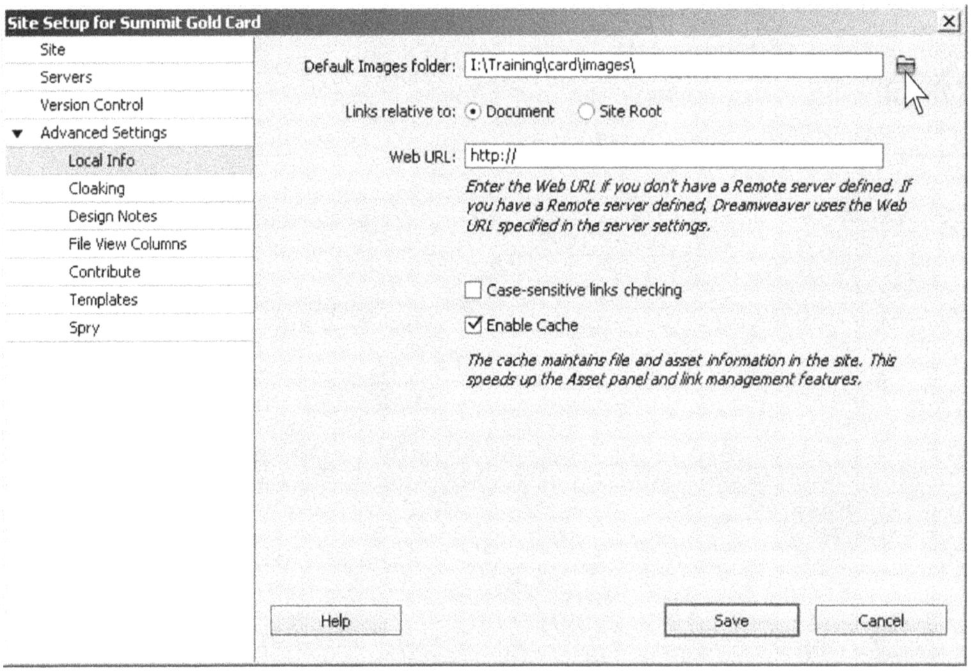

Figure 1-10: Designating a Default Images Folder

Having a Default Images Folder will make it less likely that you end up with missing images like the one shown in figure 1-11, on page 13; where an empty box is displayed instead of the image itself.

Images that you import into a web page are not embedded in the page; instead, they are referenced. If you import an image from a location outside the Local Site Folder, a reference will be created to a location that is not mirrored on the server. However, if you define a Default Images Folder, Dreamweaver will first place a copy of the image inside the Default Images Folder and then create a reference to this local version of the image; thus preventing the broken link. In the practical exercise at the end of this chapter, you will be given a chance to see this useful mechanism in action.

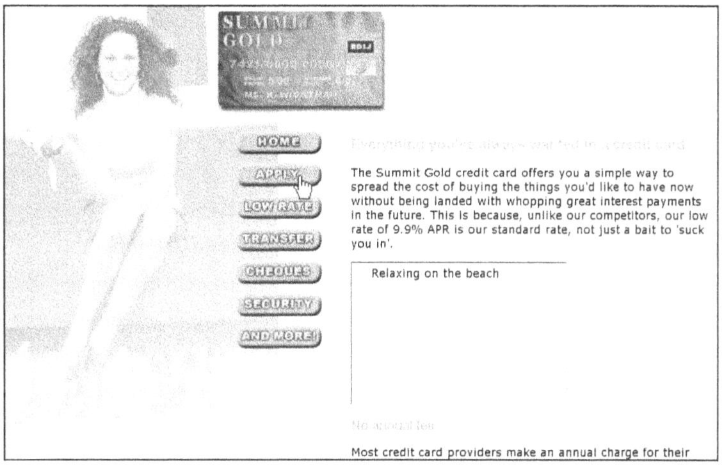

Figure 1-11: Specifying a Default Images Folder reduces the risk of "broken" images

Let's have a look at the other settings in the **Local Info** section of the **Advanced Settings** category.

Links Relative to Document/Site Root

These options refer to hyperlinks and links to images. Although all such links could be specified as absolute URLs, e.g. "http://www.somedomain.com/images/logo.gif", this would be rather restrictive and make it more difficult to transfer pages from one domain to another.

Document relative links

To allow greater flexibility, links are normally specified relative to the document that contains them. For example, suppose we want to place a hyperlink on web page called **index.htm** to a page called **products.htm** which is located in a folder called **about**, as shown in figure 1-12, below.

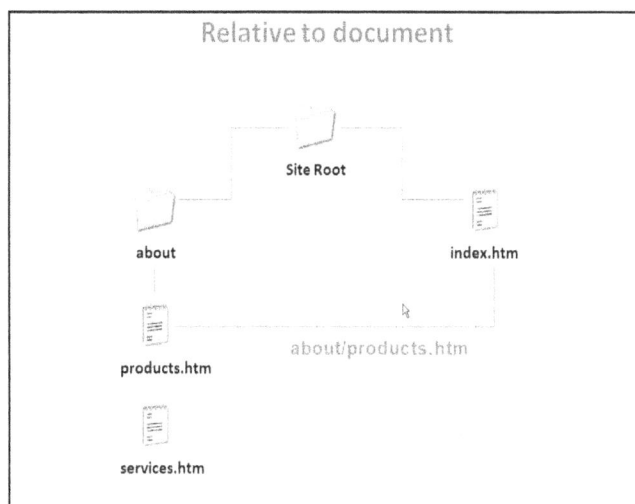

Figure 1-12: Links relative to document

Starting from **index.htm**, we need to go inside the **about** folder and there we will find **products.htm**. This means that our link would look like this:

> **about/products.htm**

By contrast, if we wanted to link from **services.htm** to **products.htm**, because both files are in the same folder, there would be no need to mention the folder name and our link would be simply:

> **products.htm**

In other words, although both links point to the same page, because the link is relative to the document containing the link, we end up with two different paths.

Site root relative links

Links which are relative to the site root are less frequently used. They always start with a forward slash (/) followed by the path to the document but always starting from the root. Thus, in both our **index.htm** to **products.htm** and **services.htm** to **products.htm** examples, the link would be the same.

> **/about/products.htm**

The link is determined only by the page to which you are linking and not the document that contains the link.

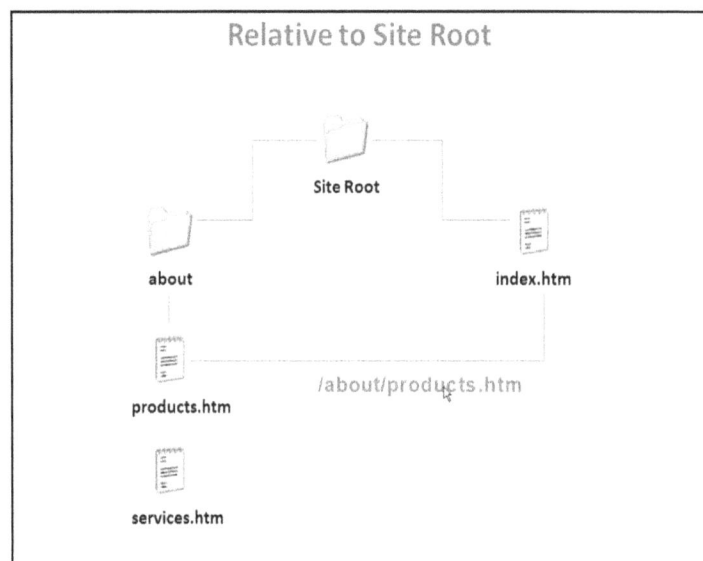

Figure 1-13: Links relative to site root

Which is better?

From the server standpoint, specifying all links relative to the site root offers greater flexibility. For example, a document containing a link to a given image can be moved to a different folder and the link to the image will still work. However, from a development standpoint, site root relative links have one major drawback: they only work when the files have been uploaded to the server. For this reason, most developers choose to specify their links relative to the document.

Case-sensitive links

The option for case-sensitive links is useful if your site is being hosted on a Linux or UNIX server since, here, the names of files and folders are case-sensitive. Dreamweaver has a feature for locating broken links; so, if a site is to be hosted on a Linux or UNIX server, this box should be ticked, so that Dreamweaver will take case into account when checking links. If the site is being hosted on a Windows server, this option should be left unchecked.

HTTP address

In this box, you would type in the URL of the site that you are developing; this will not necessarily point to the root of the site. For example, if we are working on a site called "izxtw.com" on a project relating to affiliates, we might enter the URL of the area of the site on which we are working—for example:

> **http:// izxtw.com/affiliates/**

When you specify a server, Dreamweaver will use the server information rather than the Web URL.

Enable cache

Activating this option will help Dreamweaver to manage links and other assets within your website. Let's say, for example, that you have a site with 500 pages and, for legal reasons, you are forced to rename one of your pages. If the cache facility is enabled, Dreamweaver will look in the cache to see if there are any pages which have links to the page being renamed. It will then update all of the links to reflect the new name.

Try it for yourself!

In this **Try it for yourself** exercise, we will be creating a Local Site Folder and Default Images Folder. We will then define a site and specify the key local information. After that, you will get to see first hand how Dreamweaver's Default Images Folder mechanism actually functions.

Creating a Local Site Folder

1. Go to the desktop of your computer (or any other convenient location) and
    create a new folder.

2. Rename the folder "Web Project".

When creating a website, you may need a number of support files in various formats:
Photoshop .psd files; Microsoft Word .doc or .docx files; Flash .fla files; and so on.
These native files are not web-ready and should never be uploaded to the server; but
they are relevant to the web project as a whole. So what we'll do in this simulation
is to create a few folders for support files and then create one final folder for the
web-ready files—those files which will actually form part of website. It is this last
folder which will be designated as the Local Site Folder when we define our site in
Dreamweaver.

3. Open the folder and create five sub-folders inside it: **Photoshop**, **Flash**, **Text**,
    PDF and **Website**.

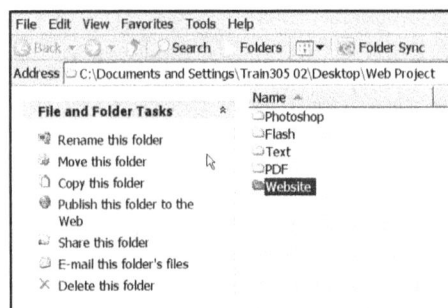

Creating a Default Images Folder

Inside our Local Site Folder, we can now create a few key sub-folders. The contents of these folders will form part of the website and will be uploaded to the server when the site is finished. One of these folders will later be designated as the Default Images Folder.

4. Open the **Website** folder and create three sub-folders inside it: **Flash**, **Images** and **PDF**. (Naturally, it is the **Images** folder which will later be designated as the Default Images Folder when we define the site.)

Defining a Dreamweaver site

We will now create a new Dreamweaver site; but we will only enter essential local information. In order to get started with a site, you only need to complete the two fields in the Site category: Site Name and Local Site Folder. In addition, however, it is recommended that you also specify a Default Images Folder. You can return to the Site Setup dialogue box at any time to enter the remaining information.

5. Back in Dreamweaver, choose **Site > New Site**; and, in the **Site Name** field, enter the text "Getting Started".

6. Click on the **Browse for folder** button on the right of the Local Site Folder box.

7. Navigate to the desktop; open the **Web Project** folder; open the **Website** folder then click the **Select** button—or the **Choose** button on a Mac.

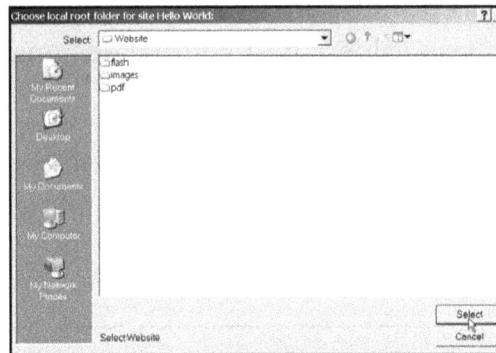

Defining the Default Images Folder

8. On the left of the Site Setup dialog, click **Advanced Settings > Local Info**.

9. Click on the **Browse for folder** button next to the **Default Images Folder** box.

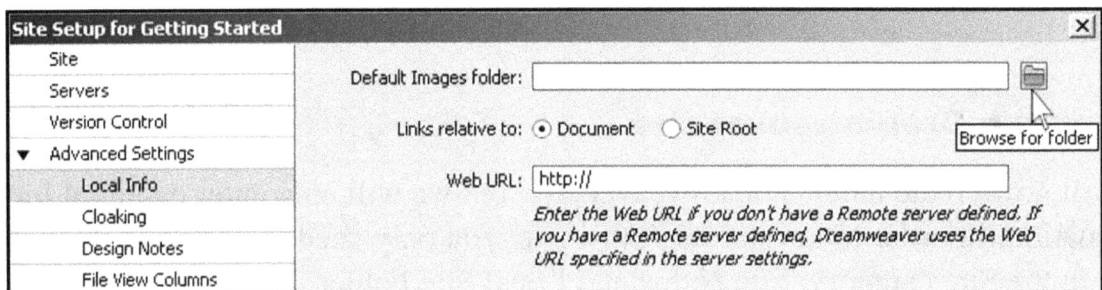

10. Navigate to the **Images** folder inside the **Website** folder; open the **Images** folder then click the **Select** button (Mac, **Choose**).

11. We don't need to flesh out the definition of our site any further; so click **Save** to close the **Site Setup** dialogue box.

The Default Images Folder in action

We will now look at the way in which the Default Images Folder functions. Basically, if we import an image from outside the Local Site Folder, Dreamweaver will automatically place a copy of the image in the Default Images Folder and then import this local copy onto the page, thus avoiding the risk of a broken image link.

12. In the Files panel (which Dreamweaver automatically opens for your convenience) click on the plus sign next to the **Images** folder to open it. Since the folder is empty, the plus sign simply disappears.

Now let's create a blank page, import an image and see what happens.

13. Click on the **HTML** link in the **Create New** column of the Welcome screen to create a blank web page.

14. Choose **File > Save** and save the file as **index.htm** in the Local Site Folder.

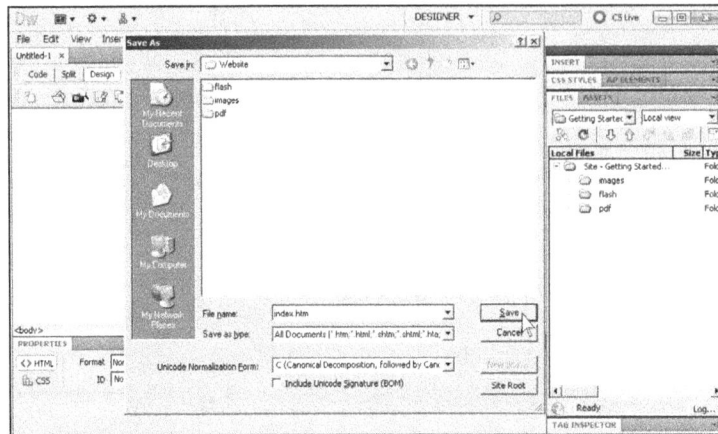

15. Choose **Insert > Image** to add an image to the blank page.

16. Navigate to any location where you have a GIF or JPEG image; for example, in the illustration below, we have used one of the Windows sample images inside **My Documents > My Pictures**.

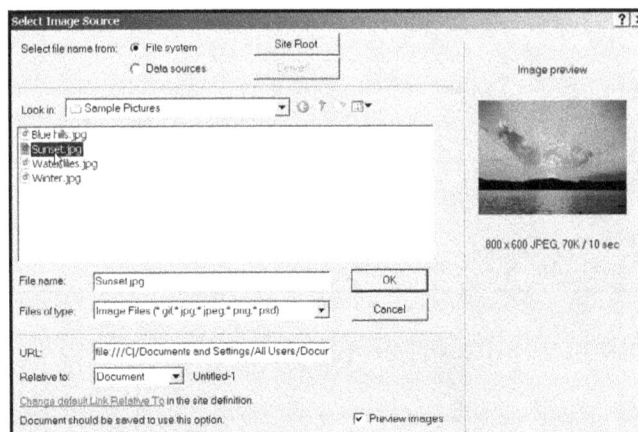

If you cannot find any images on the machine you are using, visit any website which contains royalty free images, such as **www.copyrightfreephotos.com**.

Here, you can right-click on any image and download it to your computer. However, for the purposes of this exercise, do not download the image to the Default Images folder.

Whenever an image is inserted, Dreamweaver normally displays the Image Tag Accessibility Options to enable you to enter alternate text. Alternate text is displayed whenever the image is not displayed in the browser, so that the user is still able to know something about the image. It is also read by assistive devices such as screen readers. When this dialogue box appears, you should always enter a word, phrase or sentence which describes the image.

17. Enter a word or phrase that describes the image you have just inserted and click **OK**.

18. If you now look at the Files panel, you will see that Dreamweaver has copied the file into the images folder and it is this local file which has been placed on the page. (If you do not see the file, click on the Refresh button in the top left of the Files panel.)

2. The Dreamweaver Interface

Having looked at setting up a Dreamweaver site and getting the ball rolling, in this chapter we'll take a look at the Dreamweaver environment, the arena in which you will be working your magic. Our approach will be selective, rather than comprehensive; we will focus on those elements which are essential when building basic websites; the ones you will need to use frequently.

The welcome screen

When you first launch any Adobe Creative Suite program, such as Dreamweaver, the welcome screen is displayed. It contains handy links to online resources as well as offering quick access to a number of facilities which are also available elsewhere in the program—for example, recently opened files (also available in the File menu).

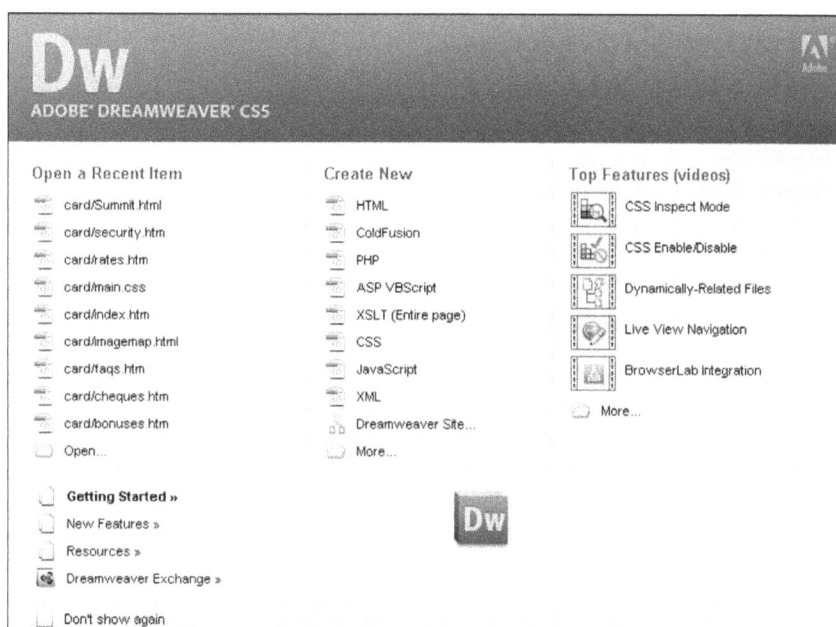

Figure 2-1: The Dreamweaver CS5 welcome screen

You can disable the welcome screen by activating the checkbox marked "Don't Show Again". You can also reinstate it at any time by visiting the General category of the Dreamweaver Preferences under the Edit menu (Dreamweaver menu on a Mac).

Floating panels

The functionality offered by Dreamweaver is accessed by a combination of menu items and options presented on floating windows called panels. To show or hide a panel, choose its name from the Window menu.

The fact that Dreamweaver offers so many panels often confuses new users. However, some panels are used far more often than others. When building basic websites, the most frequently used panels are Properties, Files, Assets and CSS Styles. These are the panels on which we will focus in this book; so, let's begin by closing all of the other panels.

Dreamweaver offers the user a number of preset workspace layouts suitable for different workflows. These can be accessed by choosing **Window > Workspace Layout**. The default layout, **Designer**, is ideal for our purposes.

Working with files and documents

When building websites with Adobe Dreamweaver, you will find yourself alternating between two main views of your web pages: Files and Document. The Files panel gives you an overview of the entire site and allows you to work with the site structure. It shows listings of the files in your Local Site Folder and on your server. When you open any document, by contrast, you work on one HTML page at a time, adding and modifying content as necessary.

The Files Panel

Each time you create a new site or modify a Site Setup, Dreamweaver will open the Files panel automatically and the site you have just created will be the active site. You can also enter site Files view at any time by choosing **Window > Files**. You can activate a particular site by choosing its name from the pop-up menu in the top left of the Files panel. Alternatively, you can choose **Site > Manage Site**, select the desired site name and click **Done**.

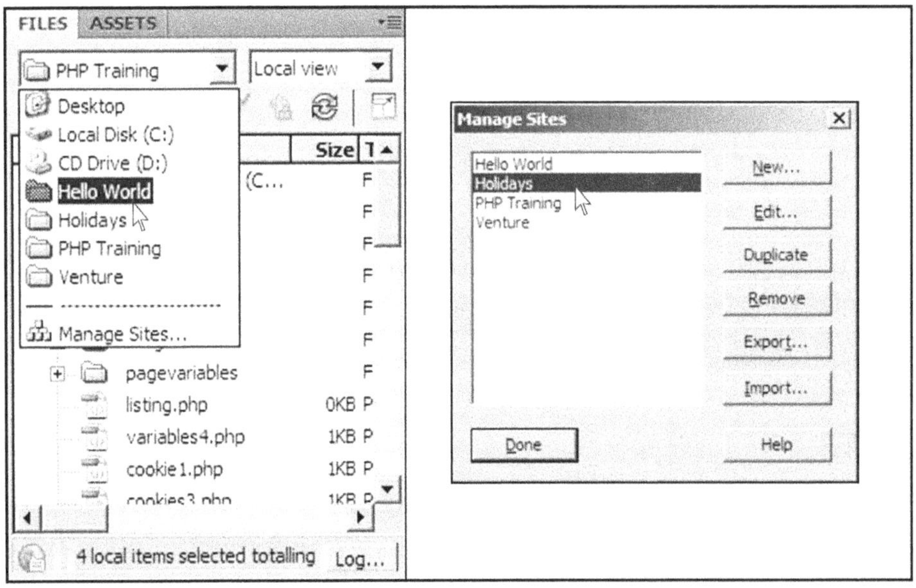

Figure 2-2: Switching between sites using the Files panel and Manage Sites dialog

The Files panel contains a good few menu options divided into sub-menus for your convenience. It allows you to work directly with the file structure of your operating system in a similar way to Windows Explorer or the Macintosh Finder. You can create, delete and rename files; create folders and move files between folders.

It is also important to remember that the site listing is a live indication of a section of one of the hard drives connected to your computer. When you delete a file or folder, you are deleting an item from that drive in real time. You cannot choose to undo the deletion at some point in the future. Similarly, when you create a file, it is placed on disk immediately; whereas, if you choose **File > New** from the main menu bar, the file created exists only in memory, until you save it.

Creating files and folders

When working in the Files panel, there are two methods of creating a new file or folder in a particular location. Firstly, you can right-click the name of a folder (or of one of the documents inside it) and choose **New File** or **New Folder** from the context menu. Secondly, you can highlight the target folder and choose **File > New File** or **File > New Folder** from the drop-down menu in the top right of the Files panel.

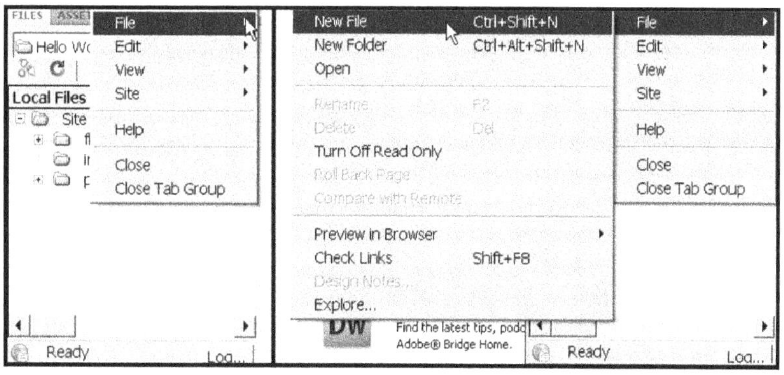

Figure 2-3: Creating a new file using the Files panel menu

When creating documents, be sure to enter the necessary file extension. For HTML documents, you may type either ".html" or ".htm"—both are acceptable. Naturally, folder names do not need an extension.

Dreamweaver CS5 has introduced a useful new feature which they stole from Adobe GoLive—a rival to Dreamweaver in the days when it was owned by Macromedia. When you create a new file, Dreamweaver now highlights only the default file name ("Untitled")—not the file extension; so you can just over-type the correct file name and press Enter. In previous versions, the entire name was highlighted; so, when you overtyped the highlighted text, you would effectively be deleting the file extension and immediately typing it back in. This will save us all a few precious milliseconds!

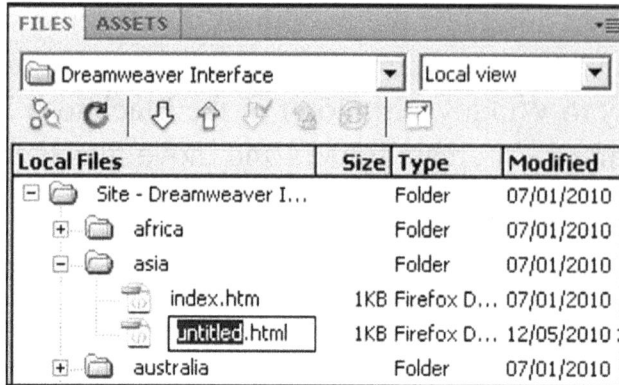

Figure 2-4: When you create a new file in the Files panel, Dreamweaver CS5 intelligently highlights just the default file name; not the extension.

When creating a bunch of files in a given folder, you can speed things up a little by using the keyboard shortcut: **Control-Shift-N** (**Command-Shift-N** on a Mac).

A plus sign (+) is shown next to each folder which contains items. To display the contents of a folder, simply click once on the plus sign, as shown in figure 2-5, below. When the contents of a folder are displayed, the plus sign changes to a minus. To hide the contents of a folder, click the minus sign.

Figure 2-5: Displaying the contents of a folder

Selecting items

To select an arbitrary range of items in the Files panel, click on the first item then, with the Control (or Command) key held down, click on each of the items you wish to add to the selection. The items being selected can be in separate folders and you may collapse and expand folders during the operation without losing the selection.

Opening files

Having selected a series of files, you can open all of them by right-clicking on one of the selected files and choosing **Open** from the context menu. To open a single file you can also simply double-click on its name in the Files panel listing.

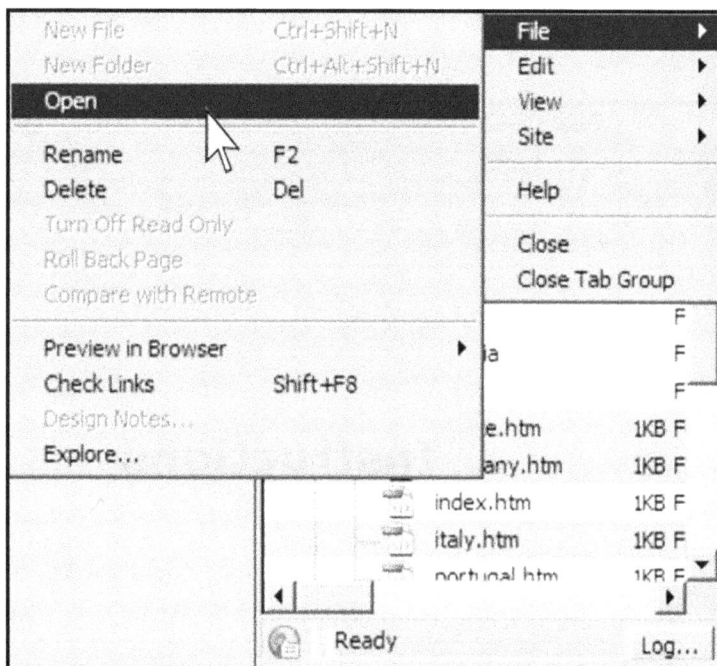

Figure 2-6: Opening several files at once in the Files panel

If the file is a web page of any description, it will open in Dreamweaver. (If it is another type of file, such as an image, the default editor for that file type will launch automatically).

Renaming files and folders

To change the name of a file or folder in the Files panel, click on it with the right mouse then choose **Edit > Rename** from the context menu. You can also press F2 or click twice on the current name of the item, taking care that the two clicks are on slightly different parts of the name (so as not to register a double-click). The name will then be highlighted, ready to be edited. If the name contains a file extension, Dreamweaver will only highlight the name; not the file extension.

Deleting files

To delete the currently selected file, press the Delete key on your keyboard or right-click on the file and choose **Edit > Delete** from the Context menu. Click **OK** when Dreamweaver checks to see if you are sure you want to delete the file.

The document window

Whenever you open a document, Dreamweaver displays it in the document window. In many ways, the document window is the central part of the Dreamweaver interface; it is here that you will add elements to your page and modify them to suit your requirements. Most of the time you will have several documents open at once. Dreamweaver displays a tab representing each page and containing its name. To activate a document, simply click on its tab, as shown in figure 2-7, below.

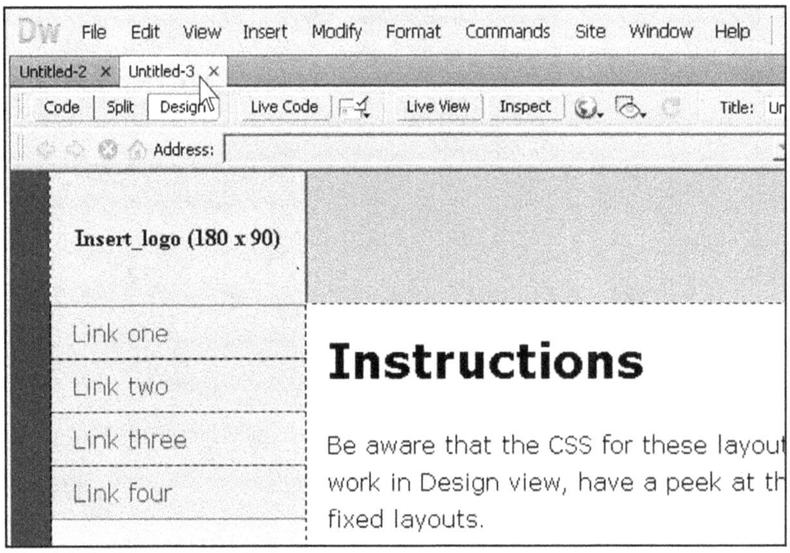

Figure 2-7: Switching between open documents

If there are any unsaved changes in a particular document, an asterisk will appear next to its name. It is important to keep an eye out for these asterisks, as this reminds you which of your pages need to be saved. If several pages need to be saved, you can use the very useful command **File > Save All** to save changes to all open documents simultaneously.

The document tabs are only displayed when the document is maximized; this is the normal default behaviour. In this mode, document windows cannot be moved or resized. To obtain a resizable document window, you can click on the Restore Down button in the top right of the window—the two little squares (▭). The window can then be moved and resized.

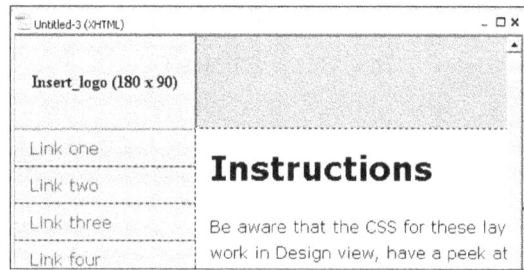

Figure 2-8: Resizing a document window

(The Restore Down button now changes to the Maximize button; which can be clicked at any time to return to the default mode, with document tabs displayed.) Working in this mode is particularly useful where you want to compare two documents side by side. Dreamweaver offers two extremely useful commands for this purpose under the Window menu: Tile Horizontally and Tile Vertically. In figure 2-9, below, two documents are displayed using vertical tiling.

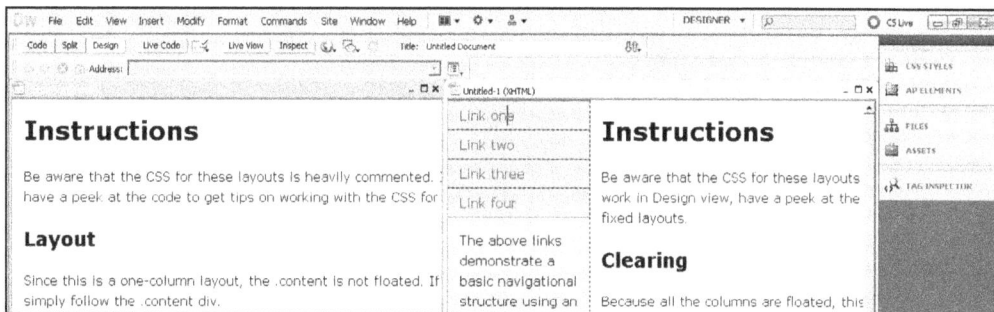

Figure 2-9: Displaying two documents side by side using Window > Tile Vertically

The Properties panel

When working on a document in Dreamweaver, the Properties panel is normally displayed at the bottom of your screen. (To show and hide it, simply choose **Window > Properties**.) It is used both to ascertain and modify the attributes of any element which is highlighted on the page and is extremely versatile. It is also context sensitive, in that it displays options which are relevant to the currently selected item. These options both offer useful feedback and allow you to make changes to the attributes of the selected element.

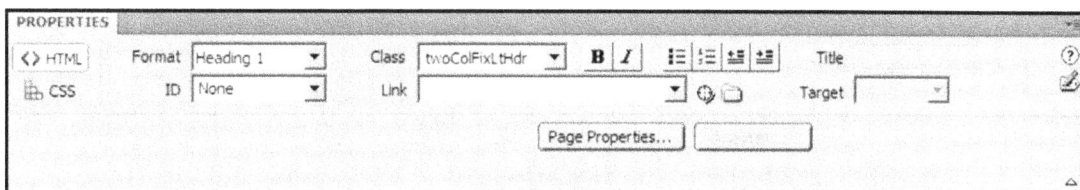

Figure 2-10: The Dreamweaver Properties panel with HTML options active

The Properties panel has two different sets of options: HTML and CSS. These may be accessed by clicking on one of the two buttons on the left of the panel. When formatting text, the HTML section contains options which allow you to assign structural attributes to your text, such as designating headings and paragraphs.

The CSS section contains options relating to the styling of elements on the page. It is used in conjunction with the CSS Styles panel.

The CSS Styles panel

Cascading Style Sheets (CSS) is the web standard which is used in tandem with HTML to control the presentation of web content within the browser. CSS controls the layout of web pages: how much of the browser should your content occupy, should it be centred in the browser, should there be a single or multi-column layout.

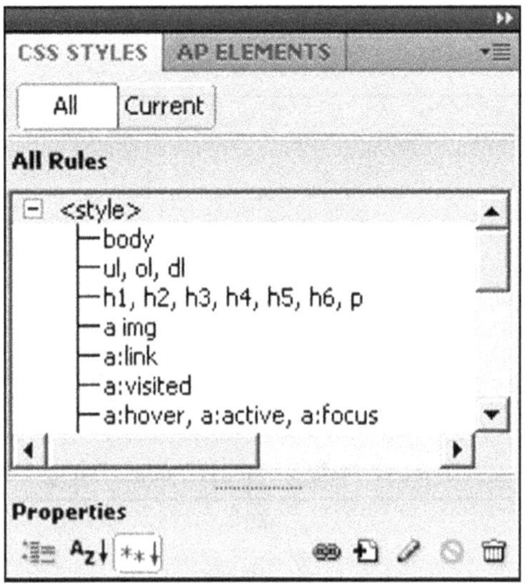

Figure 2-11: The CSS styles panel

CSS also controls the formatting of all elements on the page: fonts, colours, text alignment, indentation etc. We will start using the CSS panel in earnest in Chapter 5: CSS Essentials.

Dreamweaver toolbars

In addition to the various panels, Dreamweaver has three other floating palettes which are referred to as toolbars. To show and hide toolbars, choose **View > Toolbars**.

The Document toolbar

The Document toolbar (See figure 2-12, on page 31.) is normally displayed in the top left of the document window. The first three buttons it contains are the most frequently used: Code, Split and Design views.

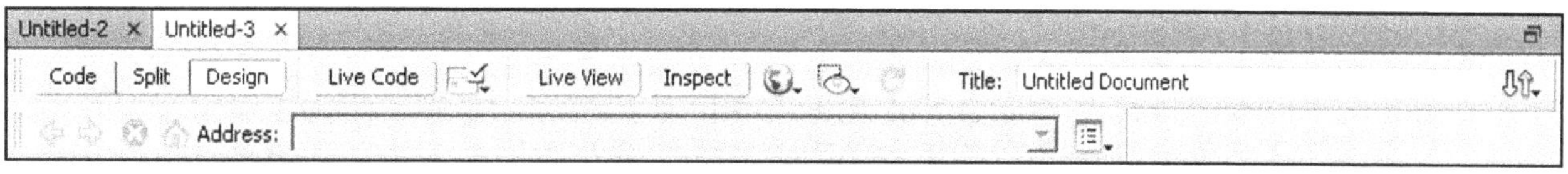

Figure 2-12: The Document toolbar at the top of the document window

The Title box is used to set the document title which will appear in the title bar of the user's browser (as opposed to the document's file name). The file management pop-up menu contains options for uploading and downloading the document as well as commands to be used when working in collaboration with others. (These options are also available in the Site menu.) The browser preview pop-up menu (See figure 2-13, below.) allows you to preview your page in any of the browsers specified using the command **Edit Browser List**.

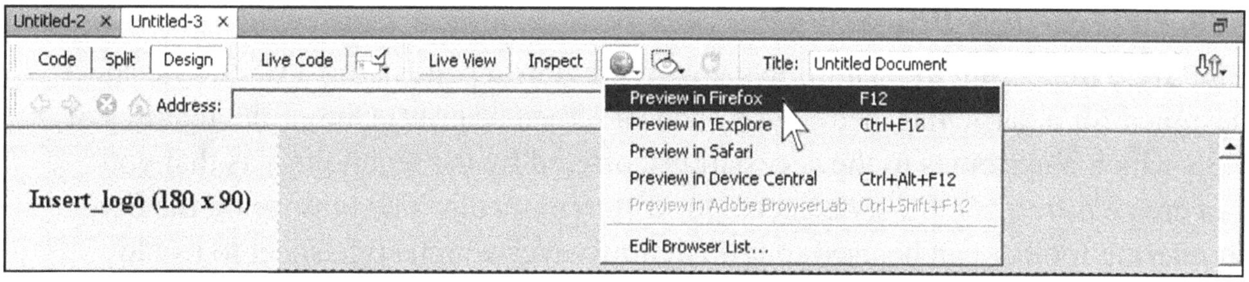

Figure 2-13: The browser preview pop-up on the Document toolbar

The document toolbar also contains options for showing and hiding visual aids and for document checking and validation.

The Browser Navigation toolbar

As well as using the Preview in Browser feature, it is possible to preview pages directly in Dreamweaver using a feature called Live View. In Live View mode, you can hold down the Control key (Command key on a Mac) and click on hyperlinks to navigate from page to page directly within Dreamweaver.

The Browser Navigation toolbar is used when working in Live View: you can use the buttons—Back, Forward and Refresh—just like you would on a browser.

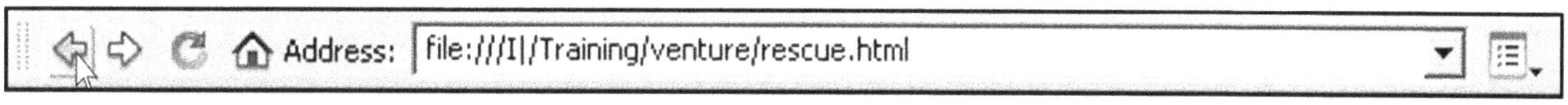

Figure 2-14: The Browser Navigation toolbar

The Standard toolbar

The standard toolbar is reminiscent of the standard toolbar in Microsoft Office 97-2003, with buttons for creating and opening files, copying, pasting, undoing and redoing.

Figure 2-15: The Standard toolbar

The Style Rendering toolbar

The Style Rendering toolbar allows you to preview a page using a CSS style sheet designed for a particular media type such as screen or print. One of the features of CSS which contributes to the accessibility offered by the technology is that you can create different CSS style sheets for different media. The buttons on the Style Rendering toolbar can be used to tell Dreamweaver which style sheet to use to preview the page.

Figure 2-16: The Style Rendering toolbar

3. Editing Web Pages

In this chapter, we will look at the fundamentals of creating web pages and adding content to them. Although Dreamweaver offers a way of working on your pages which make them seem fairly similar to documents created for print, an HTML page differs from a print document in its reliance on markup—tags which let the browser know where each element on the page starts and ends.

Let's begin by looking at how to create a new document.

Creating a new document

Dreamweaver offers a number of ways of creating new documents and beginners often struggle to see which method should be used under which circumstances.

1. One method is to go to the File menu and choose **New**. This displays the New Document dialog which allows you choose from a huge variety of useful documents which can either be blank or include pre-created content.

2. A second method is to use one of the links on the Welcome Screen which normally appears when the program is first launched. This allows you to create a new file of a given type, e.g. HTML, CSS, JavaScript etc.

3. Yet another method is to choose **New** from the menu within the Files panel.

Using File > New from the main menu bar

When we use **File > New** from the main menu bar to create a new document, Dreamweaver displays the New Document dialog and allows us to choose not only the type of document we wish to create, but also a CSS layout.

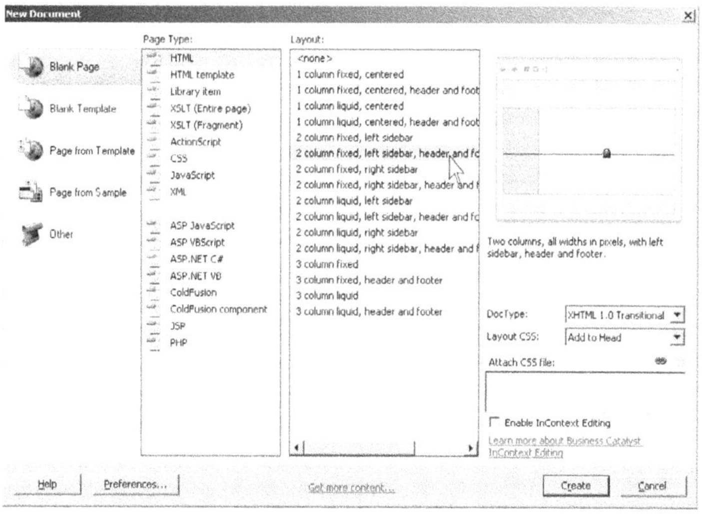

Figure 3-1: Choosing File > New brings up Dreamweaver's New Document dialog

You can use these layouts as a starting point and then customize the page to suit our own purposes.

When you first start using Dreamweaver, you will be creating basic HTML pages. So in the first column of the dialogue you would select **Blank Page**; in the second column, **HTML** and, in the third column, either **<none>** or one of the CSS layouts.

The main benefit of using this technique for creating new documents is that you get to choose and customize the document type. It is also the best method of creating Dreamweaver templates, one of the most powerful tools the program offers.

Using the Welcome screen links

The benefit of using the Welcome Screen method is speed and convenience. The Welcome Screen appears on program launch but it also reappears whenever no documents are open. To create a new HTML file, simply click on the HTML link in the **Create New** column.

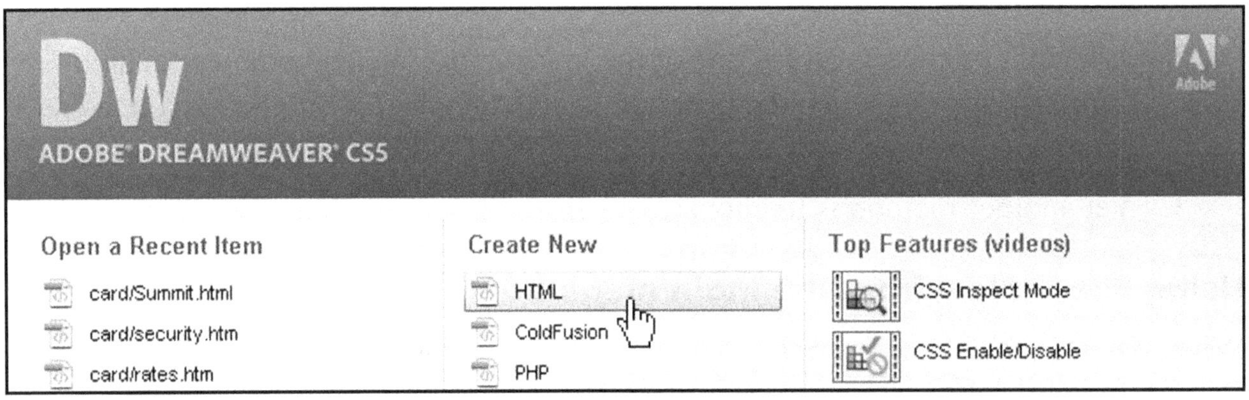

Figure 3-2: Creating a new HTML web page using the Welcome screen

Dreamweaver will create the document without displaying any dialog boxes. This method is ideal when you want to create a one-off HTML page, for example, a promotional page or email. It is also useful if you want to add a page to an existing site. It is less useful if you need to quickly create lots of pages since each page you create will also have to be saved—giving you two steps, instead of one.

You can never really make this your preferred method of creating new files since, as we have seen, the Welcome Screen is only available on startup and when all documents are closed. You can hardly be expected to be constantly closing all your documents just to display the **Create New HTML** link on the Welcome Screen!

Using File > New in the Files panel

When using either the Welcome screen or **File > New** in the main menus to create a new document, the document created is open in memory and it is then up to the user to save it in a given location. The benefit of creating documents in the Files panel is that files are created on disk straightaway but remain closed. Therefore, this method is extremely useful when creating a new site, since it allows the developer to generate the entire site structure before adding content into any of the pages.

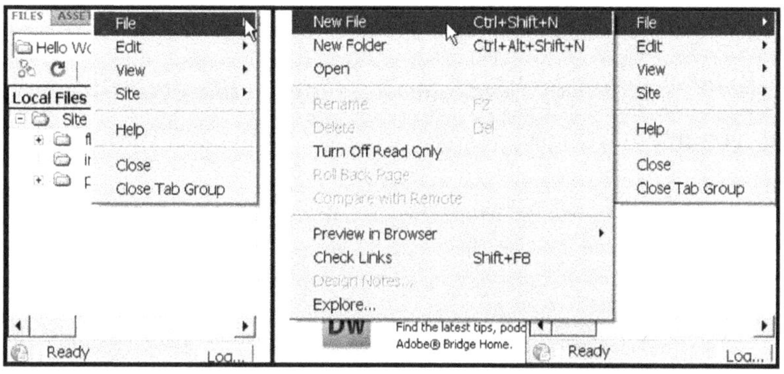

Figure 3-3: Creating a new file using the Files panel menu

Why is this useful? Well, before building a site, it is important that you have a plan of how the site will work and the pages it will contain. Creating all of these pages before adding content to any pages is a good way of minimizing the risk of creating link errors.

For example, let's say you are working on a page called "index.htm" and you want to create a link to a page called "contact.htm"; if the "contact.htm" page doesn't yet exist, you can still create the link. However, when you come to create "contact.htm", you need remember to match the name precisely to the one you used when creating the link. If you forget and call it "contact-us.htm", you will have one more error to detect and correct. If the page already existed, Dreamweaver allows you create the link by simply pointing to the file, thus removing the risk of error.

Anatomy of an HTML page

Having created your HTML page using one of the three methods described, you will either have a completely blank page or a page containing placeholder text which you can then customize.

A blank HTML page

When viewed in Design View, a blank HTML page will appear to be completely empty. However, in Code view, you will notice that Dreamweaver has created the skeleton of an HTML page complete with the essential markup.

```
<!DOCTYPE html PUBLIC "-//W3C//DTD XHTML 1.0 Transitional//EN" "http://www.
w3.org/TR/xhtml1/DTD/xhtml1-transitional.dtd">
<html xmlns="http://www.w3.org/1999/xhtml">
<head>
<meta http-equiv="Content-Type" content="text/html; charset=utf-8" />
<title>Untitled Document</title>
</head>

<body>
</body>
</html>
```

Figure 3-4: The HTML markup of a blank Dreamweaver page

HTML consists of elements which are arranged in a hierarchical structure. The structure of the "blank" page is shown in figure 3-5.

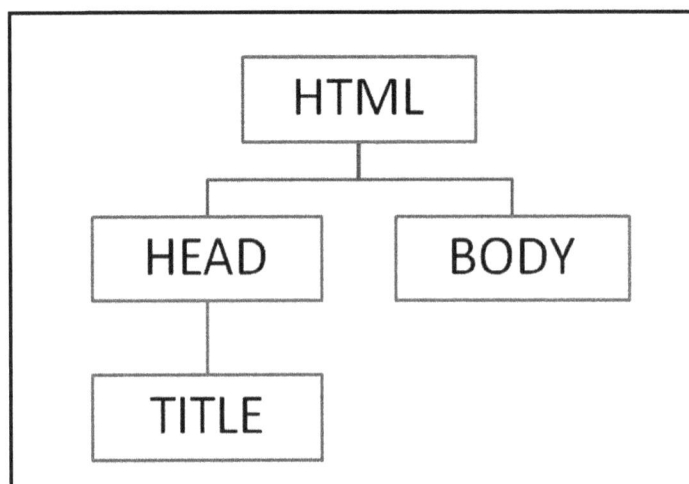

Figure 3-5: The HTML structure of a blank Dreamweaver page

The HTML element contains all other elements and is therefore shown at the top of the hierarchical diagram. While the HEAD element contains a title, the BODY element is empty and this is why nothing shows up when the page is viewed in Design View.

The good news is that, if you are not familiar with HTML markup, Dreamweaver provides tools which will allow you to learn everything you need to confidently create web pages without having to manually enter code.

Creating an HTML page based on a Dreamweaver CSS layout

1. Choose **File > New** from the main menu bar at the top of your screen.

2. Click on **Blank Page** in the first column of the **New Document** dialog.

3. Click on **HTML** in the second column (which is headed **Page Type)**.

4. In the third column (headed **Layout)** click on the layout called "**1 column fixed, left sidebar, header and footer**".

5. At the bottom of the fourth column, choose **Add to Head** from the **Layout CSS** drop-down menu. (This means that the CSS which is required to create the layout will be placed inside the HTML page, rather than in an external file.)

6. Click the **Create** button to generate the page.

7. If necessary, click on the **Design** button which is located on the Document toolbar in the top left of the document window.

The page which Dreamweaver creates for you consists of a series of **DIV** elements containing placeholder text. **DIV** is short **DIV**ision and is the element used in HTML as a container for the various items on the page: headings, paragraphs, images, etc. Understanding the structure of the page is important if you are going to be able to customize it to suit your requirements. The key facts are as follows.

- Each paragraph of placeholder text is contained inside a heading or paragraph element.

- The headings and paragraphs are, in turn, placed inside one of the **DIV** elements.

- These **DIV**s are placed inside a container **DIV** which is used to limit the content to a fixed width and to position it in the centre of the page.

- There are a total of four **DIV** elements on the page: container, header, content and footer.

- The body element is the overall container for the entire page.

The hierarchical structure of the page is shown below.

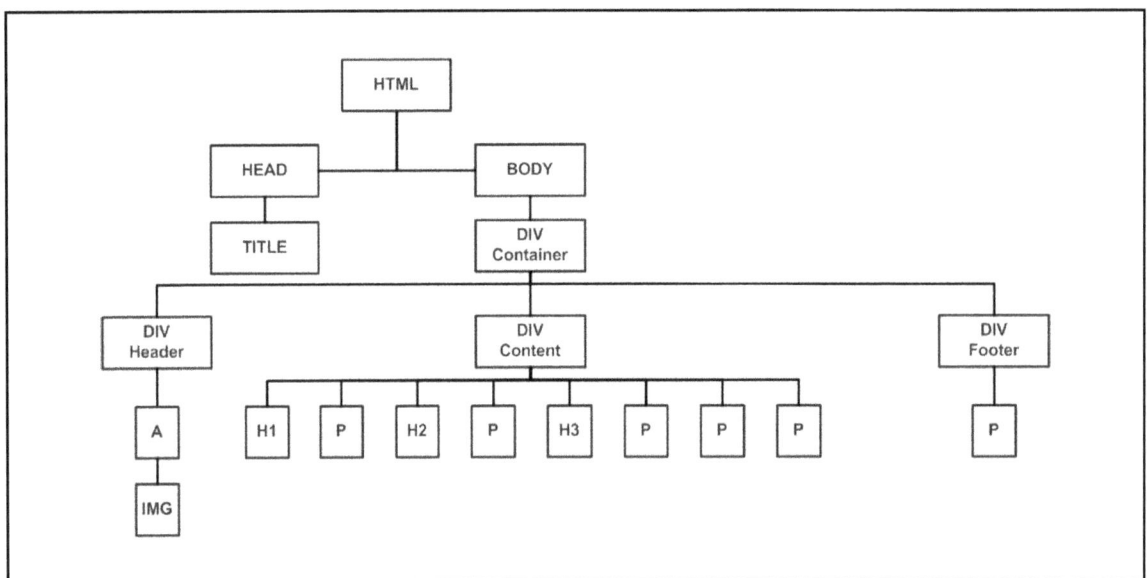

Figure 3-6: The HTML structure of a page using a one-column Dreamweaver CSS layout

Using the Tag Selector

While working in Design view, it is still possible to examine the structure of an HTML page. One of the key tools for doing this is the Tag Selector which is located in the Status Bar, in the bottom left of the document window.

8. Highlight the first item on the page, the image placeholder which bears the text "Insert_logo (180x90)". (For a description of how image placeholders work in Dreamweaver, see Chapter 6: Working with Images, page 71.)

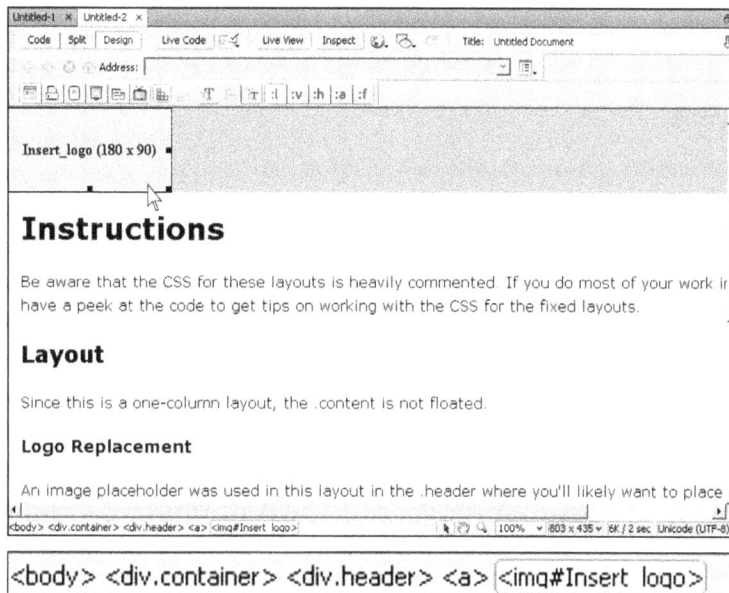

9. Look at the tags listed in the Tag Selector and notice how the order in which they are listed corresponds to the hierarchy shown in figure 3-6, on page 38. First we have the body; this contains the container **<div>**; which, in turn, contains the header **<div>**; which contains the **<a>**; which contains the **<img>** element—the image placeholder that is currently highlighted on the page.

10. Let's take another example. This time, highlight the text that reads "Instructions" in the **content DIV**; then look at the Tag Selector. Notice how the last tag listed is always the one that is currently selected.

As well as displaying the structure of tags on the page, the Tag Selector can also be used to highlight elements. This is particularly useful when editing a busy page; where clicking or dragging to select an element may be difficult.

11. Click anywhere in the header **<div>**; then, in the Tag Selector, click on the tag marked **<div.header>** to select it. Notice how the header **<div>** on the page is immediately highlighted and displayed with a yellow box around it.

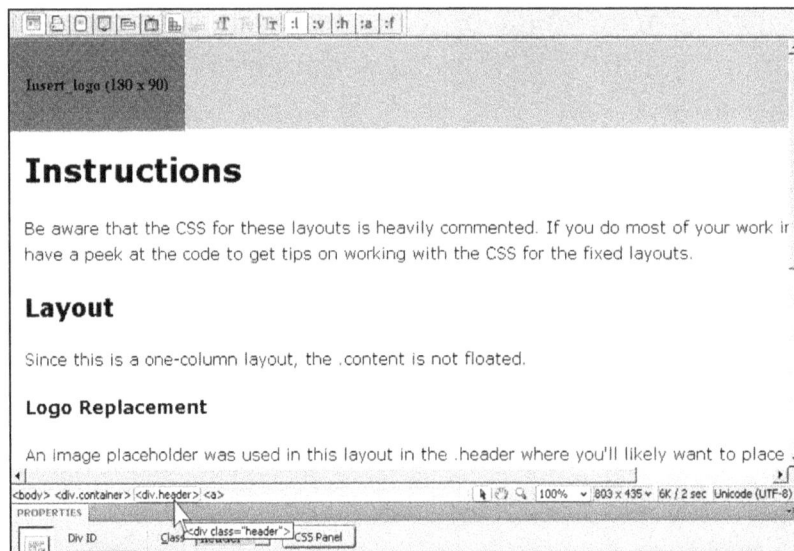

12. Continue to explore the HTML structure by highlighting different parts of the page, examining the tags displayed in the Tag Selector and comparing them to the hierarchical structure of the page shown in figure 3-6 on page 38.

Removing elements with the Tag Selector

The Tag Selector can also be used to remove elements and in a more subtle way than the Delete key. For example, the Tag Selector allows you to remove elements without necessarily removing their contents.

For example, if we click on a linked image, the Tag Selector indicates a highlighted **<img>** tag and, to the left of this, an **<a>** tag representing the link. If we no longer want the image to be a link, we can right-click on the **<a>** tag and choose **Remove Tag** from the context menu. The **<a>** element disappears from the hierarchy; but the image remains.

Figure 3-7: Using the Tag Selector to remove an HTML element

Dreamweaver and HTML

HTML is a markup language used to create documents designed to be accessed across the World Wide Web using browser software such as Internet Explorer or Firefox. The version of HTML in current use is known as XHTML, a stricter, rationalized version of the original HTML specification. One key thing to note about HTML and XHTML pages is that they describe the content and structure of the page rather than the presentation of the elements on the page.

Although you do not need to write HTML code when using Dreamweaver—since the program generates the necessary code as you work visually, it is still necessary to be aware of the elements that make up your pages. This requirement will become apparent when you come to style and position your page content. At this point, you will need at the very least to know—or to know how to find out— the name of an element. (This is where the Tag Selector becomes so useful.)

The <head> element

A web page consists of two main areas: the **<head>** and the **<body>**. The **<body>** contains all of the elements which will be displayed in the browser window and the majority of which will be visible to the user. The **<head>** element, by contrast, contains information about the web page; meta information as it is sometimes called.

The <title> element

The **<title>** element is contained within the **<head>** and should provide a broad heading which reflects the content of the page. It is extremely important that each page should have a title and that the title be pertinent to the page that contains it. Dreamweaver automatically adds a title element to every new page containing the text "Untitled Document".

The easiest way of modifying the default title in Dreamweaver is simply to enter a title in the Document Title box of the Document toolbar which is normally displayed at the top of the page.

Figure 3-8: Entering a title in the Document toolbar

The <body> element

The **<body>** element contains the visible elements of a web page; the part that visitors to your site will see in their browser. Clicking on the **<body>** tag in the Tag Selector will therefore select everything on the page.

Accessibility

A website's accessibility is a measure of how easy it is for visitors with different levels of motor, visual and auditory ability to make sense of the content on your web pages. If your website is accessible, then people using screen readers—or those who prefer not to display images as they browse, or who wish to increase the size at which text is displayed—can all gain access to the information held in your pages.

There are a number of features within Dreamweaver which help web developers ensure that their pages are accessible. By default, the program is set up to automatically offer you a series of accessibility options whenever you add an image, media element or form field to a page. There is also a built-in utility which you can use to check whether your pages contain elements which are not accessible.

Dreamweaver's accessibility preferences

To access Dreamweaver's accessibility settings, choose **Edit > Preferences** (or **Dreamweaver > Preferences** on a Mac). Next, click on the **Accessibility** category and specify the object for which you want Dreamweaver to request accessibility information: form objects, frames, media (which refers to such things as video clips, audio and Flash) and images. By default, all accessibility options are activated.

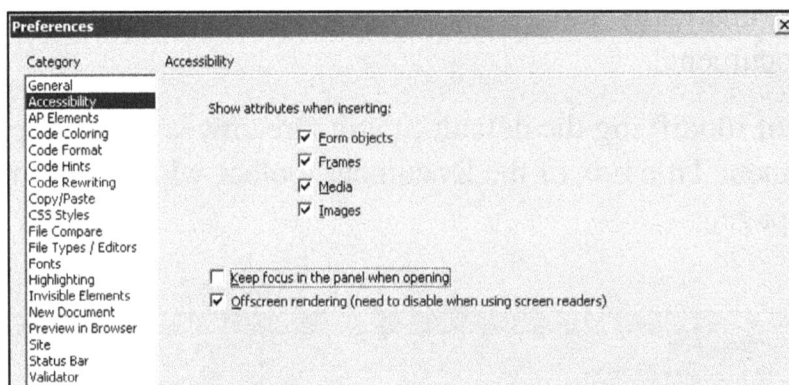

Figure 3-9: Activating Dreamweaver's Accessibility options

Once these options are activated, whenever you insert a form element, frameset, media clip or image, the dialog which Dreamweaver displays will include extra fields requesting information designed to make the element more accessible.

Supplying alternate text when inserting images

When you add an image to any page, you will see a dialog box which invites you to enter the alternate (alt) text. You should key in a brief description of the image. This alt text will be displayed in the browser if the image itself is not displayed—for example, when the user has deactivated the display of images. Screen readers will also speak your alt text whenever an image is encountered.

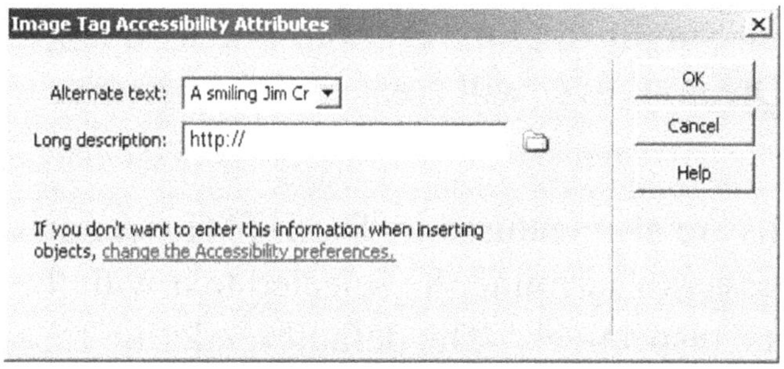

Figure 3-10: Dreamweaver's Image Tag Accessibility Attributes dialog appears whenever an image is added to a page. To make your images accessible, you should enter a brief phrase describing the content of the image.

Using the Properties Panel

Dreamweaver's Properties panel has two sections: one for HTML structural options and the other for CSS stylistic options. The two different sections are accessed by clicking on one of the two buttons on the left of the panel. (The CSS options will be discussed in Chapter 5: CSS Essentials, on page 64.)

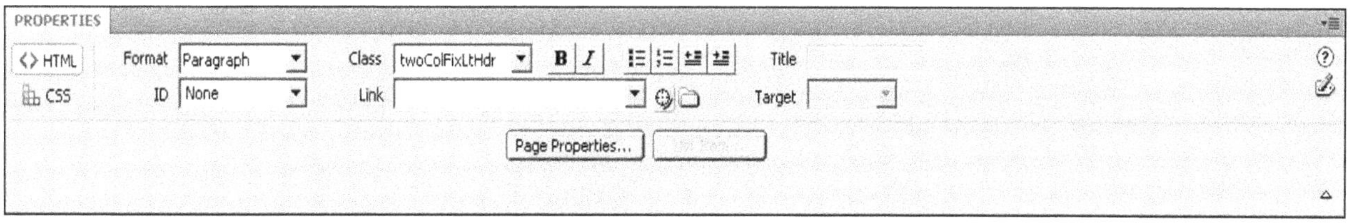

Figure 3-11: Dreamweaver's HTML Properties panel

Using The HTML Properties Panel

When formatting text, the HTML section contains options which allow you to assign structural attributes to your text. From the Format drop-down menu, you can specify whether the text is a heading (h1, h2, h3, etc.) or a paragraph (p). In the ID box, you have the option of assigning a unique ID to the item which could then be used by CSS or JavaScript to reference the item.

The drop-down menu labelled **Class** displays any CSS classes (styles) which have been defined either within the current HTML page or in a linked external CSS file.

Next we have the **Link** box, which allows you to convert the selected text into a hyperlink. Dreamweaver offers a number of ways of creating the link. Thus, for example, if the link is to an external website, you can simply enter the entire URL into the link box.

If you are linking to one of your own pages, one of the fastest techniques is to use the Point to File button. Simply drag the Point to File icon onto any page listed in your Files panel and Dreamweaver will create a link to it. (See Chapter 7: Creating Hyperlinks, page 77.)

Bold and Italic buttons are also featured in The HTML section of the Properties tab. These cause Dreamweaver to surround the selected text with the **strong** and **em** (short for emphasis) elements, respectively. The default rendering for strong is normally bold, in modern browsers, and for em, italic.

The Unordered List icon will convert the selected text into a bulleted list; while Ordered List converts it into a numbered list. The Text Outdent and Text Indent buttons can be used to promote and demote elements within lists, thus enabling you to create nested lists. (Lists are covered in Chapter 4: Working With Text; page 52.)

4. Working with Text

Text and HTML elements

Although working with text in Dreamweaver may seem pretty similar to working with text in a word processor like Microsoft Word, there are a few important differences that you should be aware of.

Text and white space

Firstly, browsers contract all white space between characters into a single space. Thus, for example, in figure 4-1, the text in the document seems to be carefully divided into paragraphs in Code view. However, in Design view, the white space created by carriage returns are replaced by single spaces and all of the text becomes one long paragraph.

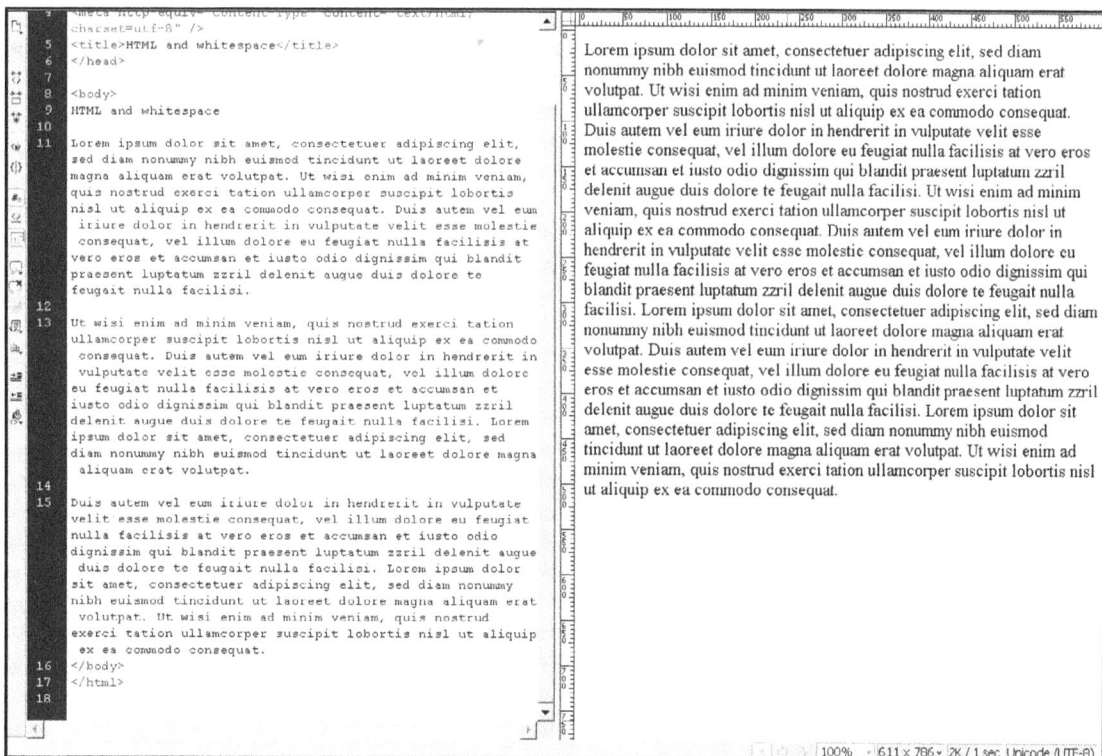

Figure 4-1: HTML contracts carriage returns into a single space.

Giving text structure

There is also the question of structure. Browsers assign a structural importance to text based on the HTML element which contains it. Text inside a heading element, such as **<h1>** or **<h2>**, is given more prominence than text contained within a paragraph element. Dreamweaver uses the paragraph element as the default container for text; so, if you create a blank page in Dreamweaver and type some text, as soon as you press Return, your text will be placed inside a paragraph element.

In order to enable the browser to display the text appropriately, the HTML code must contain tags which tell the browser where each heading begins and ends.

In figure 4-2, below, we can see the same page shown in figure 4-1 (on page 45), with the appropriate tags included; and, this time, Dreamweaver's Design view displays the text as a heading and three paragraphs.

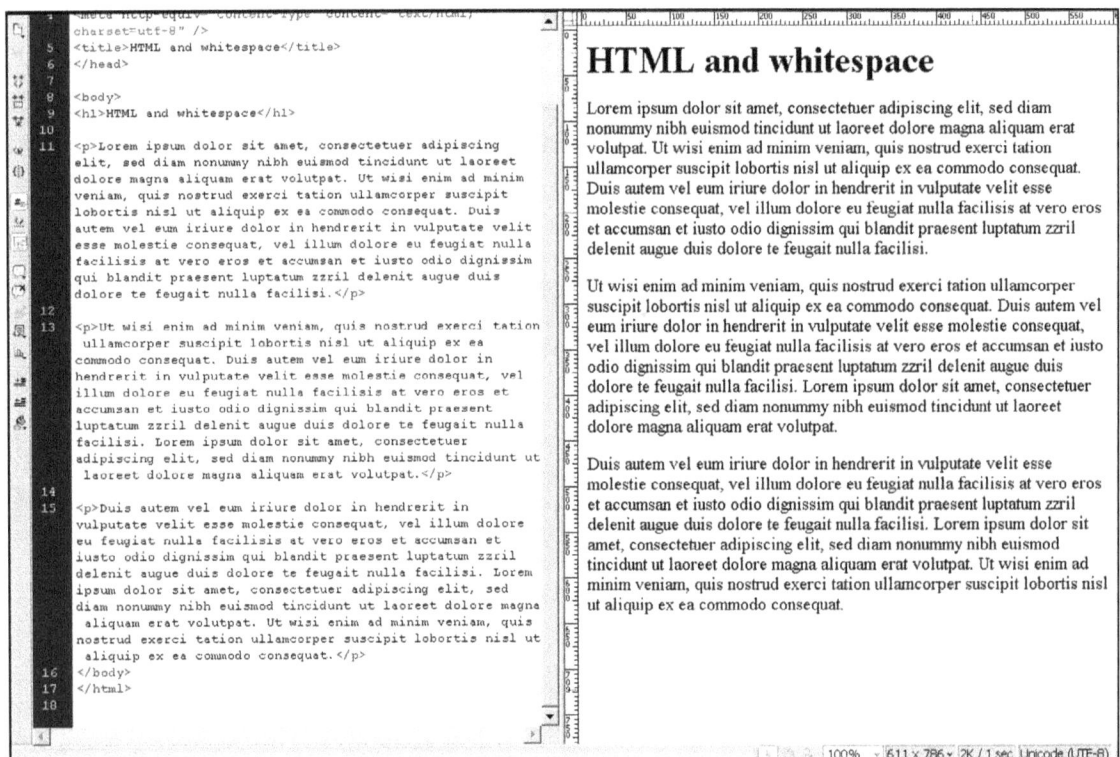

Figure 4-2: HTML tags enable web browsers to understand the structure of your text.

When editing text in Dreamweaver's Design view, users who are unfamiliar with HTML may be occasionally confused by the fact that Dreamweaver treats text as a separate entity to the element that contains it. Thus for example, in Design view, if you triple-click on a heading to select it, what Dreamweaver actually selects is the text inside the heading. The heading element itself is not selected. Once users are a little more familiar with HTML, this behaviour becomes less confusing.

A good habit to get into when working in Design view is keeping an eye on the Tag Selector. This is the area on the left of the status bar at the bottom of the document window. It displays the tags representing the elements which contain the currently highlighted item. These tags can also be used to select an element and its contents.

Thus, to select a heading, ignore the text and just click on the **<h1>** tag representing the element which encloses it.

The use of tags becomes particularly apparent when formatting text since formatting is applied to the element which contains the text rather than to the text itself. The element containing the text can be checked by looking at the tags which surround it. When working in Design view, these tags can be seen by highlighting the text and looking at the Tag Selector in the bottom left of the document window.

In Figure 4-3, below, the highlighted text is contained within an **<h1>** (heading) element and therefore the **<h1>** tag is the last one displayed in the Tag Selector. In order to control the formatting of the text, we would have to target the **<h1>** element, not the text itself.

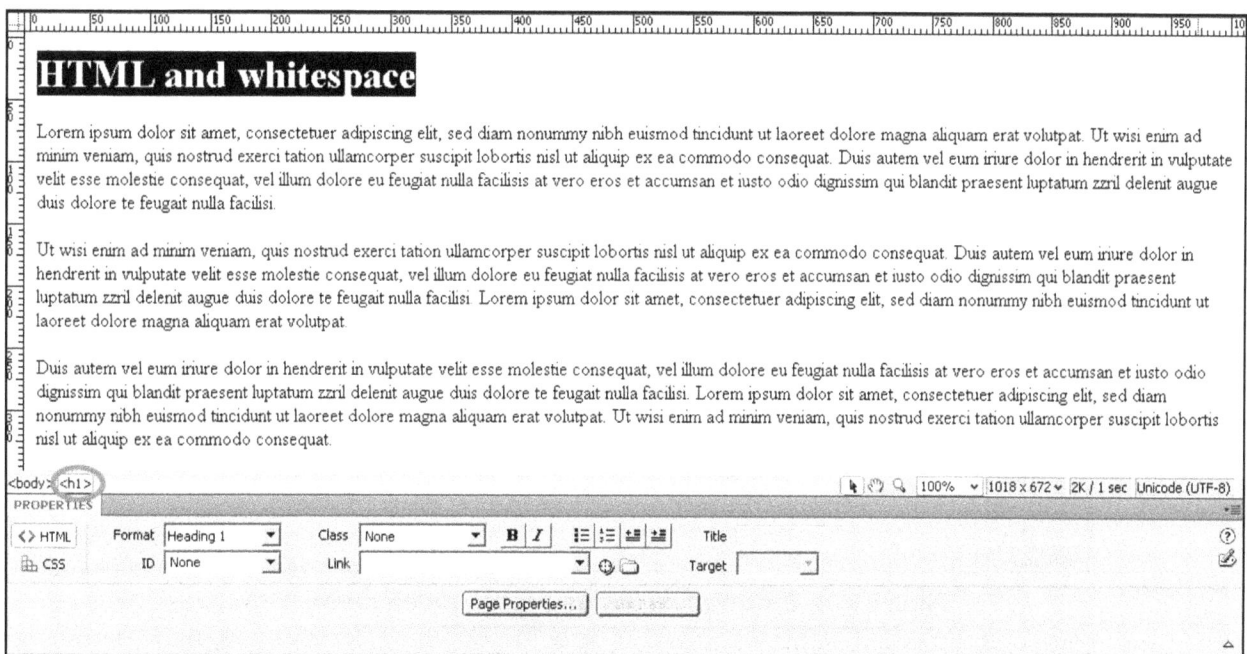

Figure 4-3: The highlighted text is contained within an <h1> element

Even though there is no CSS rule controlling the formatting of the heading, the fact that the text is inside an **<h1>** element causes both Dreamweaver and the browser to display it in a larger typeface than the paragraph below it; which is contained inside a **<p>** (paragraph) element.

Headings and paragraphs

HTML recognizes six levels of headings, **<h1>** to **<h6>**, where **<h6>** is the lowest in the hierarchy.

Converting text into a heading or paragraph

1. Highlight the text or simply click anywhere in the paragraph.

2. If the Properties panel is not visible, choose Properties from the Window menu.

3. If the CSS button on the left of the Properties panel is activated, click on the HTML button to display the HTML options.

4. Choose Heading 1, 2, 3 etc. or Paragraph from the Format drop-down menu on the left of the Properties panel.

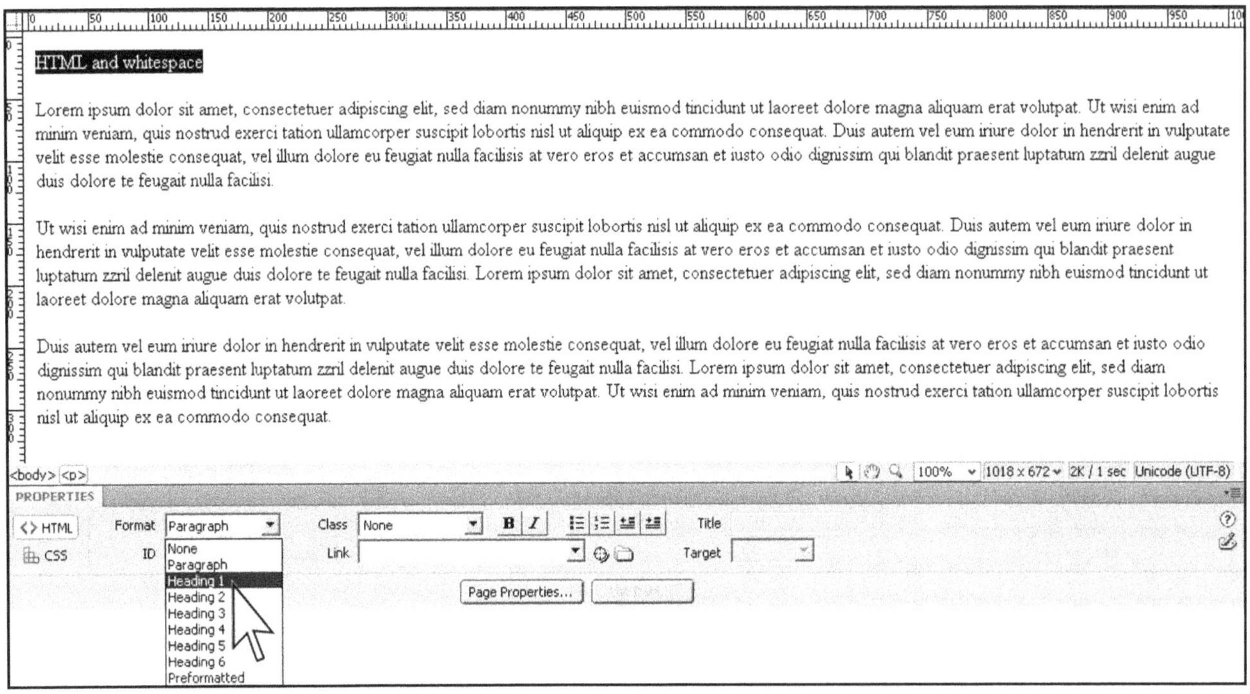

Figure 4-4: Placing text inside the \<h1> element

Copying and pasting text

When you paste text from another environment, Dreamweaver will recognise Returns and use them to split the text into paragraphs. It will also attempt to translate any formatting to its nearest HTML equivalent. Thus, if you copy some data from an Excel spreadsheet and Paste it into an HTML page in Dreamweaver, you will end up with a table containing the Excel data. Similarly, if you copy text from Word which has been formatted using Word styles such as "Heading 1", "Heading 2" and "Normal"; Dreamweaver will place all "Heading 1" text inside **\<h1>** elements, "Heading 2" text inside **\<h2>** and "Normal" text inside **\<p>** elements.

Using the Paste Special command

When you paste text copied from another environment into Dreamweaver, you sometimes get results which are less than useful. The **Paste Special** command, allows you to customize the way in which Dreamweaver handles the data being pasted.

To use the Paste Special command

1. Choose **Edit > Paste Special**, activate one of the radio buttons and click OK.

2. **Text only** will cause Dreamweaver to completely ignore line breaks and Returns, pasting the copied text as a single paragraph. This option is often useful when copying text from an email where a normal **Paste** puts line breaks at the end of each line.

3. **Text with structure** will give you text with paragraphs and line breaks but ignores all formatting.

4. **Basic formatting** (only available if copying from Excel or Word) is the same as Text with structure but, in addition, Dreamweaver preserves bold, underline and italic formatting.

5. **Full formatting** (only available if copying from Excel or Word) offers everything that **Basic formatting** does, but also preserves rich character formatting like font, size and colour.

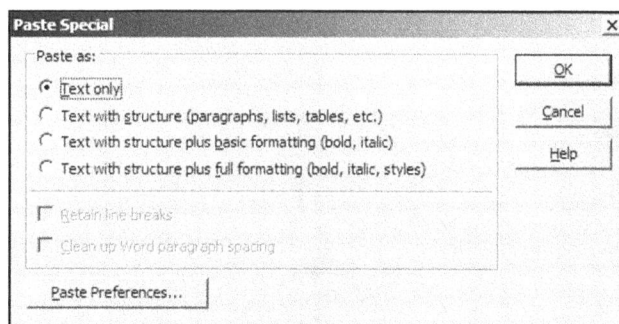

Figure 4-5: The Paste Special dialogue box

Block and inline text elements

Just as, in word processing and desktop publishing packages, there is a distinction between character and paragraph formatting; so HTML makes the distinction between block and inline elements.

Headings and paragraphs are examples of block elements. Any text placed inside these elements will be treated as a paragraph and is normally preceded and followed by a blank line. However, HTML also contains inline elements which may contain a subset of characters within a paragraph.

The strong and em elements

The strong element is used to indicate to the browser that the text it contains should be emphasized. By default, browsers will render such text in boldface. To indicate slightly less emphasis, the em element can be used. Em is short for emphasis and is normally rendered as italic by the browser.

To apply the strong and em tags to text

1. Highlight the text (a minimum of one character).

2. If the Properties panel is not visible, choose Properties from the Window menu.

3. If the **CSS** button on the left of the Properties panel is activated, click on the **HTML** button to display the HTML options.

4. Click on the **Bold (B)** or **Italic (I)** button in the centre of the Properties panel.

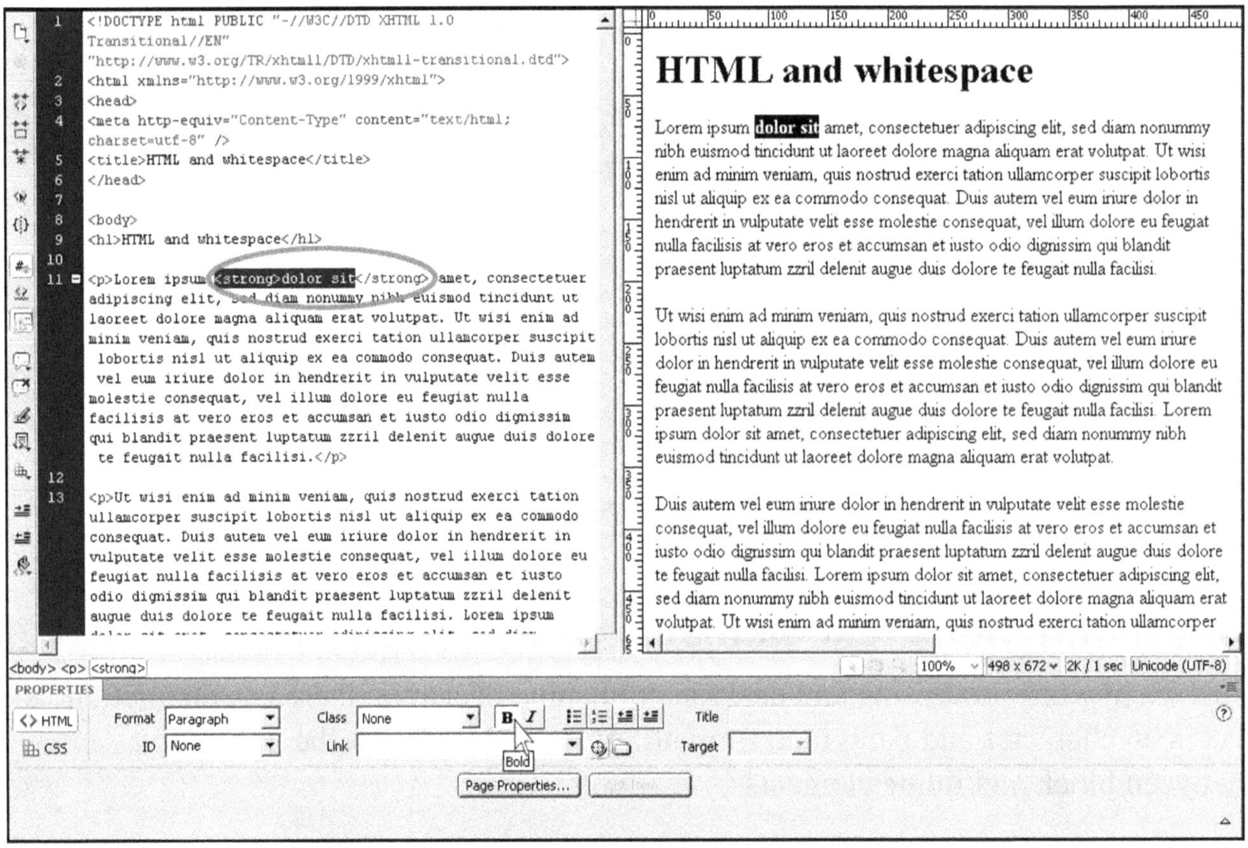

Figure 4-6: Placing text inside the strong element

When we look more closely at CSS in chapters 5 and 9, we will return to this distinction between inline and block elements, since there are some attributes (such as width and height) which can only be applied to block elements.

Special characters and character entities

You will almost certainly come across web pages where a strange symbol is displayed instead of a pound sign, euro or some other symbol. To ensure that non-standard characters are displayed correctly in the browser, HTML uses a series of special codes called character entities. When working in Code View, entities always start with an ampersand and end with a semicolon.

Commonly used character entities

Entity	Meaning
>	>
<	<
"	"
'	'
&	&
£	£

Entering entities in Design View

As you can probably guess, Dreamweaver offers users an easy and convenient way to insert entities without having to memorise a long list of codes.

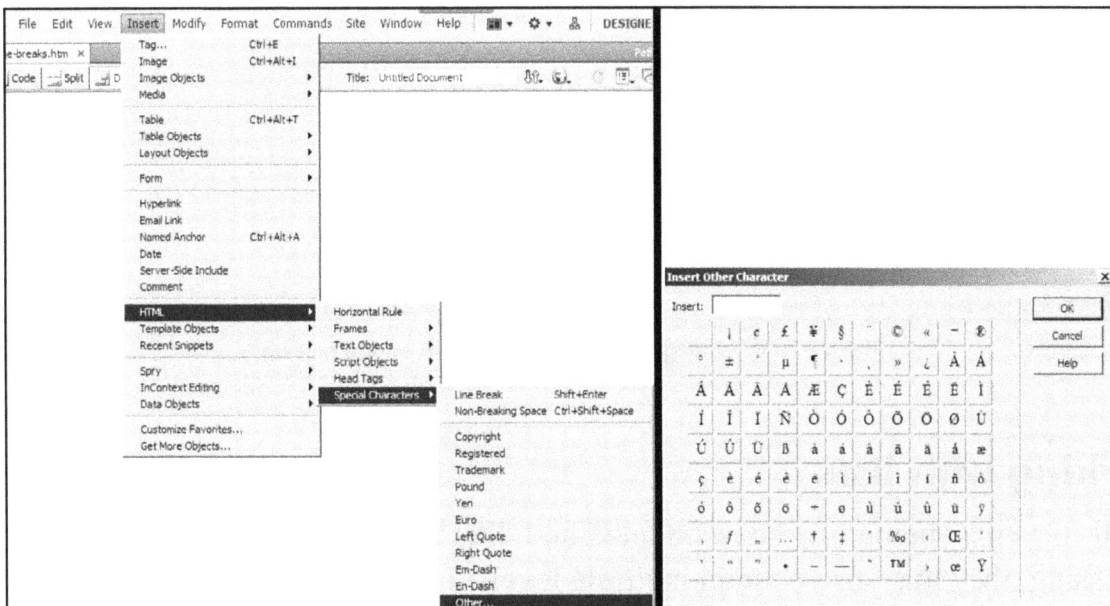

Figure 4-7: Inserting a character entity in Design View

1. Choose **Insert > HTML > Special Characters**.

2. Dreamweaver displays a list of the most commonly used character entities.

3. To access a larger list choose **Insert > HTML > Special Characters > Other**.

Non-breaking spaces

As we saw earlier, in HTML, all white space is contracted into a single space. Therefore to insert more than one space, a special character entity has to be used: it is referred to as the non-breaking space.

To insert a non-breaking space via the keyboard, type **Control-Shift-Space**. Alternatively, use **Insert > HTML > Special Characters > Non-Breaking Space**.

Line breaks

When entering text in Design View, each time you press the Return key Dreamweaver begins a new paragraph. If you need to insert a line break without creating a new paragraph, press Shift-Return instead. This causes Dreamweaver to insert the **
** (line break)—rather than the **<p>** (paragraph)—element.

In figure 4-8, below, putting a line break after each line of the address makes it a single paragraph and keeps the line spacing tight.

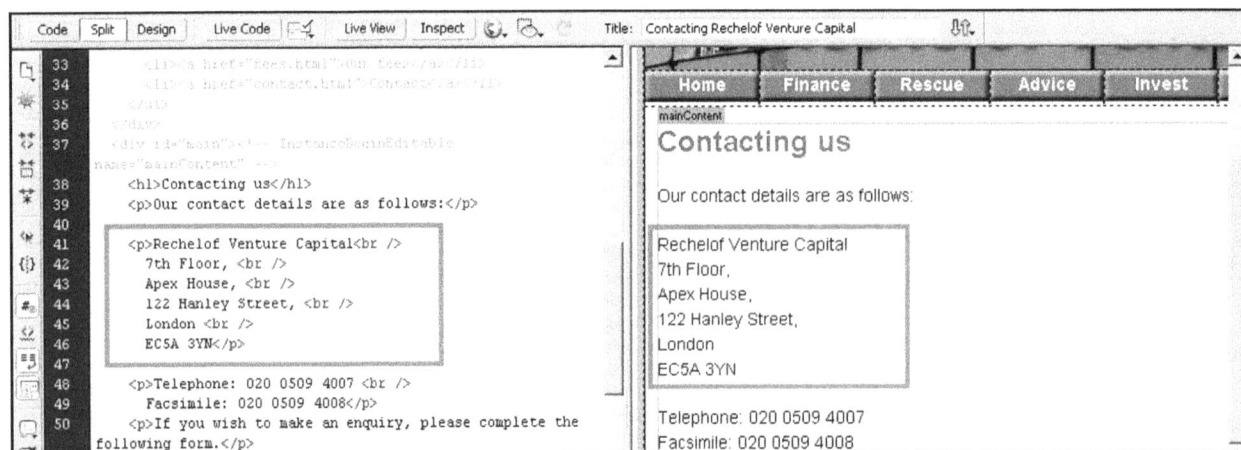

Figure 4-8: Using line breaks within a paragraph

Working with lists

HTML lists may be numbered or bulleted and, like the equivalents found in word processing, they may also contain multiple levels. In HTML, numbered lists are referred to as ordered lists and bulleted lists are referred to as unordered lists.

In Dreamweaver, a list may be created from scratch or one or more paragraphs can be highlighted and converted into a list.

To create a list from scratch

1. Click on the Unordered List or Ordered List button in the HTML section of the Properties panel.

2. Enter the text of the first paragraph.

3. Press the Enter key to create the next paragraph.

4. Dreamweaver creates an HTML list and inserts a number or bullet at the start of each paragraph.

To convert text into a list

1. Highlight the paragraph(s) which you would like to convert to a list.

2. Click on the Unordered List or Ordered List button in the Properties panel.

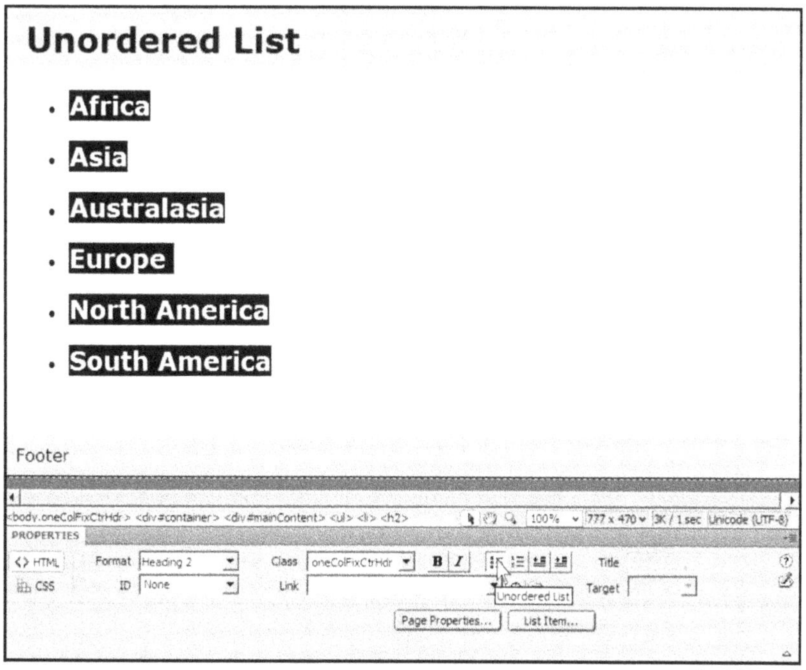

Figure 4-9: Converting highlighted paragraphs into an unordered list

Setting list properties

Dreamweaver's List Properties dialog is used to change the style of the bullets or numbers used in a list. To use this feature, simply click on any item in the list then click on the List Item button in the Properties panel. (See figure 4-10, on page 54.)

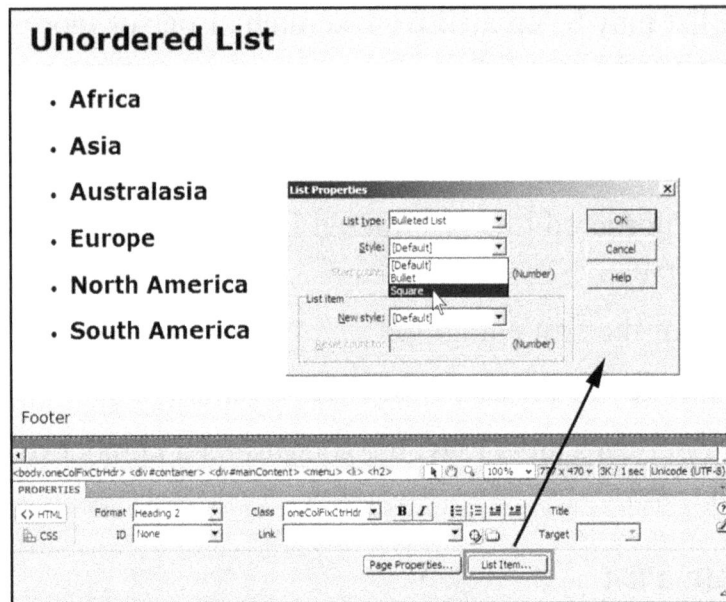

Figure 4-10: Style options for an unordered list in Dreamweaver's List Properties dialog

The **List type** drop-down allow you to set the type of list. The **Style** drop-down menu allows you to choose the style of the bullet or number that precedes each paragraph. The **New style** drop-down menu in the **List item** section at the bottom of the dialog can be used to change the attributes of an individual item in a list.

Setting the start count of an ordered list

If you insert a paragraph of ordinary text at some point in a list, you will end up with two lists: one before the paragraph and one after it. This will probably not be a problem in the case of an unordered list. However, with an ordered list, the numbering of the list below the inserted paragraph will restart at one.

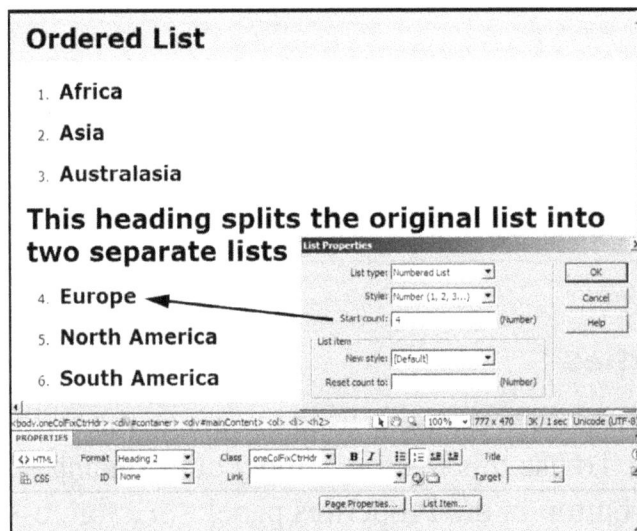

Figure 4-11: Using the Start count option with an ordered list

The **Start Count** option in the List Properties dialog can be used to solve this problem. Thus, in figure 4-11 on page 54, we can restart the numbering at 4 to make the numbers in our two list sections sequential.

Creating a nested list

Another occasion where several lists are made to work together to look like a single list is where you need to create a multi-level list; usually with different numbering or bullet styles at each level. What actually happens in HTML is that you create nested lists; each level within the list is in fact a separate list, nested inside the main list. For example, in figure 4-12, below, each block of country names nested inside each continent name is actually a separate list in its own right, nested inside the list item above it. The Indent and Outdent buttons are used to control the creation of nested lists.

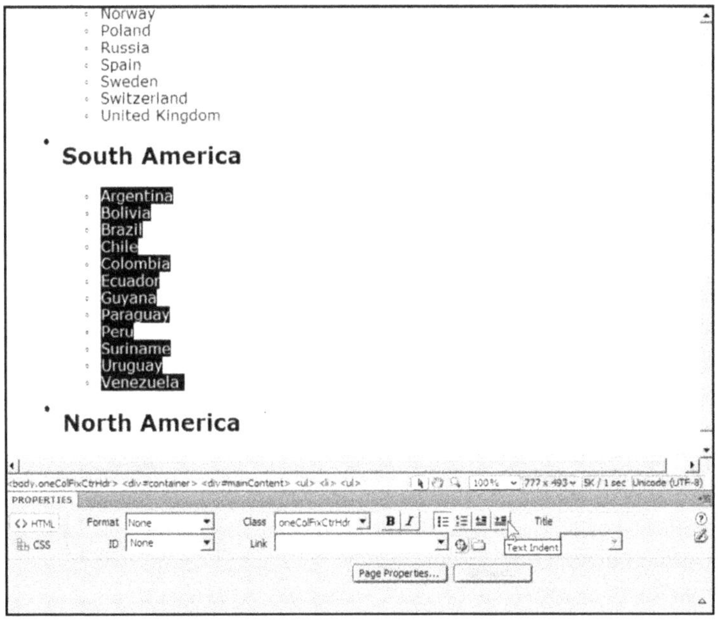

Figure 4-12: Using the Indent button to create a nested list

To create a nested list

1. Create the items which form part of the list.

2. Highlight the item(s) to be indented (nested).

3. Click on the **Indent** button in the HTML section of the Properties panel or simply press the Tab key on your keyboard.

4. Dreamweaver converts the selected items into a nested list.

5. CSS Essentials

The two key elements of most web pages are text and images and it is important that both have the right impact on visitors to our website. This is where CSS comes in. Whereas HTML defines the structural importance of our content; CSS (Cascading Style Sheets) allows us to define the layout and formatting.

In this chapter, we will give an overview of how CSS works and the tools available in Dreamweaver for creating and editing CSS rules.

What is CSS

CSS is a recommendation of the Worldwide Web Consortium (W3C) and offers web designers precise control over the formatting and layout of web pages. CSS enables you to set up default formatting rules which the browser will automatically apply to headings, paragraphs and any other elements on your pages.

CSS allows web developers to separate the content of their web pages from the style and formatting information. This means that the HTML code is not cluttered with style information and will be processed more quickly by browsers, leading to faster download times. Also, since style definitions are normally stored in external files to which all HTML pages are then linked, the appearance of the entire site can be updated by modifying the CSS file(s), without even having to open any of the HTML pages.

To edit CSS in Dreamweaver's Design view, you use the CSS Styles panel and the Properties panel. The Tag Selector is also extremely useful in specifying the object to be targeted by the CSS rule.

Location of the CSS information

CSS can be implemented in three different ways. Firstly, it can be embedded inside an HTML document, in the **<head>** area of the page. Secondly, it can be placed in an external file, with a ".css" file extension. Thirdly, CSS can be placed inline; that is to say, inside HTML tags.

The three methods are not mutually exclusive. A typical website may have one or more external style sheets, combined with internal CSS on certain pages and a few smatterings of inline CSS within one or two pages. In general, the closer the CSS is to the HTML element it controls, the higher its precedence. Thus inline styles normally take precedence over internal CSS, which, in turn, takes precedence over external CSS definitions.

Creating a CSS file

Using File > New

You can create a CSS file by choosing **File > New** and making the necessary choices in the New Document dialog. In the first column, click on **Blank Page** and, in the second column (**Page Type**), click **CSS**; then click the **Create** button.

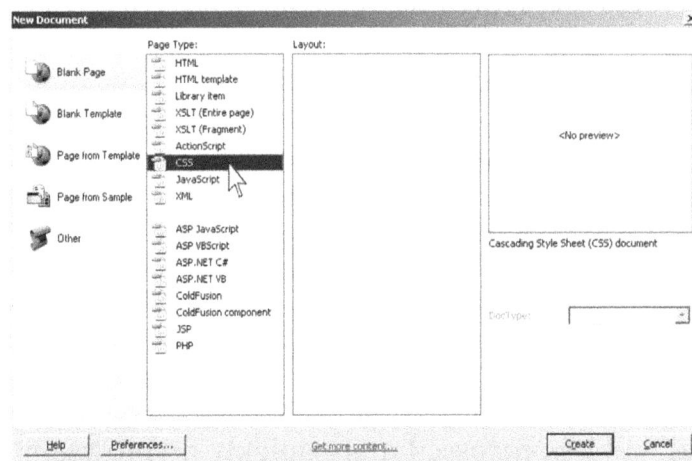

Figure 5-1: Creating a new CSS file

Using the Files panel

To create a CSS file using the Files panel, simply right-click on the folder that you want the file to go inside and choose **New File** from the context menu. You must then remember to end the file name with the extension ".css"—as opposed to ".html".

Linking an HTML page to a CSS file

External CSS files offer the greatest flexibility to web developers, allowing them to link multiple HTML pages to a single CSS file then modify the look and feel of all of these HTML pages simply by updating that one CSS file. It is also possible to use the same external CSS file on more than one website. Dreamweaver allows us to make this process even more efficient by linking a template to the CSS file. We will examine the use of templates in Chapter 10: Dreamweaver Templates. For the moment, let's look at linking a single HTML page to a CSS file.

Choose **Attach Style Sheet** from the CSS Styles panel menu to display the Attach External Stylesheet dialog. Click on the **Browse** button; locate the **.css** file then double-click on it to select it.

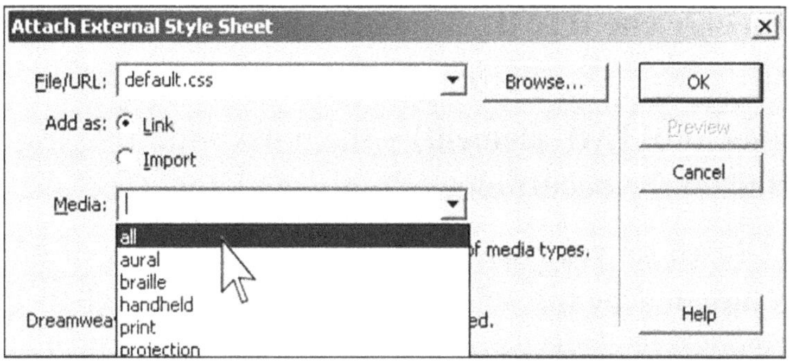

Figure 5-2: Using the Attach Style Sheet command

Media

The dialog also allows you to specify the type of media which the style sheet is designed for. By default, a single style sheet is used for all media; however, for the convenience of visitors to your website, you can designate different styles sheets for different media. The most important option is of course **Screen**; but **Print** is also worth considering for those pages which you know visitors are likely to print out.

Creating CSS rules

A CSS file is simply a repository for a set of rules which instruct the output device—usually someone's web browser—how to display the various elements in an HTML page. Each CSS rule targets a particular element or group of elements and the mechanism for this targeting process is the use of a name referred to as a selector. The selector specifies which elements will be affected by the rule.

The usual method of creating a new CSS rule in Dreamweaver is by choosing New from the drop-down menu in the top right of the CSS Styles panel. This displays the New CSS Rule dialog box shown in Figure 5-3, on page 60.

Before creating a new rule, it is often useful to use the Tag Selector to select a tag representing the element you wish to target. Thus, if you want to create a rule specifying that the page background will be pale blue and the default font for the page will be Arial, you would select the **<body>** tag, since this represents the HTML page itself. When the **Compound** selector type is used, Dreamweaver will suggest a name for the selector which is based on your selection.

The New CSS Rule dialog first asks you to specify the type of selector that you would like to use to target elements on the page. The drop-down menu offers four choices, each followed by a brief explanation of its function:

1. **Class (can apply to any HTML element)**—you make up the name of the selector and later choose which elements are affected by the rule.

2. **ID (applies to only one HTML element)**—targets only the element having the ID specified.

3. **Tag (Redefines an HTML element)**—the most wide-ranging choice; rules of this type affect every occurrence of a given element.

4. **Compound (Based on your selection)**—provides a way of narrowing the range of elements targeted by the selector; for example, all <h1> elements inside the content <div>.

Next, we have the selector name. Sometimes, this is entered automatically Dreamweeaver, based on the **Selector Type** that you choose. However, it always remains editable.

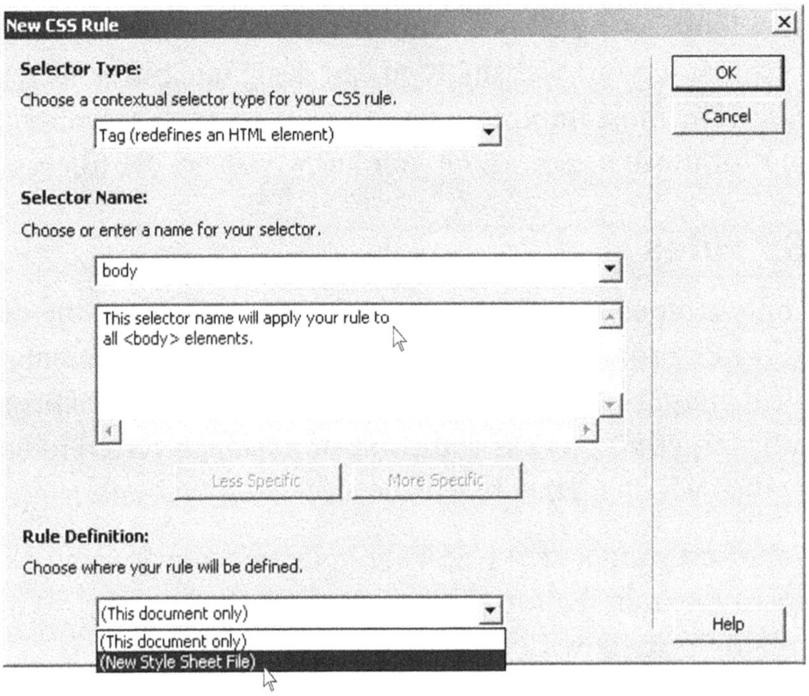

Figure 5-3: Creating a new CSS rule

Specifying the location of a CSS rule

In the **Rule Definition** section , at the bottom of the New CSS Rule dialog, Dreamweaver invites you to **Choose where your rule will be defined**. You can choose **This document only** from the drop-down menu to embed the style information in the head area of the HTML page. If, instead, you choose **Create New Style Sheet**, the new CSS rule will be placed in an external file. (Dreamweaver will allow you to specify where the file is placed.) If you would like to link an existing CSS file to the HTML page, choose **Attach Style Sheet** from the CSS Styles panel menu and click on the Browse button; locate the file then click **OK**.

Selector type

Let's look at the selector types in a bit more detail.

Tag

The most global **Selector Type** option is **Tag**. This option allows you to target every occurrence of a particular element on the page. When you choose the **Tag** option, Dreamweaver enters the name of the tag which is currently selected on the page. If this is not the tag you wish to redefine, then choose the name of another tag from the drop-down menu.

For example, if you wanted all your **<h1>** elements (main headings) to be red, regardless of their position on the page, you would set the **Selector Type** to **Tag** and enter **h1** in the **Selector Name** field.

Since this option is so global, it is normally only used to define very broad stylistic attributes such as **font-family** or **color**.

ID

The main container used in HTML page layout is the **<div>** element and each **<div>** is normally identified by a unique ID. The ID selector type is used most frequently when creating a rule specifying the layout and format of a **<div>** element. If you click on the name of the **<div>** in the Tag Selector before creating the rule, when you choose the ID option, Dreamweaver will enter the name of the **<div>** preceded by a hash (#) sign. The hash sign is a syntactical requirement in CSS and indicates that the selector is targeting an item on the page via its unique ID.

I should mention here that any HTML element on the page can be given a unique ID and targeted with an ID type selector. However, **<div>** is probably the HTML element most frequently targeted in this way.

Class

While an element with a specific ID can only occur only once on a particular HTML page, several elements on the page can be of the same class. For example let's say you want to format some of your images with a 1 pixel grey border and have the image floating on the left with text wrapping around it. You would create a CSS rule using a class selector and then apply it to any image that you wish to format in this way. Class names must always start with a dot; but, if you forget the dot, Dreamweaver will insert it for you.

Unlike rules which use the other three types of selector, CSS rules using the class selector do not automatically apply to elements on the page. In order for a class style to affect an element, highlight the element and choose the appropriate selector name from the **Class** drop-down menu in the Properties panel.

Compound

It is usually the case that formatting of a particular element may depend on its position on the page. Thus, for example, you will probably want a paragraph inside a footer to look different to a paragraph inside the main text area of the page. The most common use of the Compound selector type is to create tag and class rules that apply to a specific area of the page, usually inside a particular DIV.

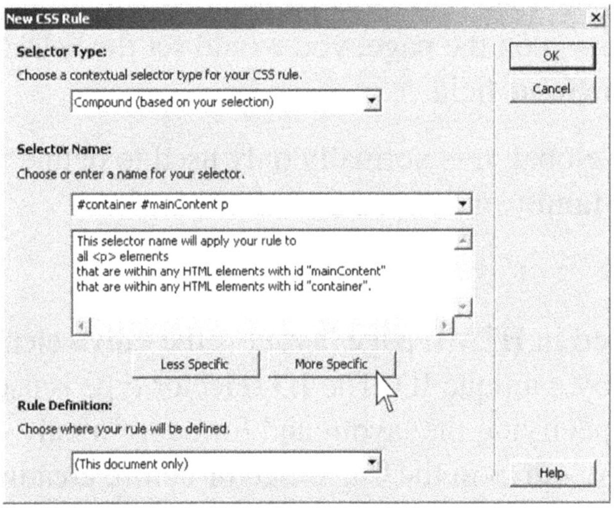

Figure 5-4: Creating a compound CSS rule

Let's say that the main **<div>** on our page is called **MainContent** and that we have a **<div>** at the bottom of the page called **Footer**; and both of them are inside a wrapper **<div>** called **Container**. To easily create a CSS rule controlling the display of paragraphs with the **MainContent <div>**, we would first select any paragraph within the **MainContent** area and then choose **New** from the CSS Styles panel menu.

When we set the Selector Type to Compound, Dreamweaver automatically enters a name in the Selector Name box which reflects the currently selected item:

body #Container #MainContent p

This name is similar to a file path: it means "paragraphs inside the **MainContent** **<div>** which is inside the **Container <div>** which is inside the page body". The box below the Selector name displays a description of the significance of the name.

Since there can only ever be one element on the page with an ID of MainContent, there is no need to be so precise. All we really need to say is:

#MainContent p

Instead of manually altering the selector name, Dreamweaver allows us to change it by clicking on the **Less Specific** and **More Specific** buttons. Thus, in the example above, we would click on the **Less Specific** button twice to remove first **body** and then **#Container** from the selector name. (See Figure 5-4, on page 62.)

Viewing CSS rules in the CSS Styles panel

If an external CSS source is associated with an HTML file, Dreamweaver will display the name of the CSS document in the CSS Styles panel whenever the HTML file is open.

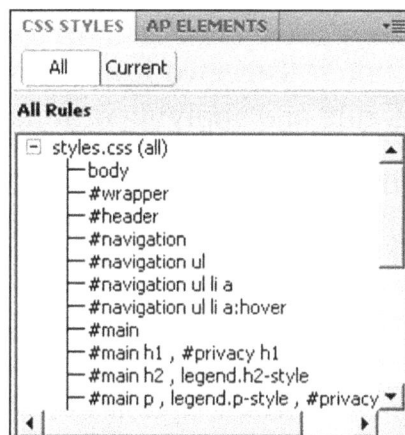

Figure 5-5: A series of CSS rules in an external style sheet (called "styles.css"), displayed in the CSS Styles panel. Rules can be created, edited and deleted via the panel.

If the CSS is being stored internally, the rules will be grouped under the heading **style**, indicating that it has been defined within a **<style>** element in the **<head>** area of the current page.

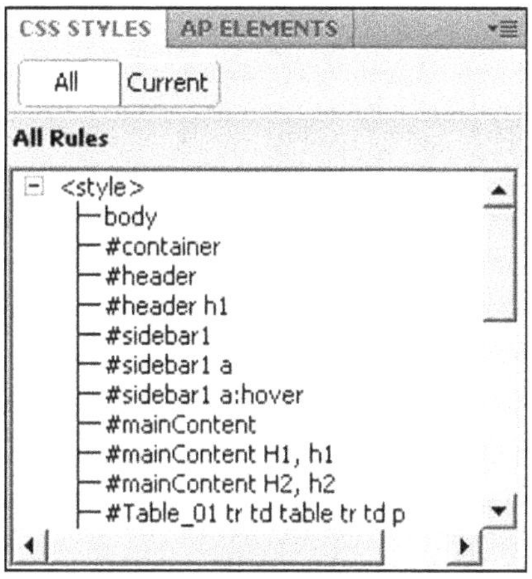

Figure 5-6: A group of rules named simple "style" denotes an internal CSS style sheet. (External style sheets are always denoted by "somthing.css").

Using The CSS Properties Panel

The Properties panel displays two sets of options: **HTML** and **CSS.** Click on the **CSS** button on the left to display the CSS options shown in Figure 5-7, below.

Figure 5-7: Dreamweaver's CSS Properties panel

The first option in the CSS section is **Targeted Rule**. This drop-down menu contains options for creating a new CSS rule and applying or removing an existing rule.

The **Font** drop-down menu in the CSS Properties panel displays a series of lists of fonts rather than a series of individual fonts; for example **Impact, Arial Black, Arial, sans-serif**. This means that if the Impact font is not present, Arial Black will be used; if Arial Black is not present, plain old Arial will be used; and, in the unlikely event that none of them are present, the default sans-serif font on that user's browser will be used. The font drop-down also contains the option **Edit Font List** which allows you to create new wish-lists of fonts and amend existing ones.

Selecting text and choosing a colour from the Properties panel brings up the New CSS Rule dialog box with the **Selector Type** set to **Class**. The Bold, Italic, and alignment buttons will also display the New CSS Rule dialog, in exactly the same way.

6. Working with Images

How images work in HTML

Images are a key element in almost all web pages and are extremely important in communicating key messages to website visitors. However, since web pages consist of purely textual markup, they are incapable of embedding images in the way that word processing documents do. Instead the HTML page contains a reference to the image which enables the browser to locate and display it as necessary.

In figure 6-1, below, the file logo.gif has been placed on the page using the HTML code:

> **<img src="../images/logo.gif"...**

but the image itself ("logo.gif") is an external file which must be uploaded to the server if it is to be displayed on the page each time it loads in someone's browser.

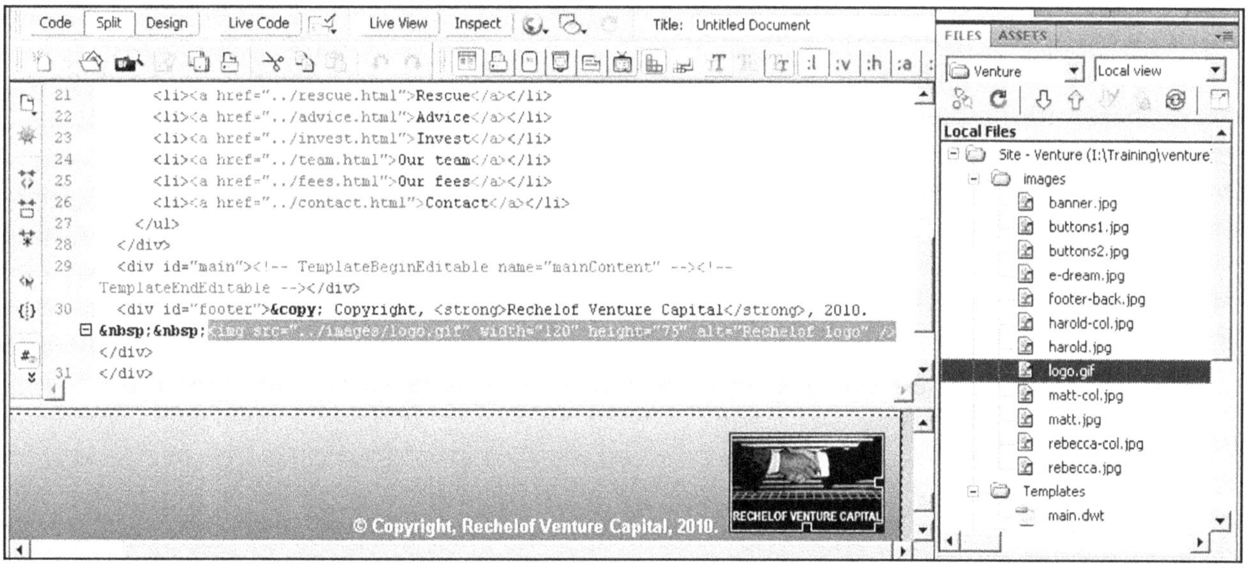

Figure 6-1 Images are always external to web pages and must be uploaded to the server as well as the page that contains them, if they are to be displayed.

Adding images to a page

Dreamweaver offers three basic methods of adding images to a web page. The standard method is to use the menu command **Insert > Image** or to click on the equivalent icon from the Insert Panel. However, Dreamweaver offers two convenient alternatives: firstly, the Files Panel and, secondly, the Assets panel.

Using Insert > Image

To add an image to an HTML page, position the cursor in the required location and choose **Insert > Image**. Dreamweaver displays the Select Image Source dialog.

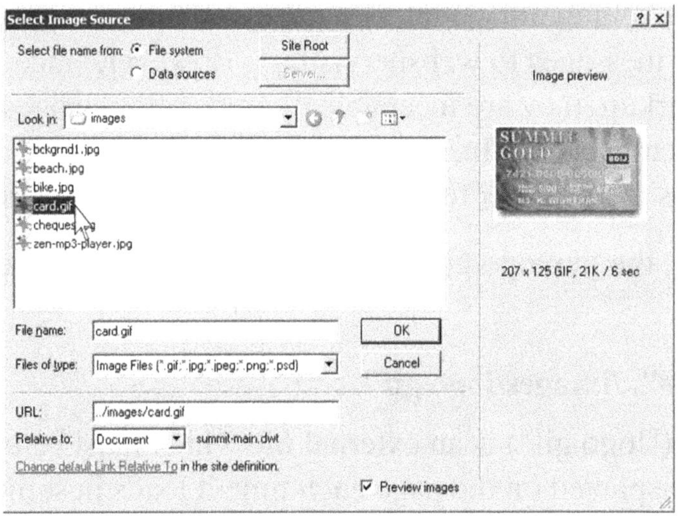

Figure 6-2 Inserting an image using Insert > Image

Naturally, the most important thing you need to do is to navigate to the image and double-click to import it. However, there are a few other options which it might be useful to explain.

Select filename from

At the top of the Select Image Source dialog are two radio buttons labelled **Select file name from**. The options are **File system** and **Data sources**. Here you will want to select **File system**. (The **Data sources** option is used to create a dynamic image when working with data-driven websites using ASP, PHP or ColdFusion.)

Navigating to the Local Site Folder

To locate the image, you will use the normal file navigation provided by your operating system. In addition, Dreamweaver provides a **Site root** button which takes you straight back to the Local Site Folder. (The Server button located underneath the Site root button is only used when building data-driven websites.)

Relative to document or site root

Images and hyperlinks inserted into an HTML page are merely referenced and the reference can have one of two starting points: the document containing the image; or the site root. The normal choice here is relative to the document. (This topic is discussed in more detail on page 13.)

Importing images using the Files panel

Dreamweaver's Files Panel offers a complete list of all the files and folders within the site—in a manner not dissimilar to Windows Explorer or the Macintosh Finder. If you know the name of the image you want to add to the page, you can simply drag it from the Files Panel directly onto your page.

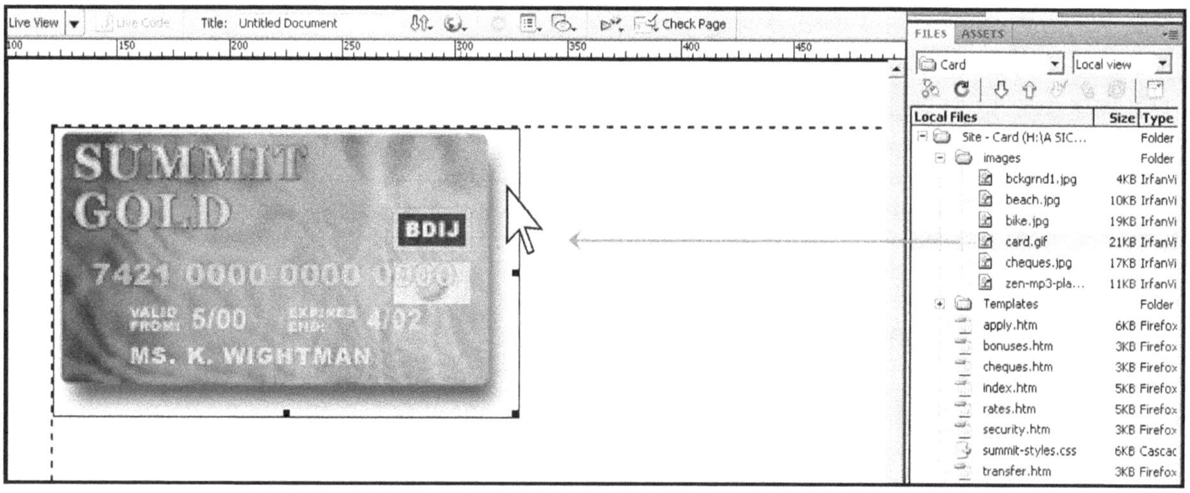

Figure 6-3 Dragging an image onto a page from the Files panel

This is perhaps the fastest method of adding images to a page and is particularly useful when adding several images to a busy page. The only disadvantage of using this technique is that the Files panel does not provide a preview of the image being inserted.

Importing images using the Assets panel

The Assets panel is basically a internal database which provides a categorized and automatically generated list of assets available—not only in the current site, but also in other sites defined on your computer. The elements it keeps track of include images, colours and Flash movies. To work with image assets, simply activate the Assets panel (using the menu command **Window > Assets**) then click on the Image category. As you highlight each image, a thumbnail preview is displayed at the top of the Assets panel. To insert an image, either drag the image onto the page or highlight the image and click the **Insert** button.

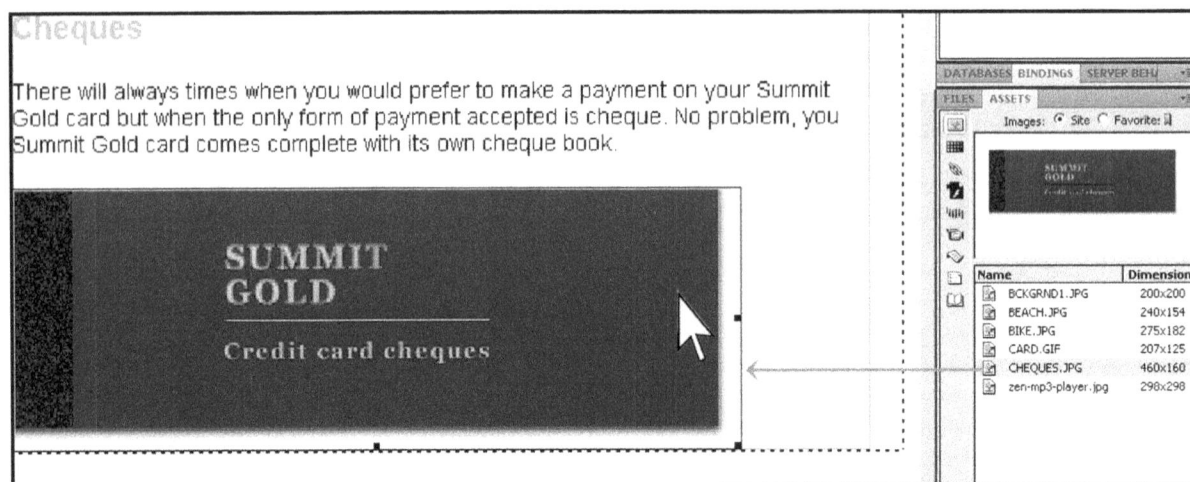

Figure 6-4 Inserting an image from the Assets panel

Avoiding "broken" images

The Default Images Folder

Some of those images that you add to your web pages may not be within the Local Site Folder of the site that you are currently working on. As we have seen, when defining your site, Dreamweaver includes the option of specifying a Default Images Folder. The folder you specify here will be used by Dreamweaver to ensure that all images you add to your pages are inside the Local Site Folder.

What if you were to use the Assets panel to add an image to one of your web pages but the image is located in a different site? No problem! Dreamweaver will automatically copy the image into the Default Images Folder and then create a reference to this local version of the image on the current page.

Copying an image to the Local Site Folder

In fact, even if you haven't defined a Default Images Folder, Dreamweaver will still offer you a chance to manually copy the image into the Local Site Folder. Whenever you insert a graphic which is not located in the Local Site Folder of the active site, Dreamweaver displays a dialogue offering you the opportunity of saving this image in the current Local Site Folder. (See figure 6-5, on page 69.)

Whenever this message appears, you should always click the **Yes** button and save the image somewhere in the current Local Site Folder—or, better still, always ensure that you have specified a Default Images Folder.

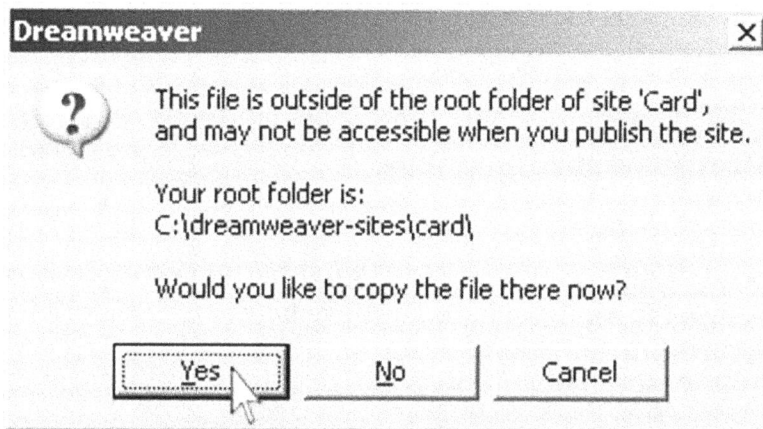

Figure 6-5: The dialog box displayed by Dreamweaver when an image is inserted from outside the Local Site Folder and no Default Images Folder has been specified

Image accessibility options

Whenever you add an image to a page, Dreamweaver will display the **Image Tag Accessibility Attributes** dialog.

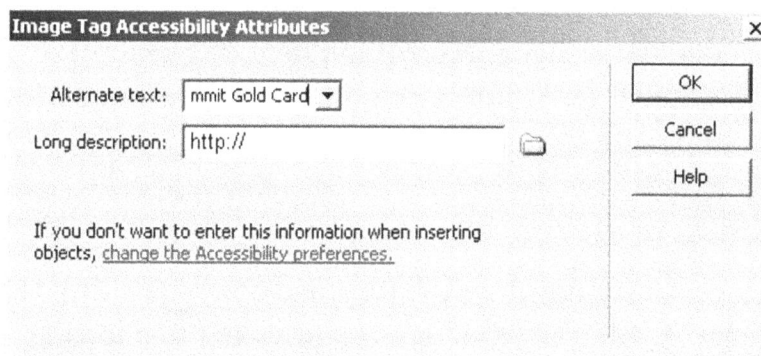

Figure 6-6: Whenever Dreamweaver's image accessibility options are displayed, you should get into the habit of entering a short description of the image in the alternate text box. This helps to make the image accessible to all your website visitors—not just those who can see it.

Alternate text

The key element in this dialog is the Alternate text (also known as alt text); this serves four main purposes.

- It is used by assistive devices to provide visually impaired users with a description of the image.

- If the user has switched off the display of images using their browser preferences, the alt tag is the only thing which will let them know what the image depicts.

- Some search engines use alt tags to gain information about the images on a web page.

- If a page is slow to load for any reason, the alt tag is temporarily displayed before the image eventually appears.

Alternate text should provide a succinct description of the image. If the image is really text saved as an image—for example, where your page needs text for some kind of special effect—the alt text should simply be the text that the image contains.

If the image is purely decorative and does not communicate information, the alt text should be set to "empty".

The Image Tag Accessibility Attributes dialog is not the only way of entering alternate text. You can edit the alt text value at any time by highlighting the image and modifying the value in the **Alt** field, in the HTML section of the Properties panel.

Long description

If the image contains a fairly complex subject or communicates a fair amount of information, it may not be possible to summarize its content in a short phrase. In this case, detailed information can be placed in a separate HTML file and a link to that file can be included in the **Long Description** field of Dreamweaver's Image Tag Accessibility Attributes dialog. Simply click on the **Browse** button (the folder icon), locate the file and double-click its name.

Image accessibility preferences

The Image Tag Accessibility Attributes dialog also contains a link to Dreamweaver's accessibility preferences. Clicking this link is equivalent to choosing **Edit > Preferences** (**Dreamweaver > Preferences** on a Mac) and then selecting the Accessibility category on the left of the Preferences dialog.

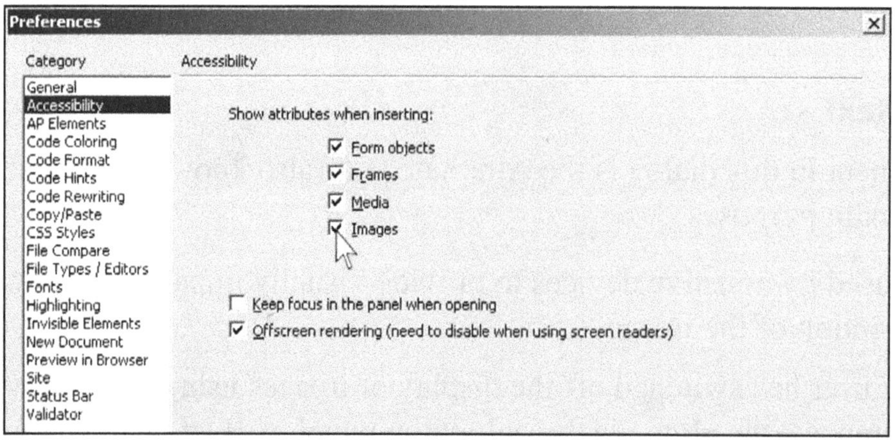

Figure 6-7: Activating image accessibility preferences

The accessibility options feature a series of check boxes headed **Show attributes when inserting**. As a general rule, it is convenient to keep the **Images** checkbox activated; but you may occasionally prefer to switch it off—for example, if you are involved in a project where someone has the job of subsequently checking all images and supplying the necessary alt tags and long descriptions.

Replacing an image

If you ever need to replace an existing image with a different one, simply double-click the existing image. A dialogue labelled Select Image Source appears. This is the same dialogue which appears when the **Insert > Image** command is used. Locate and double-click the replacement image, as per usual.

Another method of replacing an image is to use the **Point to file** button. This is the circular icon located on the right of the **Src** box (short for source) in the Properties panel. Simply drag the **Point to file** button onto the name of replacement image in the Files panel. (When using this technique, if the folder containing the image is closed, simply position the pointer over it and wait for the folder to automatically open.)

Using Placeholder images

When working on web pages, it is possible that some of the images you plan to use will not be ready. To add some semblance of completion to the page, Dreamweaver allows you to insert a placeholder image which can later be replaced when the actual graphic is ready.

Choose **Insert > Image Objects > Placeholder Image** and Dreamweaver displays the dialog box shown in figure 6-8, below.

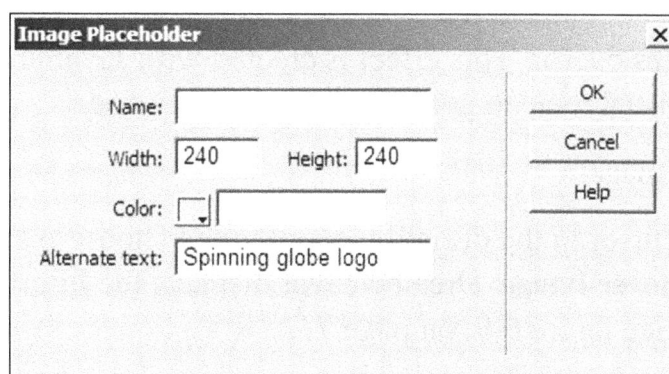

Figure 6-8: Setting options for a placeholder image

Setting the **Width** and **Height** of the placeholder image to match those of the final graphic will enable you to get a reasonable idea of the impact the graphic will have on the page, in terms of balance and layout.

As we saw earlier, it is also important to enter a short description of the image in the **Alternate text** field.

The Name field can normally be left blank. (It allows you to add a name and unique ID to an image which can be referenced by JavaScript and CSS.)

The Color option

It is probably best to avoid the **Color** option altogether. You might be tempted to choose a colour which gives a better representation of the actual image than that provided by the default grey. However, Dreamweaver adds the colour as the **background-color** attribute of the image, using an inline CSS rule; and, when the placeholder is replaced, it leaves this rule in place. This means that if you insert a GIF file with a transparent background, the colour used for the placeholder image will fill the transparent areas of the GIF!

If this does happen, follow these steps to fix the problem:

1. Click on the image to highlight it.

2. Click on the Code button in the top left of the document window to enter Dreamweaver's Code view.

3. Remove the style attribute by deleting the text:

    style="background-color: #FF0000"

(Naturally, **#FF0000** in the code above will be replaced by a hexadecimal number representing the actual colour you chose in the Image Placeholder dialog.)

Inserting rollover images

The term rollover image refers to the effect whereby an image changes appearance when the mouse passes over it. This effect is created with JavaScript. However, Dreamweaver uses visual tools to generate the necessary code.

To create a rollover image:

1. Position the cursor in the desired location; then choose **Insert > Interactive Images > Rollover Image**. Dreamweaver displays the Insert Rollover Image dialog box. (See figure 6-9, on page 73.)

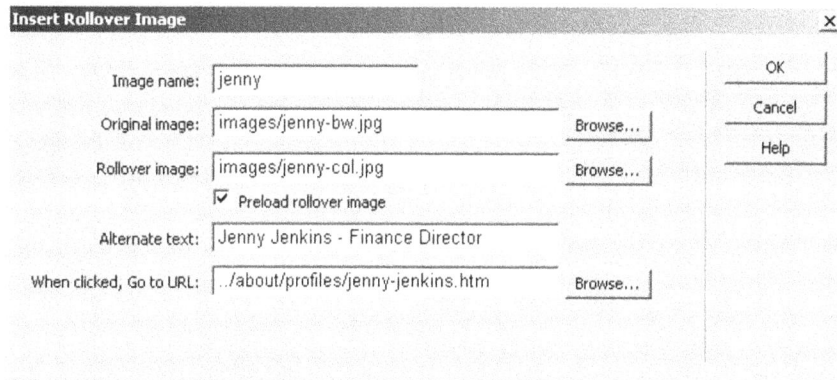

Figure 6-9: The Insert Rollover Image dialog.

2. Type in a name for the image.

3. Click the **Browse** button next to **Original Image**, then locate and double-click the appropriate image.

4. Do the same for **Rollover Image**.

5. Enter a short description of the image in the **Alternate text** box.

6. The final step is to create a hyperlink—either by clicking on the **Browse** button next to the option **When Clicked Go To URL**, then locating and double-clicking the target file; or, by entering a URL manually.

7. Creating Hyperlinks

Hyperlinks (also known as just plain links) are the lifeblood of the internet: they make accessing online information rapid, flexible and fun. Since a website is an integrated whole, it is very rare that you will need to create a page with no links on it. Each page will normally need to be connected to at least one, and more usually several, other page(s) within the site.

Links can be placed on text or images. In addition, they can be placed on hotspots within an image using an HTML feature called an image map.

There are several different types of hyperlink and Dreamweaver offers several different methods of creating them. In this chapter, we will look at the various types of hyperlink and how to create them.

The <a> element

In HTML, hyperlinks are created by wrapping the text or image inside an **<a>** element—where "a" is short for "anchor". Although Dreamweaver allows you to create links without having to type any code, it is useful to know this—particularly when you come to control the appearance of links, using CSS.

The **<a>** element is an inline element, since links often need to be slotted into the middle of a paragraph of text. (If it was a block element, the whole paragraph would always be treated as a single link.)

Types of link

As a web developer, the links that you will create can be broadly divided into the following categories:

- Links to your own web pages
- External links to other people's websites
- Links to email addresses
- Hotspot links using an image map
- Links to a specific location on a web page, as often seen on Frequently Asked Questions (FAQs) pages.

Creating links to your own web pages

When working in Design view, Dreamweaver offers two methods of creating hyperlinks:

- Using Insert > Hyperlink
- Using the Link box in the Properties panel

Using Insert > Hyperlink

To create a link using this method, highlight the text or image to which you would like to attach a hyperlink; then choose **Insert > Hyperlink**. Dreamweaver then displays the Hyperlink dialog box, which offers you a fairly comprehensive set of choices.

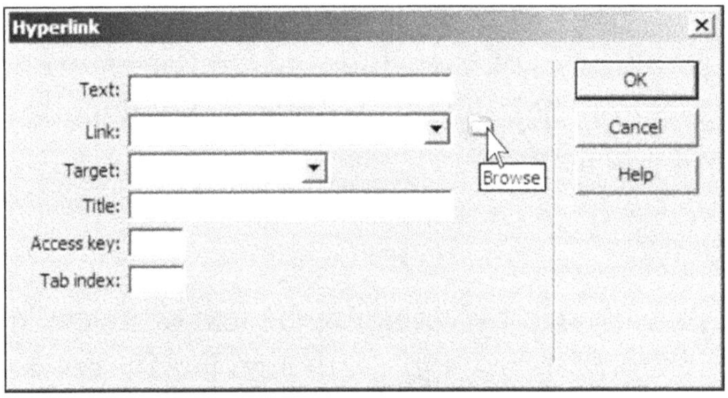

Figure 7-1: The Hyperlink dialog

Text

If you are attaching a link to highlighted text, the **Text** field displays the selected text; if you are attaching a link to an image, this field should be left blank.

Link

The Link box is where you enter the URL of the page that you wish to link to. You can either type the URL in the link box yourself or, to avoid the risk of errors, you can click on the **Browse** button (the yellow folder icon), locate the file and double-click its name.

Target

The target specifies the window in which the linked page will load. The options in the drop-down menu are reserved HTML terms which relate to framesets, an outmoded element which permits the display of several pages in different frames within the same browser window. The default (obtained by leaving this field blank) is that the linked page will load in the same window as the original. Choosing the option **_self** will produce the same result.

The only target option that is commonly used is **_blank**, which will cause the page to load in a separate window. This is useful when you are creating links to other people's websites, since it helps to minimise the risk that visitors will click on the link and not bother returning to your site.

Title

The **Title** attribute is (optionally) used to clarify the nature and purpose of a hyperlink—whenever clarification becomes necessary. For example, if you had a series of snippets on a listing page, each followed by hyperlinked text saying "More Info", you could use the title attribute to clarify the topic on which each link supplied more information.

Access key

The **Access Key** field allows you to enter a keyboard equivalent (consisting of a single letter) which can be used to select the link in the browser.

Tab index

The **Tab Index** field allows you to enter a number specifying the tab order in which hyperlinks can be selected via the keyboard.

Using the Properties panel

The **Link** box in the Properties may at first appear to be simply a subset of the **Hyperlinks** dialog. There is a field in which you can type the link yourself and a **Browse** button which allows you to navigate to the linked file and have Dreamweaver create the link for you. Also, the **Target** drop-down menu is located just below the Link box.

Using the Point to file button

However, there is one extra tool next to **Browse** button—a circular icon called the **Point to file** button; and it can be a big time-saver. (See figure 7-2, on page 78.)

To use the Point to file button:

1. If necessary, resize and reposition the Files panel and the document window until they are both visible next to each other.

2. Highlight the text you wish to convert into a hyperlink.

3. Drag the **Point to file** icon into the Files panel directly onto the file to be linked. As you drag, an arrow will appear stretching from the **Point to file** button to the document you drag to.

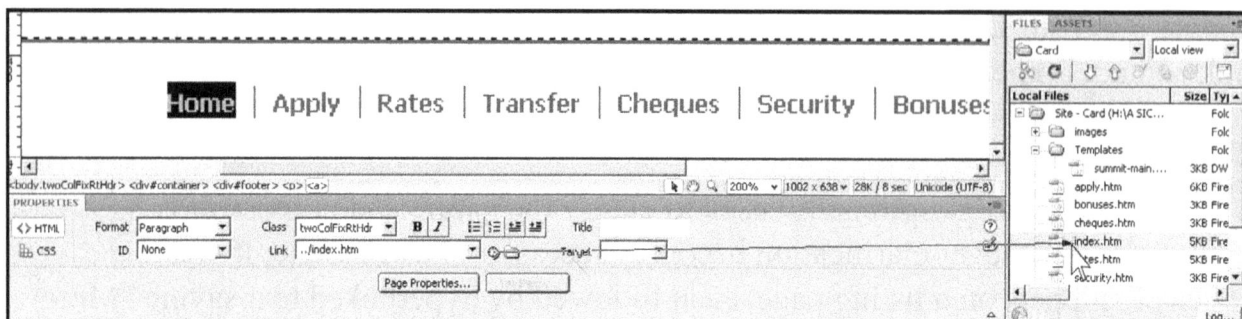

Figure 7-2: Using the Point to file button to create hyperlinks.

Needless to say, the **Point to file** and manual link creation techniques can also be used when attaching hyperlinks to images. Images which have been hyperlinked can normally be distinguished from other images by a border which appears around them in a colour which matches the link colour for that page.

Dreamweaver normally suppresses this border by automatically setting the border attribute of the **<img>** element to zero. To do this manually yourself, highlight the image then type a zero in the **Border** field of the Properties panel.

Creating links to other people's websites

To create links to an external website, use either the **Insert > Hyperlink** command or the Properties panel, as just described. Naturally, however, you cannot use the Browse or the **Point to file** buttons, since the page you are linking to is not located in your Local Site Folder. Instead, you must enter the link yourself in the link box, always making sure to start with "http://", for example:

http://www.trainingcompany.com

If you start the link merely with "www.", your link will not work when the page is uploaded to your server.

Setting the target to **_blank** is often a good idea when linking to external web pages. This is particularly true when linking to a large website like Adobe or Apple. Your visitors will always find plenty to interest them and may not bother to return to your site. By having the link open in a separate browser window or tab, your page remains available on their screen.

Creating email links

Email links can be created either by entering the URL in the Link box of the Properties panel or using the **Insert > Email Link** menu command.

Using Insert > Email Link

To use the menu command, highlight the text or graphic which you want to convert into a link and choose **Insert > Email Link**. If you are creating a text link, the highlighted text will appear in the **Text** field. If you are adding the link to an image, the **Text** field should be left blank.

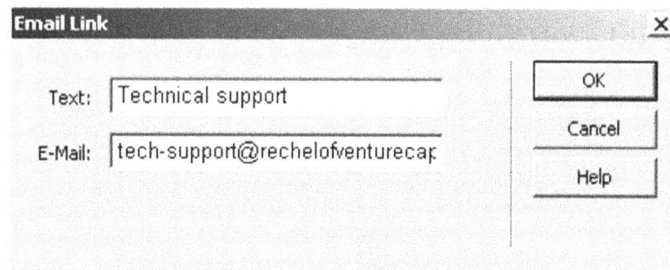

Figure 7-3: Creating an email link using Insert > Email Link

Sometimes, the text you want to appear on the page is the email address itself. If you highlight an email address and choose **Insert > Email Address**, Dreamweaver will (very intelligently) place the email address in both the **Text** and **E-mail** boxes. So all you need to do is click the **OK** button.

Using the Properties panel

To create an email link using the Properties panel, highlight the text or graphic and enter an email address in the **Link** box. However, this time, you must prefix the email address with **mailto:**, as shown in figure 7-4, below.

Figure 7-4: Creating an email link using the Properties panel

The **mailto:** prefix is required to distinguish the email link from a web link. (When you use **Insert > Email Link**, the **mailto:** is added to the code automatically, behind the scenes.)

Adding parameters to an email address

The following code (which should be written as one long string in the Link box of the Properties panel) will pre-populate the subject, cc (carbon copy) and body fields of the mail message, as shown in figure 7-5, below.

mailto:example1@trainingcompany.com?subject=Enquiry
&body=Please send me information on the following:
&cc= example2@trainingcompany.com

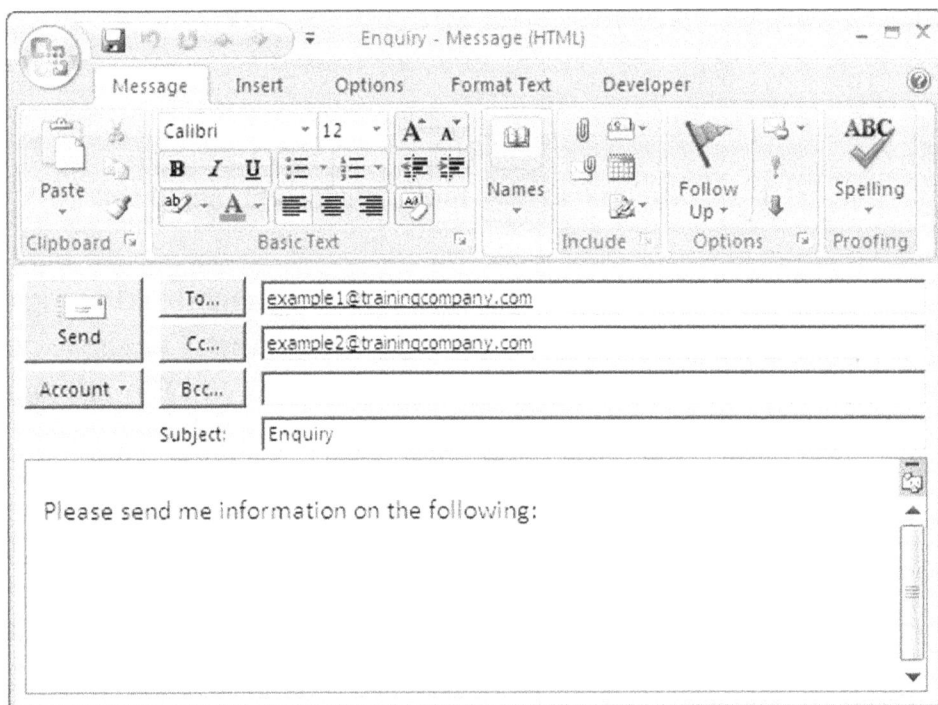

Figure 7-5: An Outlook message generated by an email link with parameters.

Creating an image map

An image map is a collection of invisible hotspots superimposed on an image each of which can have its own hyperlink and alternate text. Dreamweaver makes the creation of image maps really simple by providing drawing tools which become available in the Properties panel whenever an image is highlighted. The hotspots which comprise the image map can be rectangular, circular or polygonal and Dreamweaver provides a tool for each shape—just like a drawing program. There is also a selection tool for highlighting and modifying hotspots.

To create an image map

1. Select the image to which you want to attach the map.

2. Enter a name in the **Map** field on the left of the Properties panel.

3. Click on one of the hotspot tools: rectangle, circle or polygon.

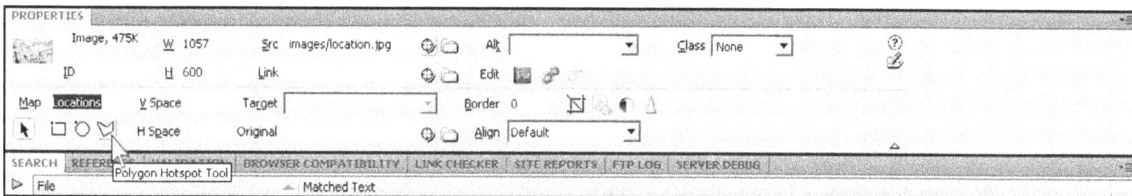

Figure 7-6: To create a hotspot, click on the tool which will generate the appropriate shape. The Polygon Hotspot Tool offers the most flexibility.

4. Draw the hotspot using the appropriate technique.

   • To draw a rectangle or circle: click, hold and drag over the part of the image you wish to encompass.

   • To draw a polygon: click and release; move the cursor to another point; click again; move again; click again; and so forth.

5. If the shape needs to be tweaked and modified, click on the Pointer hotspot tool. You can then drag a hotspot to move it or drag the anchor points to change the shape of the hotspot.

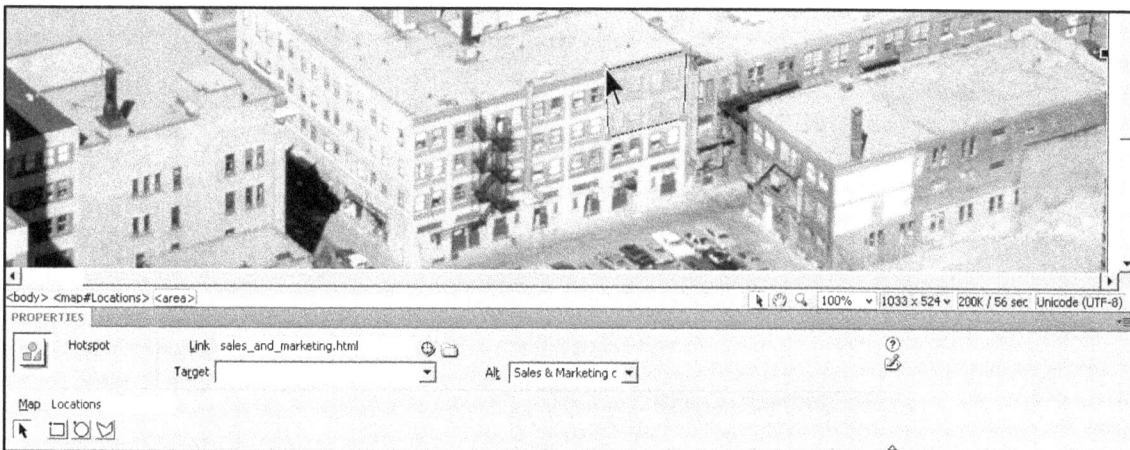

Figure 7-7: Using Pointer Hotspot tool to modify a polygonal hotspot.

Making hotspots accessible

As soon as you start to draw a shape, Dreamweaver displays a dialog reminding you to enter alternate text describing the part of the image under that particular hotspot.

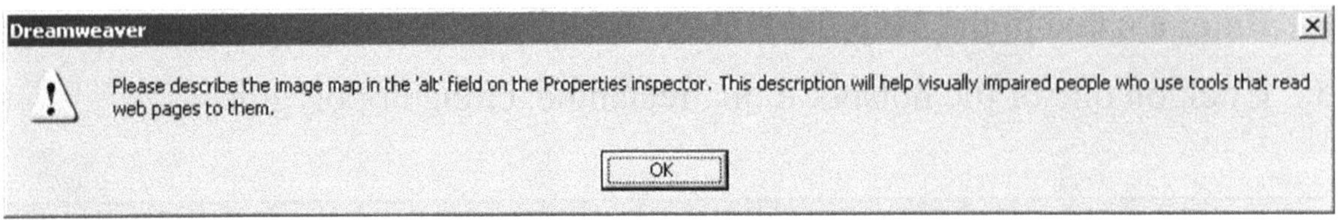

Figure 7-8: Dreamweaver's hotspot accessibility warning. Each hotspot you create should have its own alternate text, describing its content.

6. Specify the page or URL you would like the hotspot to link to.

7. If you would like the linked page to open in a new browser window, set the **Target** property to **_blank**.

8. In the **Alt** field, be sure to enter a description of the image content within the hotspot—not a general description of the image; just the bit under the hotspot.

9. To create other hotspots on the same image, simply repeat steps 3 to 8 above.

Using named anchors

Named anchors are destinations within an HTML page which can be targeted by hyperlinks—thus enabling web developers to create links to a specific point on a page. By far the most common use of this technique is to create a "Back to top" link. Another very common use is the creation of Frequently Asked Questions (FAQs) pages, where all the content is on the same page.

Using named anchors is always a two step procedure: first you create a named anchor at a given point on the page; then you create a hyperlink to that named anchor.

To create a named anchor

1. Position the cursor at the location that you want skip to.

2. Choose **Insert > Named anchor.**

Figure 7-9: Inserting a named anchor—a destination associated with a specific point on an HTML page to which a hyperlink can then be created.

3. Enter a name (without spaces or special characters) and click **OK**.

To create a link to a named anchor

1. Highlight the text what you wish to convert into a hyperlink.

2. Choose **Inert > Hyperlink**.

3. Click on the drop-down menu next to the Link field and choose the named anchor that you wish to link to. You will notice that each name is prefixed with a hash sign (#): this is a requirement in HTML.

Figure 7-10: The Insert Hyperlink dialog makes it easy to create a link to a named anchor. The Link field features a drop-down menu containing all the named anchors on the current page.

Try it for yourself!

In this **Try it for yourself** exercise, we will use named anchors to set up a typical Frequently asked questions page.

Setting up a new site

1. Choose **Site > New Site**.

2. Enter the name "SummitGold" in the **Site name** box.

3. Click on the **Browse for folder** button next to the Local Site Folder box.

4. Navigate to the root of the training folder and double-click on the folder called "card" to open it; then click on the **Select** button (Mac, **Choose** button).

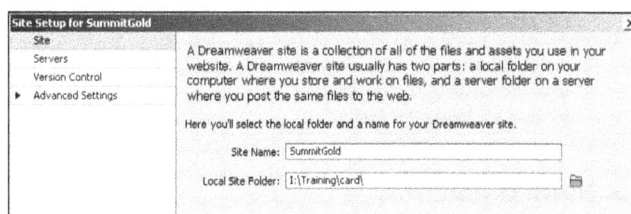

5. Click on the **Advanced Settings > Local Info** category, on the left of the Site Setup dialog.

6. Click on the **Browse for folder** icon next to the **Default images folder** box.

7. Open the "images" folder then click on the **Select** button (Mac, **Choose** button).

8. Click **Save** and then **Done** to complete the site setup.

The page structure of a typical FAQs page

9. In the Files panel, double-click on the file "faqs.htm" to open it.

You will notice that the (dummy) questions are arranged at the top of the page and are followed by the answers. Each answer is preceded by a repetition of the question. We need, firstly, to insert named anchor at the start of each answer; and, secondly, to convert each question at the top of the page into a hyperlink to the appropriate named anchor.

Each answer is also followed by a **Back to top** link. These links are all identical, since they all lead to the same point on the page. Hence, we will only need to create the link once; we can then **Copy** and **Paste** it as many times as required.

Creating a named anchor

10. Scroll down the page to the answers section.

11. Click to position the cursor immediately in front of the first answer.

12. Choose **Insert > Named Anchor**.

13. Enter the name "Question1" and click **OK**.

Creating a link with the Point to file button

Notice that Dreamweaver inserts a yellow marker to represent the (invisible) named anchor. This enables you to interact with the object in Design view—for example, you can create a link to the named anchor by dragging the nifty **Point to file** button onto the yellow marker.

1. Scroll back up to the top o the page and highlight the first question.

2. Leaving the text highlighted, scroll down the page to make the yellow marker visible.

3. In the Properties panel, drag the **Point to file** button onto the yellow marker representing the named anchor.

Dreamweaver inserts the link **#Question1** in the **Link** box of the Properties panel.

Using Insert > Hyperlink

1. Scroll down the page and click to position the cursor immediately in front of the second answer.

2. Choose **Insert > Named Anchor**.

3. Enter the name "Question2" and click **OK**.

4. Scroll back up to the top of the page and highlight the second question.

5. Choose **Insert > Hyperlink**.

6. Choose **#Question2** from the drop-down menu on the right of the **Link** box.

7. Create named anchors and links for the remaining questions, using your preferred method.

Creating the Back to top links

To create a **Back to top link**, we follow the same procedure; just making sure that, when we insert the named anchor, it is the first element on the page.

1. In the Tag selector—in the bottom left of the document window, click on the **<body>** tag to highlight everything on the page.

2. Press the left cursor key on your keyboard (<--).

3. Choose **Insert > Named Anchor**.

4. Enter the name "top" and click **OK**.

5. Scroll down the page and highlight the first occurrence of "Back to top".

6. Choose **Insert > Hyperlink**.

7. Choose **#top** from the drop-down menu on the right of the **Link** box.

8. Highlight the link you have just created and choose **Edit > Copy**.

9. Highlight the next occurence of "Back to top"—the one that follows the answer to question 2.

10. Choose **Edit > Paste** to replace the plain text with the hyperlinked version.

11. Repeat steps 9 and 10, as necessary to convert all occurrences of "Back to top" into hyperlinks.

And that's it!

12. Press F12 (Mac: Option F12) to preview the page in your primary browser and test out the links.

8. Tables

HTML tables were once extensively used for page layout, since the inherent grid structure of a table offered a useful mechanism for accurately positioning elements within the browser window. The problem with this approach was in the code it generated: copious and hard to maintain, it entangled the actual content of the page, making it hard for search engines to find and for screen readers to navigate.

Table-based web page layout is now a thing of the past and has been replaced with CSS-based layout, which allows the separation of content from presentation and is a much more efficient approach all round. However, tables are still an important element in web development—only, now, they are only used for the purpose for which they have always been intended; namely, the display of any information which lends itself to tabular presentation.

In this chapter, we will look at how tables are created; how to import tabular data; and how to modify the structure of a table. We will end the chapter with a practical exercise on creating a table and controlling its appearance with CSS.

Creating a table

To create a table, choose **Insert > Table**, make your choices in the Table dialog then click OK. The table dialog contains three sections: **Table Size**, **Header** and **Accessibility**.

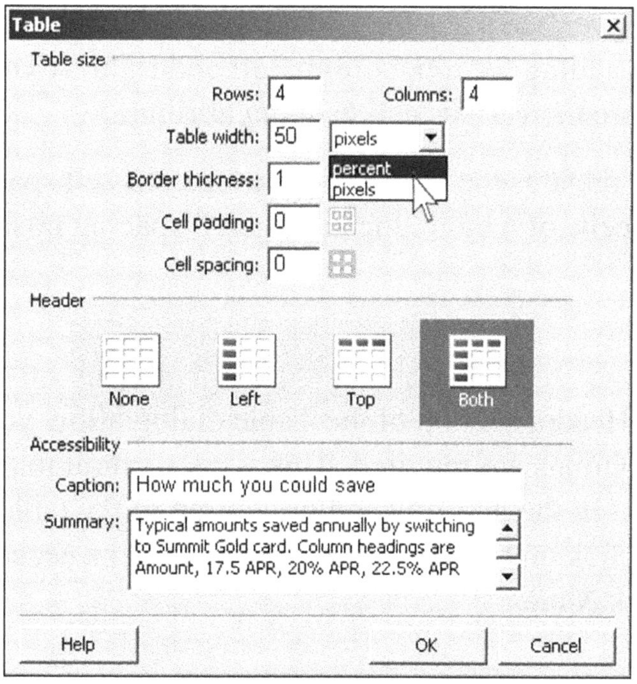

Figure 8-1: The Table dialog

Table size

Rows/Columns

Enter the number of rows and columns required—if you know in advance. However, Dreamweaver makes it easy to add and delete rows and columns at a later stage.

Table width

In HTML, table widths can be expressed in absolute or relative terms—using either pixels or percentages, respectively. Using pixels allows you to fix the layout of the table and present your data in a predictable fashion. If you use a percentage, e.g. 50%, this will make the table shrink or expand to fit 50% of the space available in its container (usually a DIV element).

These two methods of expressing widths also apply to page layout as a whole and the method used for page layout will often dictate the method used for describing table widths.

Border thickness

The **Border thickness** box allows you to specify whether the internal and external borders of the table will be visible, by entering a width in pixels. If you want the table borders to be hidden (and only its contents visible), enter a value of zero.

Cell padding/ Cell spacing

Cell padding is used to specify the internal margin of the cells in a table, the space between the text and the edge of the cell. It offers similar result to using the padding attribute in CSS. However, CSS has the advantage of allowing you to specify different amounts of padding for top, bottom, left and right. If you plan to use CSS padding, you can ignore the HTML cell padding attribute.

Whereas cell padding dictates the space inside each cell, cell spacing is the amount of space between the cells of a table. Increasing cell spacing pushes cells apart and makes them smaller.

Header

The four icons in the Header section of the Table dialog allow you to specify whether header rows and/or columns are required. This is a structural matter rather than a stylistic one. If the text in the first row and/or column of the table represents headings rather than data then click on the **Left**, **Top** or **Both** icon, as necessary: if the table has no headings, then click **None**.

Accessibility

Dreamweaver's Table dialog offers two fields in the **Accessibility** section: **Caption** and **Summary**.

Caption

The table caption is visible in the browser window and should provide a brief description of the nature of the table.

Summary

Unlike the caption, the summary is an attribute of the **<table>** element and is not visible. Its primary role is to provide a description of the table and its structure to assistive devises such as screen readers and should therefore always be supplied.

Importing tabular data

If the data you want displayed in a table already exists, Dreamweaver allows you to import it, either via the clipboard or from disk.

Copying and pasting from Excel

To import tabular data from and Excel or Word, you can simply highlight and copy the data in the original program, switch over to Dreamweaver and choose **Edit > Paste**. Dreamweaver will normally paste the data as a table, ignoring any stylistic attributes which were attached to the table in the other environment.

To dictate more precisely how Dreamweaver Pastes in the tabular data, you can also use **Edit > Paste Special**.

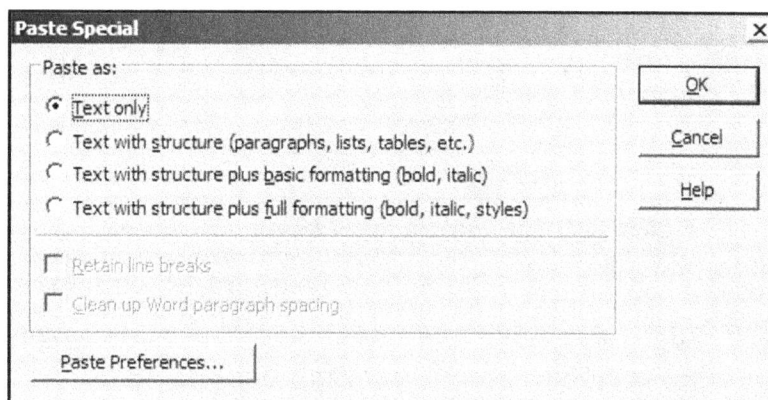

Figure 8-2: The Paste Special dialogue box

- The **Text only** option will ignore the tabular nature of the data and Paste everything as one paragraph.

- **Text with structure** will Paste the data as a simple table with CSS styling.

- **Text with structure plus basic formatting** will Paste a table with bold and italic text preserved. This is achieved using **<strong>** and **<em>** tags, respectively.

- **Text with structure plus full formatting** will reproduce the styling of the original Excel spreadsheet or Word table using embedded CSS. Dreamweaver will create class styles with names like "Excel1", "Excel2", etc.

As a general rule, **Text with structure** is the most convenient option. The table can then be styled using your own CSS rules rather then those automatically created and named by Dreamweaver.

Importing Excel files from disk

Copying and pasting is often the best way of grabbing Excel data because you are able to highlight exactly those cells which contain the information you want to import. However, since not everyone has Excel, Dreamweaver also allows you to import Excel files from disk. Simply choose **File > Import > Excel Document**.

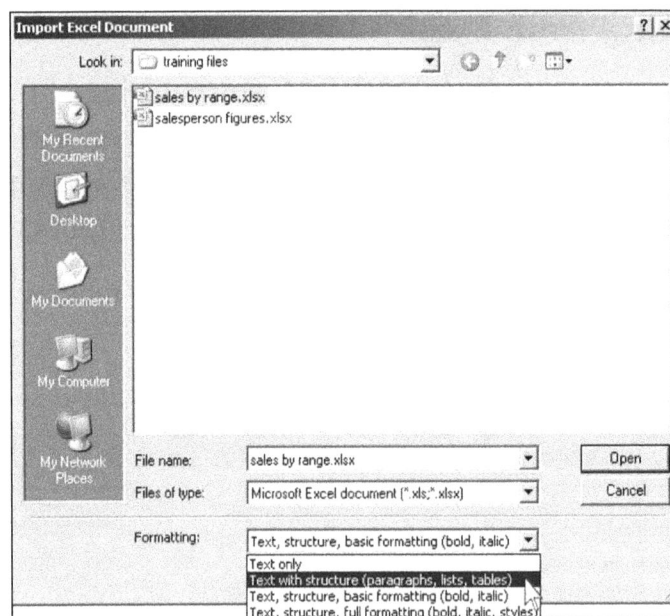

Figure 8-3: The Import Excel Document dialog

At the bottom of the Import Excel Document dialog, the **Formatting** drop-down allows you to choose between the same formatting options found in the **Paste Special** dialog.

Dreamweaver imports the entire Excel worksheet as a single table. If the Excel file contains several worksheets, it only imports the first one.

Importing delimited data from disk

In addition to importing Excel files, Dreamweaver also has the ability to import any delimited file—tab-delimited and comma-delimited being the two most popular types. To use this facility, choose **File > Import > Tabular Data**.

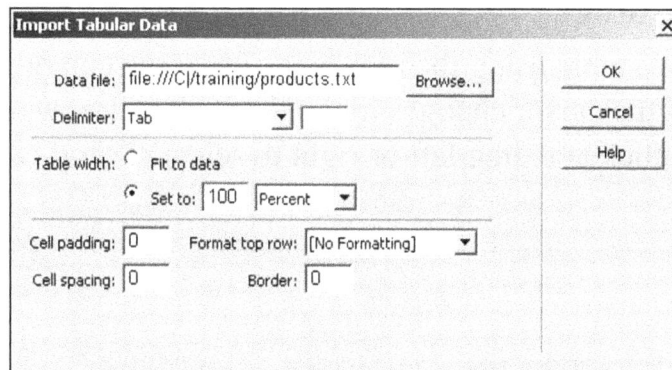

Figure 8-4: The Import Tabular Data dialog

- Click on the **Browse** button, locate the file and double-click or manually enter the file path in **Data File** box.

- Specify the delimiter used in the file you are importing. The delimiter is the character used to mark the end of each column of data. Either choose an option from the **Delimiter** drop-down menu or enter a character in the adjacent text field.

- Next, in the **Table Width** section, you can optionally specify the width you want for the table. If you choose Fit to Data, the table width will be unspecified and determined solely by its contents. Alternatively, you can choose the **Set to** option and specify a width for the table using either pixels or percentage as the unit of measurement.

- You can also specify the cell padding, cell spacing and border width, just as you can when using **Insert > Table**.

- You should avoid using the **Format Top Row** drop-down menu since the **Bold** and **Italic** options cause Dreamweaver to place <b> (bold) and <i> (italic) tags around each heading. These tags are now deprecated in HTML; it would be more useful if Dreamweaver offered you the chance to turn the top row into header rows as it does when you use **Insert > Table**.

Manipulating tables

If you are using tables, it is almost certain that you will need to chop and change your original table design from time to time. So, let's look at some of the techniques you will need to master, beginning with techniques for selecting elements within a table.

Selecting tables

There are four main techniques for making selections within tables: clicking and dragging on table elements; using the Tag Selector; using the Table Widths; and using the **Control-a** (Mac, **Command-a**) keyboard shortcut.

Clicking and dragging

To select a column in a table using the mouse, position the cursor directly at the top of the column. When the cursor changes into a thick black arrow, either click once to select the column or click and drag left or right to select several columns.

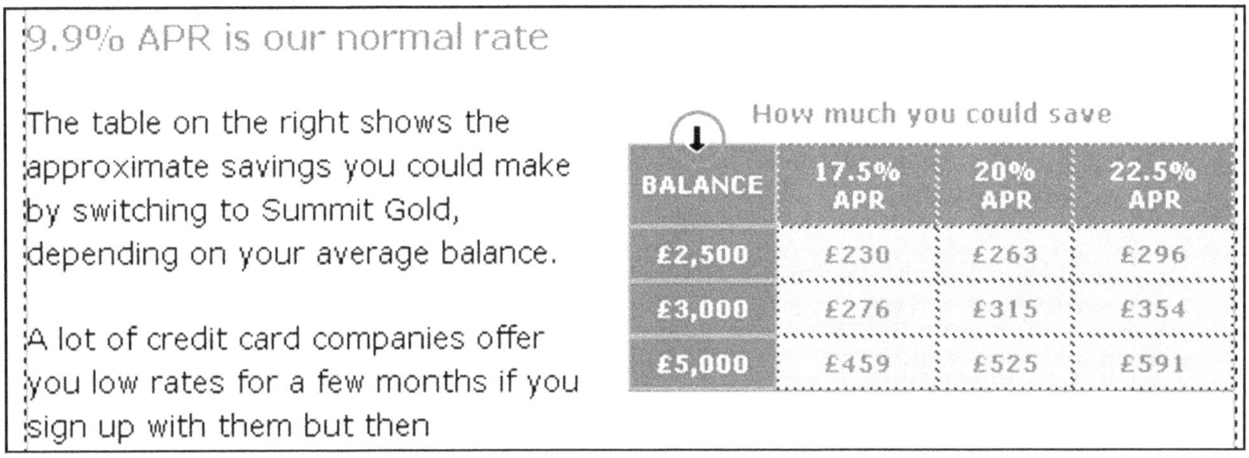

Figure 8-5: Selecting columns with the mouse requires dexterity and patience!

Rows can also be selected in a similar manner; this time, the cursor must be placed on the left edge of the row. The only problem with this technique is that you have to position the cursor in exactly the right place before it changes. You may, for this reason, decide that it's more trouble than its worth.

A simpler way of making selections within a table is to drag across the cells that you wish to select. To select a row or column, just drag across all of the cells it contains.

To select an entire table using the mouse, simply click once on its bottom or right border. When clicking and dragging with the mouse, there is always the danger of inadvertently changing table dimensions. The other three methods of making selections—which we will examine shortly—all avoid this risk.

Selecting non-contiguous cells

It is also possible to select a non-contiguous range of cells (cells which are not adjacent to each other) by holding down the Control key on Windows (or the Command key on Mac) while clicking on each of the cells you wish to highlight.

Using the Tag Selector

The Tag Selector is located in the bottom left of the document window and displays the hierarchy of tags associated with the currently selected item. It is particularly useful for selecting table cells which contain images.

To select a table cell containing an image using the Tag Selector, first click on the image to select it. The last four tags displayed on the Tag Selector will then be **<table>**, **<tr>**, **<td>** and **<img>**. (If there is a hyperlink attached to the image, the tags would be **<table>**, **<tr>**, **<td>**, **<a>** and **<img>**.) To select the cell, click on the **<td>** tag. ("td" stands for table data and represents the cell containing the image; "img" is of course the tag which represents the image.)

Figure 8-6: Using the Tag Selector to highlight a table cell containing an image

As well as the name of the tag, the Tag Selector also displays any CSS styles associated with the element. Thus, in figure 8-6, the Tag Selector shows:

<table.tgreen1> <tr> <td.tgreen5> <a>

indicating that a class style called "tgreen1" has been applied to the table and a class named "tgreen5" to the table cell.

The Tag Selector can be used to select a single table cell, a table row or the entire table. To select a cell, click a **<td>** tag; to select a row, click a **<tr>** tag; and click the **<table>** tag to highlight the entire table.

The Tag Selector does not enable you to select columns or multiple cells (apart from every cell in a particular row).

Using Table Widths

Table Widths is a visual aid offered by Dreamweaver which displays useful information about the table and provides options for making table selections. To activate or deactivate this feature, choose **View > Visual Aids > Table Widths**.

When Table Widths is active, each time you highlight any part of a table, a green bar is displayed above the table consisting of two rows. The top row displays the width of the entire table and the second row displays the width of each column.

If the width of the table or column has been expressed in pixels, Dreamweaver displays the width then shows the equivalent width as a percentage in brackets. If the width has been expressed as a percentage, the width shown will be followed by a percent sign and the equivalent pixel width will be shown in brackets. (If no widths have been entered for a table or column, no figure is displayed.)

Next to each width, a tiny arrow is displayed; which, when clicked, displays a drop-down menu allowing you to select the table or column. (See figure 8-7, below.) The menus also allow you to clear any widths and heights associated with the table or column as well as insert rows and columns. It does not, however, allow you to work with the rows in a table.

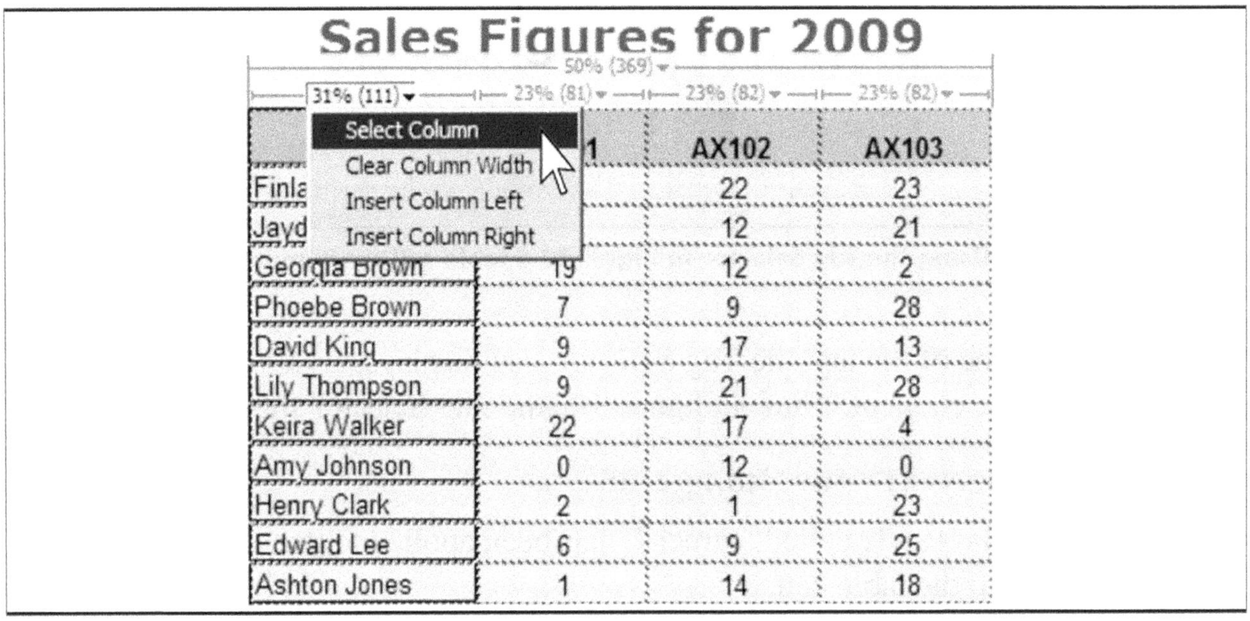

Figure 8-7: Using Column Widths to select a table column

Using the Control-a keyboard shortcut

Control-a (**Command-a** on Mac) is a universal keyboard shortcut for the **Select All** command found in the **Edit** menu of most software programs. When working with tables in Dreamweaver, this keyboard shortcut allows you to select first the active table cell and then the entire table.

Say you are entering text in a cell and type **Control-a**, the active cell will be selected. Type **Control-a** a second time and the entire table will be selected.

Inserting and deleting rows and columns

The options for inserting and deleting rows and columns can be found either by choosing **Modify > Table** or by right-clicking in a table cell and choosing **Table** from the context menu.

The **Insert Row** and **Insert Column** options will insert a row above, or a column to the left of, the active cell. **Insert Rows or Columns** offers the most flexibility, as it displays a dialog box which allows you to choose whether to insert **Rows** or **Columns** and whether they should be **Above/Below** or to the **Left/Right** of **the Selection**.

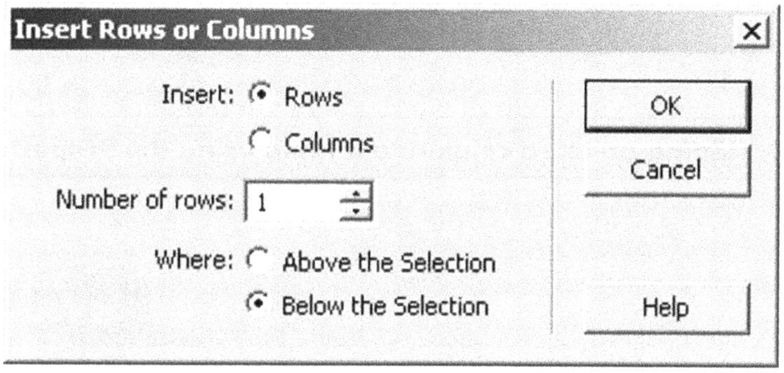

Figure 8-8: The Insert Rows or Columns dialog

The Table Widths column drop-down menu also contains options for inserting columns to the left or right of the current column. (See figure 8-7, on page 94.) You can also add a row to the bottom of a table by highlighting the bottom right cell of the table and pressing the Tab key—the old Microsoft Word trick.

As well as using **Modify > Table > Delete Row/Column** to delete rows and columns, you can also simply highlight the row(s) or column(s) to be deleted and then press the Delete key on your keyboard.

One final trick: if you want to add or delete rows or columns at the end of the table, simply select the table and modify the **Rows** and **Cols** boxes in the Properties panel as required. Enter a new figure in either the **Rows** or **Cols** boxes—or both, then press the Enter key. Increase the current number to add rows at the bottom or columns on the right; decrease the number to delete rows from the bottom or columns from the right.

Figure 8-9: Adding an extra column to a table using the Properties panel

Try it for yourself!

In this walk-through exercise, we will be creating the table shown below, controlling its position and appearance using CSS.

If the **SummitGold** site is not your current site, then choose **SummitGold** from drop-down menu in the top left of the Files panel to switch back to that site.

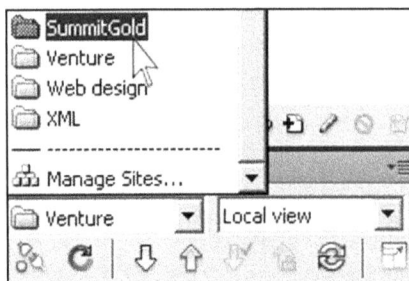

Inserting the table

1. In the Files panel, double-click on the file "rates.htm" to open it.

2. Position the cursor immediately following the heading " 9.9% APR is our normal rate".

3. Choose **Insert > Table**.

4. Set both the number of both **Rows** and **Columns** to 4.

5. Set the Table width property to **50 percent**.

6. Set the **Border** thickness to 1.

7. Set both the **Cell Padding** and **Cell Spacing** properties to zero.

8. In the **Header** section, click on **Both**.

9. In the **Accessibility** section, enter the **Caption** "How much you could save".

10. Finally, in the **Summary** box, enter the text: "Typical amounts saved annually by switching to Summit Gold card. Column headings are Balance, 17.5% APR, 20% APR, 22.5% APR. Row headings are 2500, 3000 and 5000."

11. Click **OK** then enter the information shown below into the table.

Styling the table

We will now create three CSS styles to format and position the table: one to control the table itself; one to format the header row and column; and one to format the body rows. Since we do not necessarily want all our tables formatted in the same way, let's create a class rule for the **<table>** element.

Creating a class rule for the table

1. Choose **New** from the drop-down menu in the top right of the CSS Styles panel.

2. Set the **Selector Type** to **Compound**.

3. In the **Selector Name** field, enter the name **table.tableright**.

4. Click **OK**.

By prefixing the name with "table", we are stipulating that this class can only apply to the **<table>** element. If we had simply called it **.tableright**, it could be applied to any element.

5. Click on the **Box** category on the left of the CSS Rule Definition dialog.

6. Set the **Float** property to **Right**.

7. In the **Margin** section, set the **Left** margin to "20 px" and the **Bottom** to "10 px".

8. Click on the **Border** category.

9. Set the **Type** property to **Solid**.

10. Set the **Width** to "1 px".

11. Set the **Color** to "#BC3961", which matches the navigation buttons used on this page.

12. Click **OK**.

Apply the class to the table

13. Click anywhere in the table.

14. In the Tag Selector, click on the **<table>** tag to cleanly select the entire table.

15. In the Properties panel, choose **tableright** from the **Class** drop-down menu.

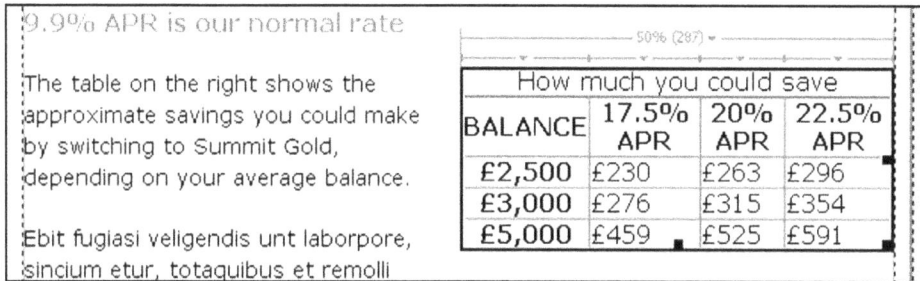

The table should now float to the right and display a border.

Creating a CSS rule for the table caption

16. Choose **New** from the drop-down menu in the top right of the CSS Styles panel.

17. Set the **Selector Type** to **Compound (based on your selection)**.

18. Set the **Selector Name** to **table.tableright caption**.

19. Click **OK**.

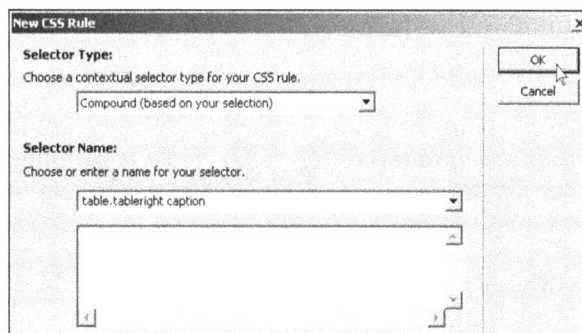

20. In the **Type** category of the CSS Rule Definition dialog, set the **Font-size** property to "0.9 em".

21. Set the **Font-weight** property to **bold**.

22. Set the **Color** to "# BC3961"—the same colour we used for the table border.

23. Click on the Box category.

24. In the **Margin** section, switch off the **Same for all** setting and change the **Bottom** margin property to "5 px".

25. Click OK.

The table should now look like this.

9.9% APR is our normal rate

The table on the right shows the approximate savings you could make by switching to Summit Gold, depending on your average balance.

Ebit fugiasi veligendis unt laborpore, sincium etur, totaquibus et remolli

How much you could save

BALANCE	17.5% APR	20% APR	22.5% APR
£2,500	£230	£263	£296
£3,000	£276	£315	£354
£5,000	£459	£525	£591

Creating a CSS rule for the header cells

When we created the table, we specified that both the first column and first row would be headers.

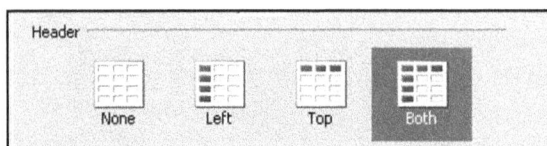

What this means, in HTML terms, is that these cells will use the **<th>** element—table header; while the other cells will use **<td>**—"table data". Therefore, to format the header cells, we simply need to create a CSS rule targeting all **<th>** elements inside **<table>** elements of the **tableright** class.

If you are new to web development and are asking: "How am I supposed to know that kind of thing?"; remember our old friend the Tag Selector—in the bottom left of the document window. When you need to style an element on the page and you are unsure of its name, just highlight the element and look at the Tag Selector. The last tag listed will be the name of the element.

26. Choose **New** from the drop-down menu in the top right of the CSS Styles panel.

27. Set the **Selector Type** to **Compound**.

28. Set the **Selector Name** to **table.tableright th**.

29. Click **OK**.

30. In the **Type** category of the CSS Rule Definition dialog, set the **Font-size** property to "0.7 em".

31. Set the **Font-weight** to **Bold**.

32. Set the **Color** to "#FFF" (by choosing white from the pop-up palette).

33. Click on the **Background** category.

34. Set the **Background-color** to "#BC3961".

35. Click on the **Box** category.

36. Set the **Padding** property to "6 px", leaving the **Same for all** box checked.

37. Click **OK**.

Creating a CSS rule for the body cells

Finally, to format the body cells of the table, we need to create a CSS rule targeting all **<td>** elements inside **<table>** elements of the **tableright** class.

38. Choose **New** from the drop-down menu in the top right of the CSS Styles panel.

39. Set the **Selector Type** to **Compound**.

40. Set the **Selector Name** to **table.tableright td**.

41. Click **OK**.

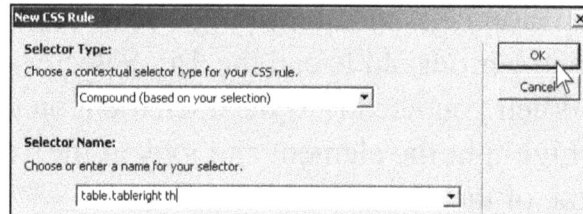

42. In the **Type** category of the CSS Rule Definition dialog, set the **Font-size** property to "0.7 em".

43. Set the **Font-weight** to **Bold**.

44. Set the **Color** to "#BC3961".

45. Click on the **Background** category.

46. Set the **Background-color** property to "#F2D7DF"—a lighter tint of the "#BC3961" colour we used for the text.

47. Click on the **Box** category.

48. Set the **Padding** property to "6 px", leaving the **Same for all** box checked.

49. Click OK.

That completes the table.

50. Press F12 (Mac: Option F12) to preview the page in your primary browser. It should look like this.

9. CSS Page Layout

So far, we have mainly encountered CSS page layout via the preset layouts provided by Dreamweaver. In this chapter, we will look at the nuts and bolts of using CSS to position your page content.

DIV Roles

As we have seen from our examination of Dreamweaver's CSS layouts, page content is normally placed inside DIV elements rather than directly on the page. Several DIVs are normally required to build the page, each performing a certain role within the layout.

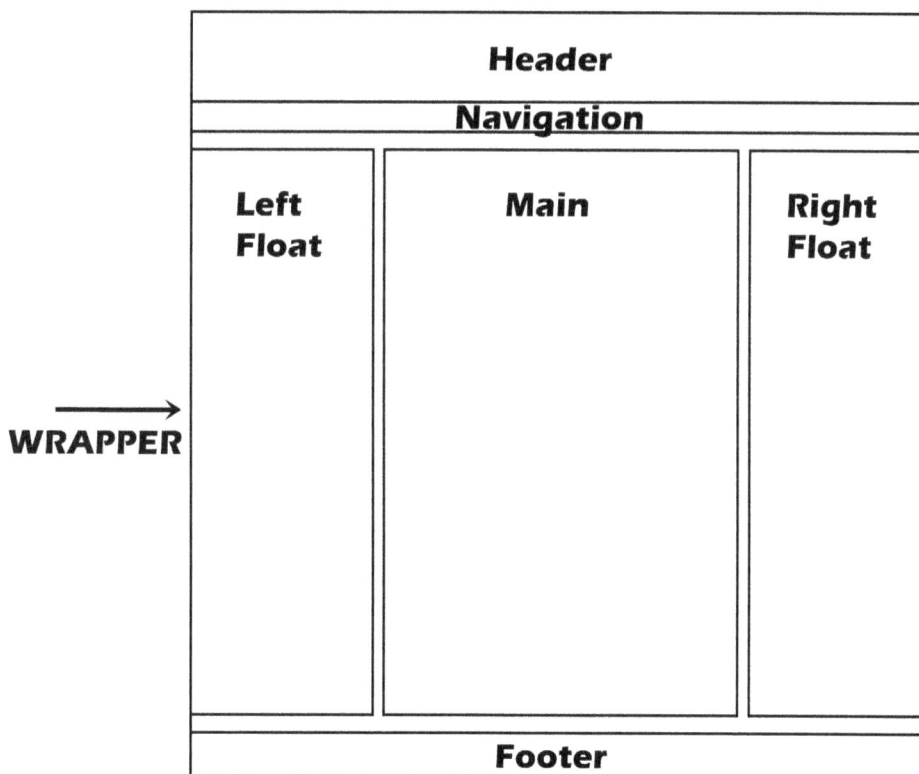

Figure 9-1: Each DIV in a CSS Page Layout performs a specific role

The wrapper DIV

This is the DIV which contains all the other DIVs within the layout. Designers use it to give an overall shape to the entire page by providing it with two key attributes: a width and position within the browser (left, right, or centre). In the Dreamweaver layouts, this DIV is always named **container**.

The header DIV

Most web pages benefit from having a header at the top of the page with key branding information like a logo, banner, slogan, phone number, etc. This can all be placed in the header DIV which is normally the first DIV to be placed inside the wrapper. In the Dreamweaver layouts, this DIV is always named **header**.

The Main DIV

The Main DIV is where you will place the bulk of the page content—the important stuff. Each page within a site will have unique content in this area, whereas the content in some of the peripheral DIVs, such as headers and footers, may be similar or even identical for many pages. In the Dreamweaver layouts, this DIV is always named **content**.

Left and Right Floating DIVs

Having a DIV floating to the left or right of the main content creates what is commonly referred to as a two column layout. Having one DIV floating to the left of the main content DIV and another on the right creates a three column layout—as shown in figure 9-1, on page 103. In the Dreamweaver layouts, these DIVs are always named **sidebar1** (left) and **sidebar2** (right).

The terms "two column" and "three column" are really misnomers in that they imply two or three columns of equal weight—which is not usually the case. The main DIV is normally the principal column, with the other two containing supplementary material such as links, headlines and promotional matter. (This is a trend rather than a rule—and, in any case, perhaps with the advent of paper thin monitors, designers will start creating web page layouts which mimic newspaper columns and we'll be able to hold our folded monitor in one hand and a beer in the other!)

The footer DIV

The footer DIV, if used, will typically contain information such as a copyright notice and secondary links. In the Dreamweaver layouts, this DIV is always named **footer**.

The navigation DIV

Another common use for a DIV is to act as a horizontal navigation bar containing links to the key pages in a given site. The Dreamweaver layouts do not include a horizontal navigation DIV.

Creating your own CSS layouts

To create your own CSS layout, you should begin by creating a CSS file which will hold all the rules required to control and position your page content. Each HTML page that uses this layout can then be linked to this page. (If you need a reminder of how to do this, see Chapter 5: CSS Essentials—page 58—for a description of how to create a CSS file and link an HTML page to it.)

Inserting DIV elements

When creating a hierarchy of DIVs, you need to be able to ensure that each new DIV you create is going in the right place. For this reason working in either Code or Split view is often useful. When working in Design View, it is sometimes difficult to see what's going on—though , as usual, Dreamweaver does give you some help.

To insert a DIV, position the cursor in the required location and choose **Insert > Layout Objects > DIV tag**. The **Insert DIV Tag** dialog appears.

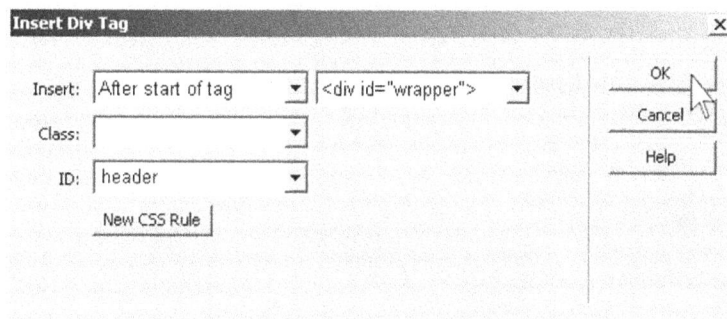

Figure 9-2: The two drop-down menus at the top of the Insert DIV Tag dialog allow you to specify the location of the DIV you are creating, in relation to existing elements on the page.

The two **Insert** drop-down menus at the top of the dialog help you to ensure that the DIV you are inserting ends up in the right place. From the first drop-down, you choose where you would like the new DIV to go in relation to the DIV specified on the second drop-down—which automatically displays a list of all of the DIVs on the page, as well as the **<body>** element.

Assigning IDs and classes to a DIV

Each DIV that you create can be assigned either with an ID or a class. IDs should be assigned to DIVs which are unique to each page; DIVs which may be repeated on the page should be associated with a CSS class. For example, in the preceding section, each of the DIVs mentioned (container, header, etc.) performs a unique function within the page layout and will therefore normally only occur once on each page.

When this is the case, the DIV is normally assigned an ID. If we were creating a DIV which is designed to contain an image and a caption, we would assign it a class name, so that we can use it as many times as required on each page.

You will notice that the DIVs in the Dreamweaver CSS layouts are all identified by class names rather than IDs. This choice was made so as to offer users the flexibility of using some DIVs more than once on the same page.

Creating a CSS rule

The Insert DIV Tag dialog also contains a button which enables you to create a CSS rule for the DIV straightaway. Although this is convenient, it has one drawback: if you use this feature, the DIV will not have been created when you are defining your rule. This means that you will not be able to click on the **Apply** button to get a preview of what the DIV will look like.

Try it for yourself!

Time for some practice! In this exercise, we'll create a basic CSS layout consisting of four DIVs: a wrapper, a header, a main section and a footer.

Creating a new site

1. Choose **Site > New**.
2. In the Site Setup dialog, enter the name "**Chapter 9**".
3. Click on the **Browse** button next to Local Site Folder, locate and double-click the **Chapter09** folder then click **Select**.
4. Click on the **Advanced Settings > Local Info** category, on the left of the Site Setup dialog.
5. Click on the **Browse for folder** icon next to the **Default images folder** box.
6. Locate and double-click the **images** folder inside the **Chapter09** folder—or highlight the folder then click **Select**, or **Choose** on a Mac.

7. Click **OK** to close the Site Setup window.

Creating the CSS page

8. Right-click in the Files panel and choose **File > New** from the context menu.

9. Enter the file name **styles.css**.

10. Create a second file in the same way; this time, enter the name **layout1.htm**.

Linking the HTML page to the CSS file

11. In the Files panel, double-click the file **layout1.htm** to open it.

12. In the CSS Styles panel (**Window > CSS Styles**), choose **Attach Style Sheet** from the panel menu.

13. Click on the **Browse** button; locate the file **styles.css** and double-click its name.

14. Choose **All** from the **Media** pop-up menu then click **OK**.

Creating the wrapper DIV

15. From the main menu bar, choose **Insert > Layout Objects > Div Tag**.

16. In the **ID** field, enter the name **wrapper**.

17. Click **OK** to create the DIV element.

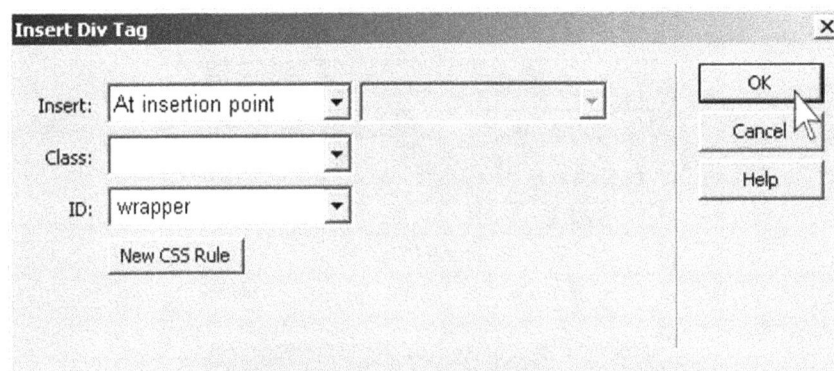

Creating a rule for the wrapper DIV

18. Choose **New** from the CSS Styles panel menu.

19. From the **Selector Type** drop-down menu, choose **ID**.

20. Enter the name **#wrapper** into the **Selector Name** field.

21. Choose **styles.css** (the css file you created earlier) from the **Rule Definition** drop-down menu at the bottom of the dialog.

22. Click **OK**.

23. Click on the **Box** category on the left of the CSS Rule Definition dialog.

24. Enter a **width** of "760 px" (pixels). We do not need to enter a height, since the height of the DIV will be determined by its content.

25. Set the **Padding** to zero all round.

26. In the **Margins** section, uncheck the **Same for all** checkbox then set the **Left** and **Right** margins to **auto**. This will align the DIV to the centre of the browser window.

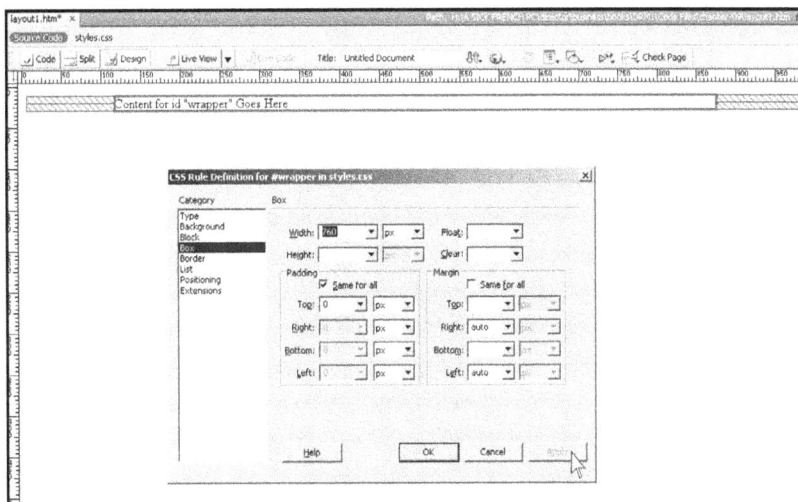

27. Click the **Apply** button to see the effect of those settings on the wrapper DIV.

28. Click **OK**.

Creating the header DIV

29. Delete the placeholder text which Dreamweaver placed inside wrapper DIV ('Content for id "wrapper" Goes Here').

30. Choose **Insert > Layout Objects > Div Tag**.

31. In the Insert section, choose **After tag** and **<div id="wrapper">** from the two drop-down menus.

32. In the **ID** field, enter the name **header**.

33. Click **OK** to create the DIV element.

```
Insert Div Tag                                          [x]
                                                    OK
  Insert:  After start of tag   ▼   <div id="wrapper">  ▼
                                                  Cancel
  Class:                         ▼
                                                   Help
    ID:  header                  ▼

          New CSS Rule
```

Creating a rule for the header DIV

34. In the Tag Selector, click **<div#header>** to select the **header** DIV you have just created.

35. Choose **New** from the CSS Styles panel menu.

36. From the **Selector Type** drop-down menu, choose **Compound (Based on your selection)**.

37. Dreamweaver will enter **#wrapper #footer** in the **Selector Name** field. Click once on the **Less Specific** button to change the name to **#header**.

38. Make sure that the **Rule Definition** drop-down menu at the bottom of the dialog is set to **styles.css**.

39. Click **OK**.

40. In the **Type** category of the CSS Rule Definition dialog, set the **Font-family** to **Arial, Helvetica, sans-serif**.

41. Set the **Font-size** to "2.25 em". This is roughly equivalent to 36 pixels; but using ems for measuring type makes the type more accessible to users of older browsers. (One em is equivalent to the default font-size setting on each person's browser.)

42. Set the **Line-height** to 100 pixels.

43. Choose white from the **Color** pop-up palette.

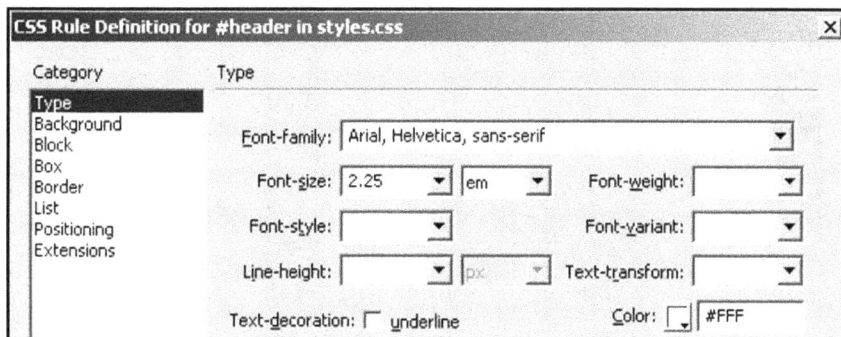

44. Click on the **Background** category on the left of the CSS Rule Definition dialog.

45. Set the **background-color** property to dark blue (or any dark colour).

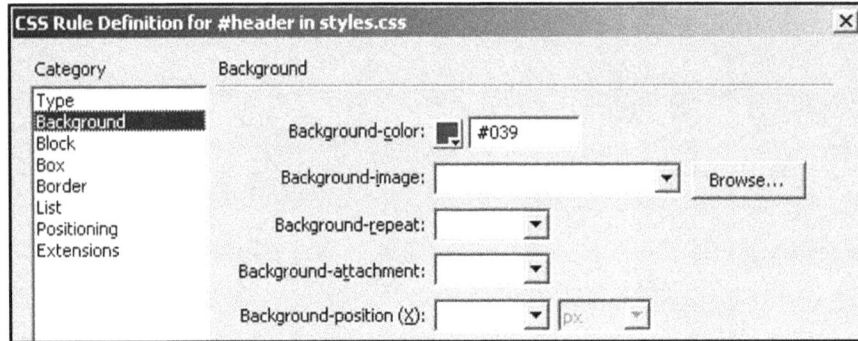

46. Click on the **Block** category.

47. Choose **Center** from the **Text-align** drop-down menu.

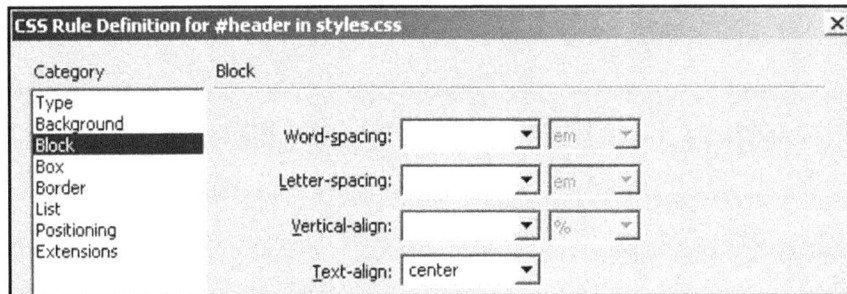

48. Click on the **Box** category.

49. Enter a **height** of "100 px".

50. Set the **Padding** to zero all round (leaving the **Same for all** box checked).

51. In the **Margins** section, uncheck the **Same for all** checkbox then set the **bottom** to 20 pixels. This will prevent the text in the main area from being too close to the header.

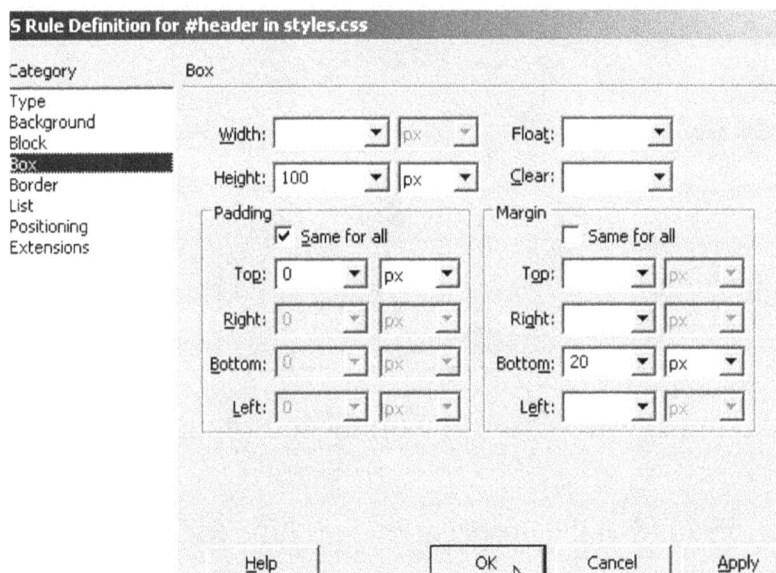

52. Click OK then change the placeholder text in the header DIV to read "Basic Page Layout".

Creating the main DIV

Now we need to create the main DIV inside the wrapper but after the header. Here's how to ensure that the main DIV ends up in the right place.

53. Choose **Insert > Layout Objects > Div Tag**.

54. Choose **After tag** and **<div id="header">** from the two drop-down menus at the top of the dialog.

55. In the **ID** field, enter the name **main**.

56. Click **OK** to create the DIV element.

Creating a rule for the main DIV

57. In the Tag Selector, click **<div#main>** to select the **main** DIV you have just created.

58. Choose **New** from the CSS Styles panel menu.

59. From the **Selector Type** drop-down menu, choose **Compound (Based on your selection)**.

60. Dreamweaver will enter **#wrapper #main** in the **Selector Name** field. Click once on the **Less Specific** button to change the name to **#main**.

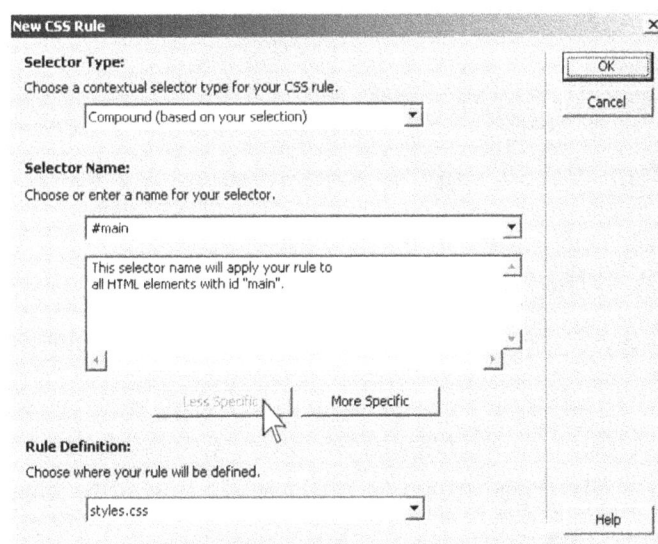

61. Make sure that the **Rule Definition** drop-down menu at the bottom of the dialog is set to **styles.css** then click **OK**.

62. Click on the **Box** category.

63. Set the left and right **Padding** to 10 pixels (uncheck the **Same for all** checkbox). Click **OK**.

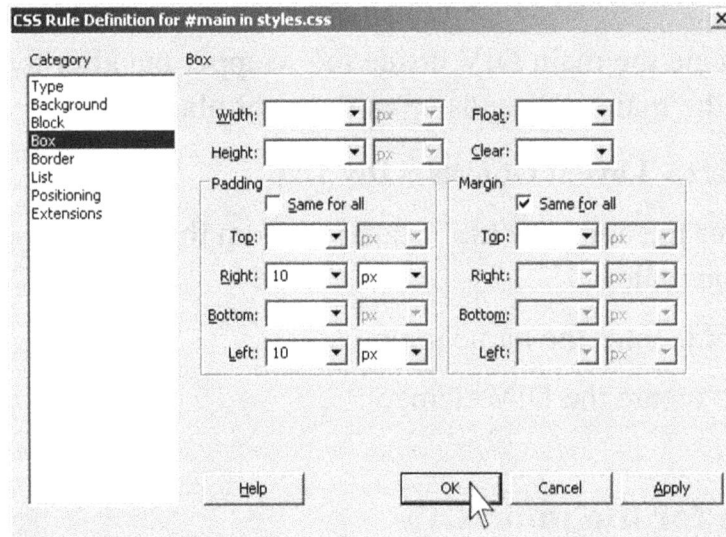

Creating the footer DIV

64. Choose **Insert > Layout Objects > Div Tag**.

65. Choose **After tag** and **<div id="main">** from the two drop-down menus at the top of the dialog.

66. In the **ID** field, enter the name **footer**.

67. Click **OK** to create the DIV element.

Creating a rule for the footer DIV

68. In the Tag Selector, click **<div#footer>** to select the **footer** DIV you have just created.

69. Choose **New** from the CSS Styles panel menu.

70. From the **Selector Type** drop-down menu, choose **Compound (Based on your selection)**.

71. Dreamweaver will enter **#wrapper #footer** in the **Selector Name** field. Click once on the **Less Specific** button to change the name to **#footer**.

72. Make sure that the **Rule Definition** drop-down menu at the bottom of the dialog is set to **styles.css** then click **OK**.

73. Set the **Font-size** to 0.9 em, **Line-height** to 30 pixels and choose white from the **Color** pop-up palette.

74. Click the **Background** category on the left of the CSS Rule Definition dialog.

75. Set the background colour to the same colour used for the header background. To do this, click on the **Color** pop-up then—ignoring the palette completely, move the cursor over the background of the header (which you should be able to see behind the dialog) and click to sample the colour.

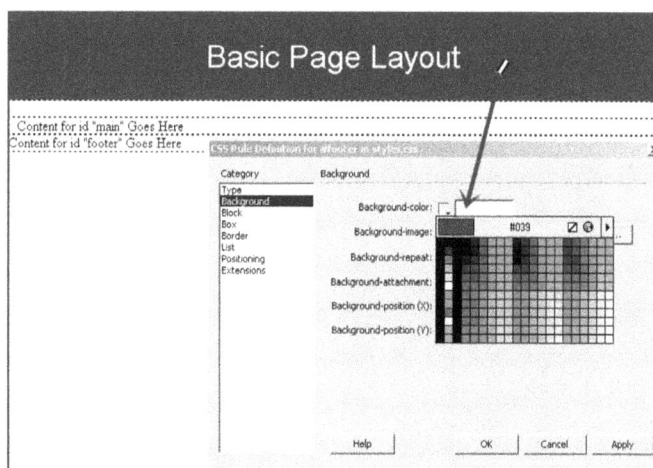

76. Click on the **Block** category.

77. Choose **Center** from the **Text-align** drop-down menu.

78. Click on the **Box** category.

79. Enter a **height** of 30 pixels.

80. Set the **Padding** to zero all round (leaving the **Same for all** box checked).

81. In the **Margins** section, uncheck the **Same for all** checkbox then set the **top** to 20 pixels. This will prevent the text in the main area from being to close to the footer.

82. Click OK then change the placeholder text in the header DIV to read "Copyright, ZYX Company Limited".

10. Templates and Library Items

Adobe Dreamweaver templates constitute one of the most powerful features of the program, enabling you to control and update the appearance of an entire site. This chapter looks at how to set up, implement and modify templates.

Templates facilitate site management by allowing you to modify and update several pages at once. A template is a web document (HTML, ASP, ASP.NET, etc.) which contains a combination of locked elements and editable regions. When creating a new document, if you opt to base it on a template, the page will inherit all of the locked elements which the template contains. You individualize the page by modifying the content of the editable regions. If you later modify the template, all of the pages which are based on it can be automatically updated.

Creating A New Template

You can create templates from scratch or you can take an existing document and convert it into a template.

To create a template from scratch

1. Choose **New** from the **File** menu. This displays the **New document** window.

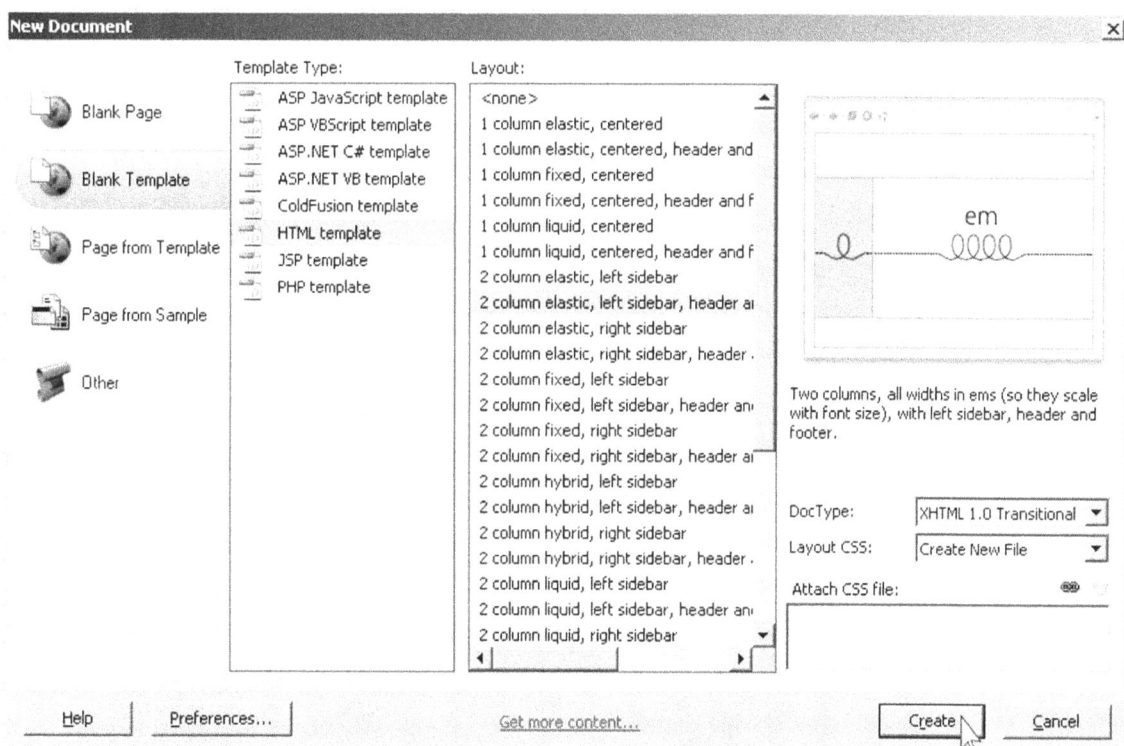

Figure 10-1: Creating a new HTML template

1. Click on **New Template** in the first column of the **New document** window.

2. In the second column, specify the **Template Type** (HTML, ASP, etc.). For a basic site, without any database-driven elements, you would choose **HTML**.

3. In the third column, optionally choose one of Dreamweaver's preset CSS layouts or click **None** to start with a blank page.

4. If you choose one of the CSS layouts, in the forth column, you must specify whether the necessary code is placed in the head of the document, in a new CSS file or an existing one.

5. Click **Create** to generate your new template.

You can also take a regular HTML document and convert it into a template.

1. Open the document which you wish to convert into a template.

2. Choose **Save As Template** from the **File** menu.

3. Type in a name for the new template and click Save.

Figure 10-2: The Save As Template dialog

When you create your first template in any site—or, to be more precise, when you save it—Dreamweaver creates a special **Templates** folder on the root of the Local Site Folder. All templates are automatically stored in this folder.

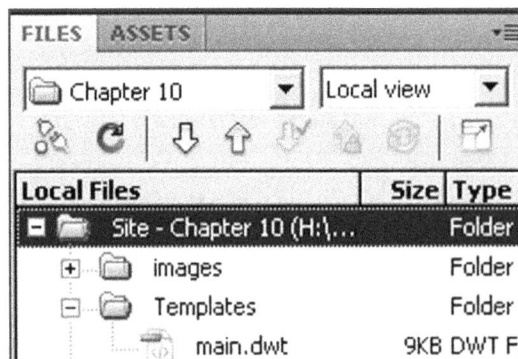

Figure 10-3: The Dreamweaver Templates folder is created automatically

If you don't see the **Templates** folder after creating a template, click on the **Refresh** button in the top left of the Files panel.

Creating the locked regions of a template

By default, all of the elements that you place on a template will be locked. They will appear on each page based on the template but cannot be modified. Locked regions are typically those areas of the page which contain items that repeat on all pages such as logos, copyright notices and navigation bars.

To create locked regions

1. If the template is not open, in the templates folder, double-click the name of the template you wish to edit. It will have the file extension ".dwt" (Dreamweaver template).

2. Create all of the elements that you wish to appear on every page.

That's it! All of these elements will remain locked and unchangeable on all pages based on the template. (In other words, you never need to lock anything you place on a template; all template content is locked by default.)

Adding Editable Regions To A Template

Having created the locked regions of the template, you must then specify which areas of the page will be editable.

To define an editable region

1. Place the cursor in the part of the page (usually inside a DIV element) which you want to make editable.

2. Choose **Insert > Template Objects > Editable Region**.

3. Enter a name for the editable region and click **OK**.

Placeholder text

Each editable region which you create is marked by a text label. This text can be modified at will. If you are creating templates for other people to use, you may find it useful to replace the original placeholder text with a message which will benefit the users of the template.

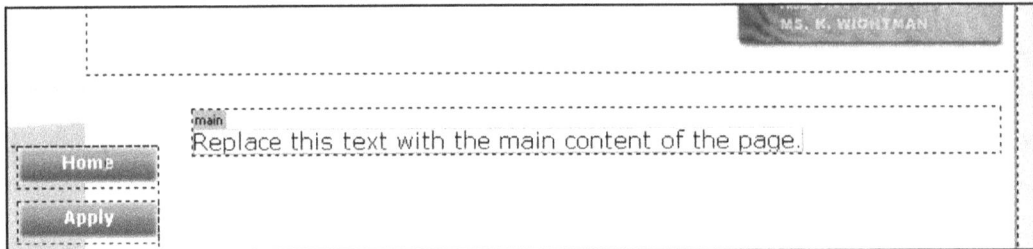

Figure 10-4: Placeholder text inside an editable region can be used to provide a kind of "idiot's guide" for anyone using a template.

Deleting editable regions

When deleting editable regions, it is not enough simply to delete the placeholder text which marks the editable region.

1. Choose **Unmark Editable Region** from the **Template** sub-menu of the **Modify** menu.

2. Click on the name of the editable region which you wish to unmark then click **OK**.

3. Note that this last operation does not delete any placeholders in the editable region. These still have to be deleted manually.

Using graphic placeholders

It can sometimes be useful to use a graphic element as an editable region placeholder. To do this, simply highlight the graphic and choose **Insert > Template Objects > Editable Region**. Enter a name for the region and click **OK**. Dreamweaver creates the editable region and leaves the image inside it. A Dreamweaver image placeholder is ideal for use in this scenario. (Image placeholders are described in Chapter 6: Working With Images, page 71.)

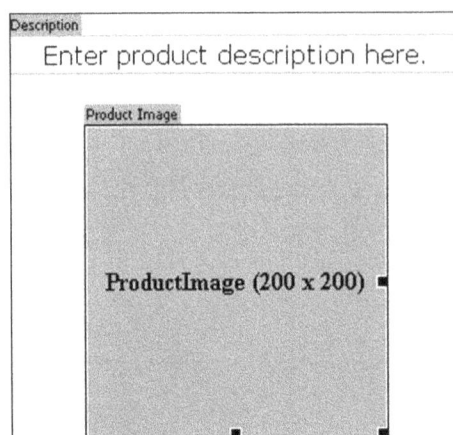

Figure 10-5: Using a graphic placeholder in an editable region

Using a template

Templates can be used in two ways: firstly, a new page can be based on a template and, secondly, a template can be applied to an existing page.

Creating a new page based on a template

To create a new page based on a template

1. Choose **File > New** to display the **New Document** dialog.

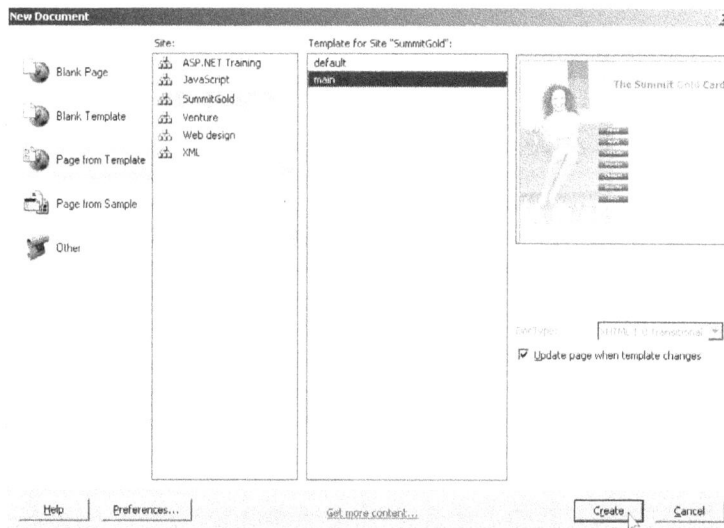

Figure 10-6: Creating a new page based on a template

2. In the first column of the New document window, click on **Page from Template**.

3. In the second column of the New document window, make sure that the name of the site you are working on is highlighted.

4. In the third column, click on the name of the template on which you would like the new page to be based.

5. Finally, in the fourth column, make sure that the option **Update page when template changes** remains checked.

6. Click the **Create** button.

The option **Update page when template changes** is what gives templates their true power. It means that if you have two hundred pages based on a template, you can change all of them simply by modifying the template.

Applying a template to an existing page

To apply a template to an existing page

1. Open the page in question.

2. Choose **Modify > Templates > Apply Template to Page**.

3. When the Apply Template dialog appears (See figure 10-7, below.), double-click the name of the template you wish to associate with the page.

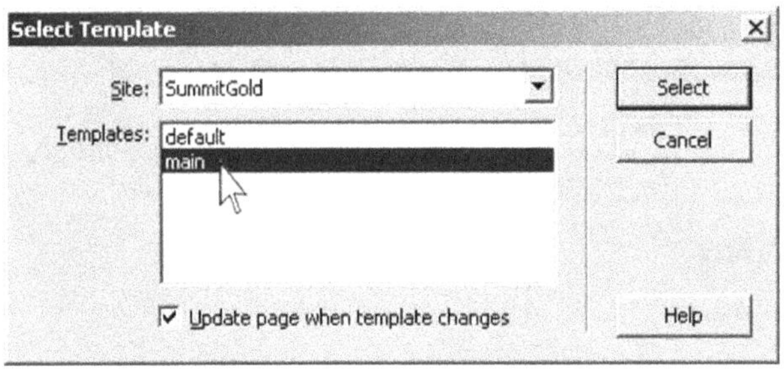

Figure 10-7: Applying a template to a page using the Modify > Templates > Apply Template to Page command

Dreamweaver's Assets panel provides an alternative method of applying a template to a page.

1. Choose **Window > Assets** to make the Assets panel available.

2. Click on the **Templates** button on the left of the Assets panel.

3. Highlight the name of the template you want use.

4. Click the **Apply** button.

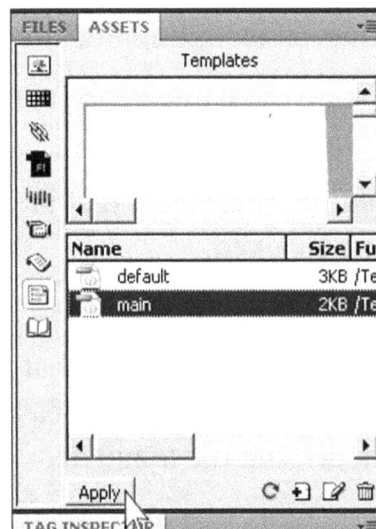

Figure 10-8: Applying a template to a page using the Assets panel

Alternatively, you can simply drag the template name—or the template preview displayed at top of the Assets panel—directly onto the page. This technique is particularly useful if you want to apply a template to several documents quickly.

Editable Region Display

When a template has been applied to a page, the name of the template is displayed in the top right and the name of each editable region is shown above the appropriate area of the page. The editable region labels compromise the WYSIWYG display of your page slightly, by pushing elements down. To switch off the display of template and editable region names, choose **View > Visual Aids > Invisible Elements**. Use the same command to reinstate them. (The keyboard shortcut for this is **Control-i**, or **Command-i** on a Mac.)

Replacing a graphic placeholder

Graphic placeholders are ideal for marking an area of a page where an image is to be inserted. Each time the template is used, a different image can be substituted for the placeholder.

To replace a graphic placeholder

1. Create or open a page based on a template.

2. Double-click the graphic placeholder.

3. Navigate to the image which will replace the placeholder.

4. Double-click the name of the image.

Another way of replacing an image is to use the Point to File button next to the **Src** (source) box in the HTML section of the Properties panel. Simply drag the Point to File icon directly onto the name of the replacement image in the Files panel. When you release, Dreamweaver will update the image source.

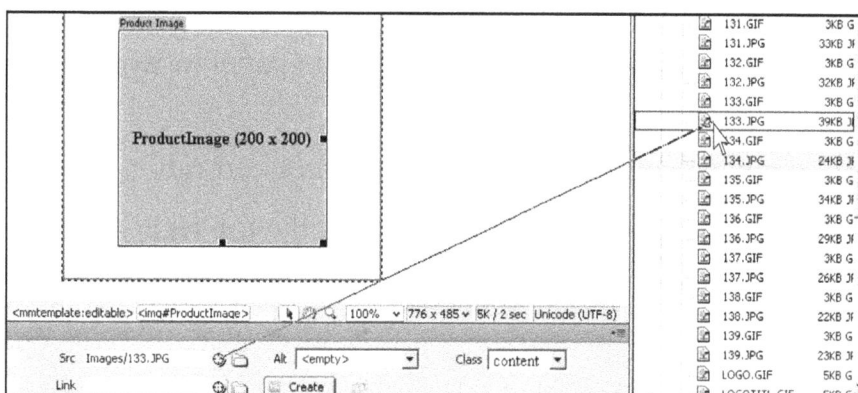

Figure 10-9: Replacing an image using the Point to file button

Detach from template

There will always be pages which you need to treat as independent and which you do not want controlled by a template. Obviously, you can simply avoid attaching a template to such pages in the first place. However, you will sometimes find it useful to apply a template to a page to obtain formatting elements and then to detach the page from the template. To detach a page from its template, choose **Modify > Templates > Detach from Template**.

Using Library Items

Dreamweaver's Assets panel offers another way of creating content which can be updated across several pages: library items. Whereas templates act as master pages controlling the content of multiple pages within a site, library items contain web fragments which you may insert anywhere you like, on any page you like. As with templates, if you update the library item, you can simultaneously update all the pages into which you have inserted that item.

Library items and templates are a Dreamweaver feature and are not part of the Worldwide Web Consortium's specifications. This may make them unattractive to some developers. However, bear in mind that they do not require the use of any non-compliant code or techniques. They simply use innocuous HTML comments to identify elements which Dreamweaver will recognise as belonging to templates or library items. If you decide to stop editing your pages in Dreamweaver, template and library markup will simply cease to be recognized; it won't do any harm.

Library items offer a great way of adding such elements as navigation panels, headers and footers to a page and being able to update the item right across the site simply by updating the original library item. The advantage they have over templates is that you only need to insert the library item on those pages that require it.

To create a library item

1. Choose **Window > Assets** to display the Assets panel.

2. Click on the last icon on the left of the Assets panel to work with Library assets.

3. Highlight the page content that you wish to convert into a library item.

4. Choose **New Library Item** from the menu in the top right of the Assets panel—or simply click the **New Library Item** button in the bottom right of the Assets panel.

Figure 10-10: Creating a new library item

As well as converting existing page content into library items, you can simply create a blank library item and then add content to it. To do this, simply choose **New Library Item** from the Assets panel menu while no content is highlighted on the current page—in fact, you don't even need to have a page open.

Editing library items

You can edit a library item at any time by simply double-clicking the name of the item in the Library section of the Assets panel. The library item opens in a window similar to an HTML document window. However, since you will often be editing elements out of context, you will often not be able to see the item as it will appear when inserted into a page.

As soon as you save the changes you have made to a library item, Dreamweaver will offer you a chance to update all instances of the item on all pages into which it has been inserted.

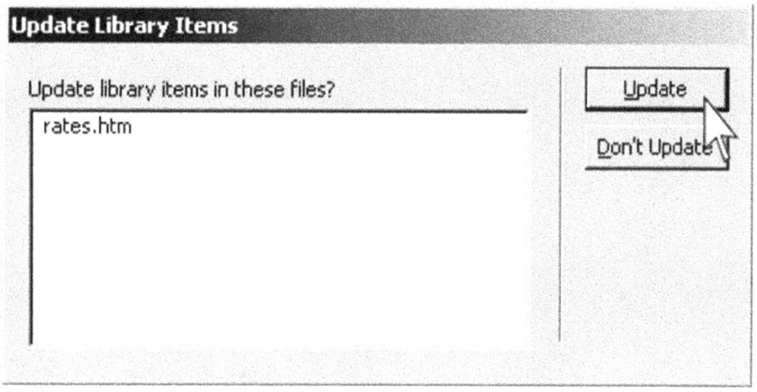

Figure 10-11: Updating pages which use a library item

11. Dreamweaver Website Creation Cycle

Now that we have looked at the key elements that go together to make up web pages, we can now discuss the business of building a basic web site. Of course, there is no limit to the potential complexity of a web site and Dreamweaver itself is a very sophisticated piece of software with some fairly advanced functionality. However, our aim in this book is to help you to gain mastery of all the basics. So, in this chapter, we will focus on the key steps necessary to create a basic web site—using Dreamweaver as your development environment.

We will be breaking down the process of building a site into a 12 step process. However, I'm not suggesting that this is the only way of building Dreamweaver web sites—for example, it involves the use of templates; and not everyone is a fan of templates. The intention is that you can use these steps to get you started; build a few sites; then, as you gain more experience, develop you own way of doing things—and, basically, outgrow what you are about to learn.

Steps involved in building a Dreamweaver website

The process of creating a basic site within Dreamweaver can be summarized in the 12 steps shown below.

1. **Plan and design**

2. **Create Local Site Folder**

3. **Create Default Images Folder**

4. **Define Dreamweaver site**

    a. **Local information**

    b. **Server information (when available)**

5. **Create all files and folders**

6. **Create template**

7. **Create CSS file**

8. **Link CSS file to template**

9. **Add content to template**

    a. **Create locked content**

    b. **Define editable region(s)**

  c. **Create CSS rules**

 10. **Apply template and add content to individual pages**

 11. **Test site**

 12. **Upload site to server and go live**

1. Plan and design

Before you start, you should have a clear idea of what information you want to display in your website and the options that will be available to visitors. It's best to start with an achievable goal—a project that you can realistically bring to a satisfactory conclusion. Don't attempt an "all singing, all dancing" e-commerce site as your first project.

Planning and design can be done using a pencil and paper. However, you will almost certainly need access to graphics tools such as Adobe Photoshop and Illustrator to collate and optimize all available relevant graphics such logos and photos showing key personnel, services or products—or whatever your site requires.

2. Create Local Site Folder

Before you are ready to start defining your Dreamweaver site, you should create a folder whose sole purpose in life is to contain the various files which will constitute the website you intend to create—your version of the site, the version that you develop and test and which only you can see.

Create a folder in any convenient location and don't put anything in this folder but the files relating to your site. Once you have completed your project, the contents of the Local Site Folder will mirror the live version of your site.

3. Create Default Images Folder

The Default Images Folder is a folder you create inside the Local Site Folder and which you later designate as the default location for images. This will help prevent you ending up with missing images on your pages. (This process was described in Chapter 1: Getting Started, page 12).

4. Define Dreamweaver site

To create a new site in Dreamweaver, choose **Site > New Site**. The key elements that you need to define are shown below.

Site Category

Site Name

In the **Site** category on the left of the dialog, enter a name for the site.

Local Site Folder

The second field in the **Site** category allows you to specify the Local Site Folder that you created in step 2. Simply click on the **Browse for folder** button, navigate to the folder, open it then click on the **Select** button (or **Choose** button on Mac).

Servers category

If you have already signed up with a hosting company, this is the category which allows you to enter the details which will enable Dreamweaver to connect to the server and upload files to make them live. (This process is described in Chapter 13: Site Management and Checking, page 238.)

Advanced category > Local info

Default Images Folder

In this section you should specify the Default Images Folder that you created in step 3, by clicking on the **Browse for folder** button.

5. Create all files and folders

Before actually putting any content in your pages, you should ensure that all the pages you mapped out in your original plan have been created and saved. Instead of creating and then completing each page individually, it is best to create and save every single folder and every single page in your design.

The reason for this approach is that it will help prevent the creation of links that don't work properly. Basically, using this method, whenever you come to create a link, the page you are linking to will already exist in the correct location within your site structure. To create a link to any page, you can then simply browse for it or use the **Point to file** tool; and Dreamweaver generates the correct link automatically.

6. Create template

There are still a couple more steps that you should perform before you are ready to actually start work on the page content; to get the most benefit from a program like Dreamweaver, you should create at least one template. Templates allow you to maintain a consistent look and feel throughout the site.

7. Create CSS file

The other key element which will enable you to create themed and consistent pages is CSS. For the greatest flexibility, the normal practice is to create an external CSS file which will hold the rules controlling the layout and formatting of all the pages in the site.

8. Link CSS file to template

The rules in the CSS file will control the layout and formatting of all elements on the template. To achieve this, the template must be linked to the CSS file.

9. Create and style template content

a. Create locked content

Locked content refers to those elements which will be reproduced on all pages based on the template but which can only be edited on the template itself. Typically, this will be items such as logos, navigation links, banners and footers.

b. Define editable regions

Editable regions are those areas of the template which will be modifiable on pages based on the template. Each time you apply the template to a page, you can put unique content in the editable regions. A template must have at least one editable region to be of any use.

c. Create CSS Rules

The layout of the content of the template is achieved by creating CSS rules to control the positioning and formatting of the elements on the page. These rules will be stored in the external CSS file created in step 7. Since the template is linked to the CSS file, all pages based on the template will also be linked to the CSS file.

10. Add content to pages

Having finished your template and your CSS file, you are ready to build the web pages that will constitute your site. Simply open each page, choose **Modify > Templates > Apply Template to Page** and then add the text, images, etc. that make up the unique content of that page.

11. Test your website

Whenever you build a new website, you can almost guarantee that you will make mistakes and that there will be errors within the site that need to be fixed before it goes live. Adobe Dreamweaver has a number of tools for helping you to locate such errors and correct them. The program allows you to perform browser compatibility checks, locate broken links, orphaned files and locate syntax errors within your code.

Testing your website should be an on-going part of building the site and not just an isolated step which is performed after the site has been built. Every page that forms part of the site should function correctly in all its aspects in all of the browsers which the site is designed for. Using Adobe Dreamweaver's various reports is a great way of ensuring that your site is error-free.

The tools available in Dreamweaver for testing and validating are described in Chapter 13: Site management and checking.

12. Upload site and go live

Once you are happy that everything checks out OK, you can think about going live. If you have not already done so, you will need to enter server information to enable Dreamweaver to connect to the server. Uploading a site is done using the Files panel.

The process of uploading files to a server is described in Chapter 13: Site management and checking.

Try it for yourself!

Just to reassure you that the process of creating a basic website in Dreamweaver is really simple, we will spend the remainder of this chapter creating a site using the 12 step process just outlined.

Step 1. Plan and design

This will be a very short step, since it has already been completed for you!

The site that we will be building is shown on page 132. It is a mini-site with 8 pages, corresponding to the eight navigation buttons shown below the header. The site features a fictitious company called Rechelof Venture Capital and, naturally, none of the products, services or personnel referred to in the site actually exist.

The site has been designed for an 800 by 600 screen resolution and has a single column layout.

Step 2. Create Local Site Folder

The Local Site Folder to be used for this site already exists. In the training folder, locate the folder called "venture". As you will see, it contains a single folder which, in turn, contains all of the images required by the site.

The training folder itself also contains a plain text file called "venture.txt" which contains all of the text required on all of the pages within the site. Double-click on the file to open it with your default text program. The text for each page is followed by a separator line.

When you come to add content to the pages, you can simply copy the appropriate text from this file and paste it into each page.

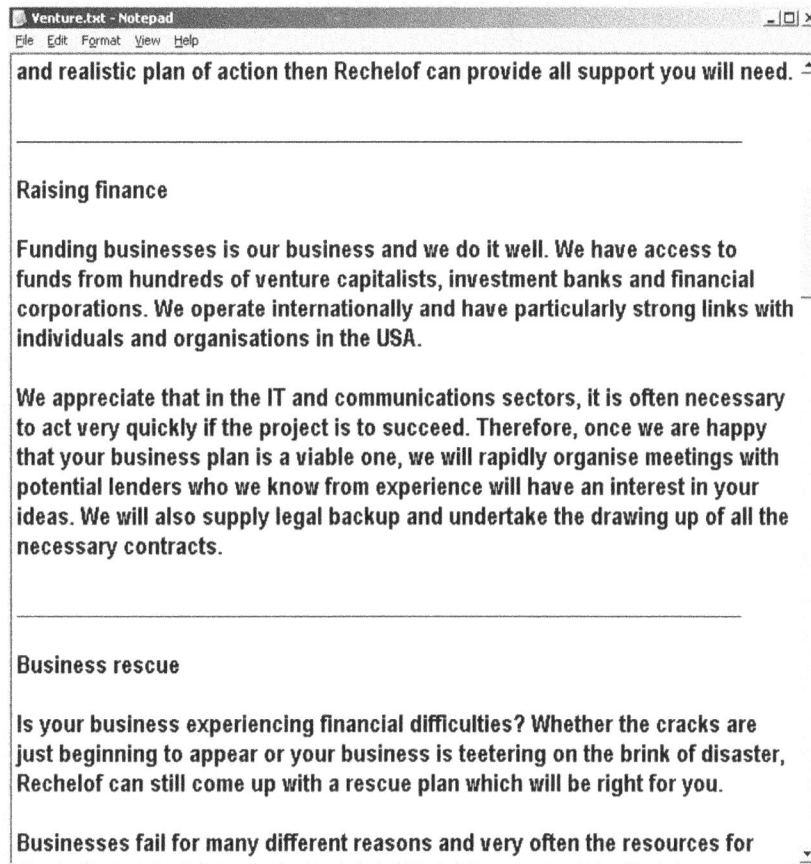

Step 3. Create Default Images Folder

1. As with the Local Site Folder, the Default Images Folder required by our site already exists. It is the folder called images inside the "venture" folder referred to in step 1.

Step 4. Define Dreamweaver site

1. Back in Dreamweaver, choose **Site > New Site**.

2. In the **Site** category of the Site Setup dialog, enter the name "Venture".

3. Click on the **Browse for folder** icon next to the Local Site Folder field, open the "venture" folder inside the training folder then click the **Select** button.

4. Click on the **Advanced Settings** section on the left of the dialog to expand it.

5. Click on **Local info**.

6. Click on the **Browse for folder** icon next to the **Default Images Folder** box; open the **images** folder inside the **venture** folder then click the **Select** button.

7. Click **OK** to complete the site setup.

Step 5. Create all folders and files

1. From the Files panel menu, choose **File > New File** or simply right-click on the Local Site Folder and choose **New File** from the context menu.

2. Enter the file name "index.htm" and press Enter.

3. To create the second new file, try using the keyboard shortcut: **Control-Shift-n** (**Command-Shift-n** on a Mac).

4. Enter the file name "finance.htm".

5. Use the same techniques to create the 6 remaining files required by the site, making sure that all of the files are placed on the root rather than inside the **images** folder. The remaining files are: "rescue.html", "advice.html", "invest. html", "team.html", "fees.html" and "contact.html".

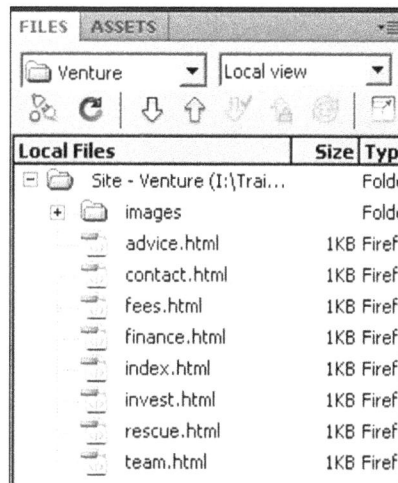

Step 6. Create template

1. Choose **File > New** from the main menu bar to display the New document window.

2. In the first column of the New Document dialog, click **Blank Template**.

3. In the second column, choose **HTML Template**.

4. In the third column, click **None**.

5. Click the **Create** button.

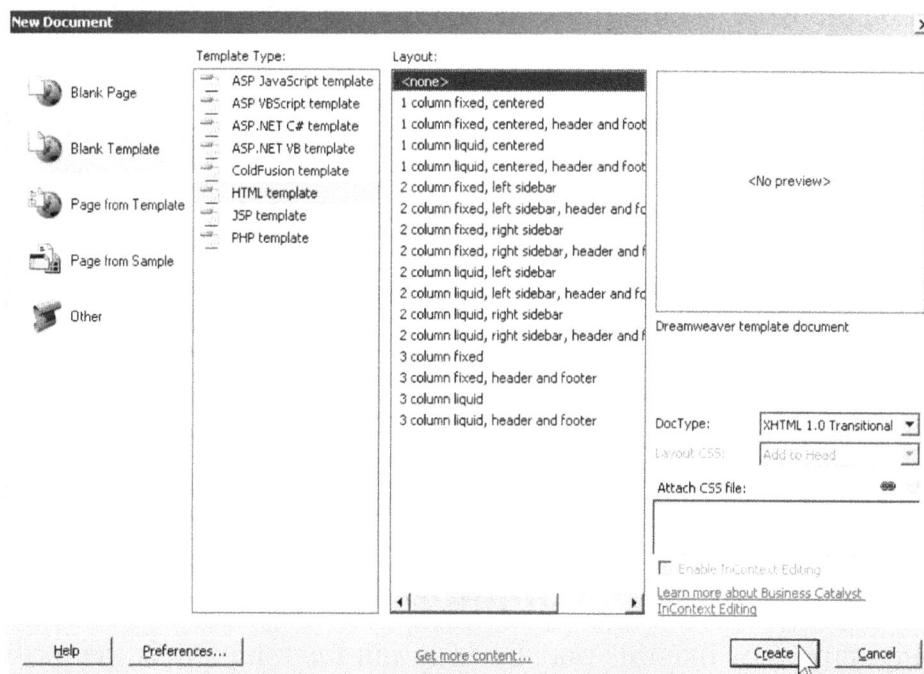

6. Choose **File > Save As Template** (Note that this is a separate command from the usual **File > Save As** command.).

> **Save As Template**   ×
>
> Site: Venture ▼   Save
>
> Existing templates: (no templates)   Cancel
>
> Description:
>
> Save as: main   Help

7. In the **Save as** field, enter the template name "main" and click OK.

Step 7. Create CSS file

1. From the Files panel menu, choose **File > New File** or simply right-click on the Local Site Folder and choose **New File** from the context menu.

2. Enter the file name "styles.css", taking care to delete the default ".html" file extension.

Step 8. Link CSS file to template

1. (Choose **Window > CSS Styles**, if necessary.) Click in the top right of the CSS Styles panel to display the panel menu; then choose **Attach Style Sheet**.

2. Click on the **Browse** button, locate and double-click "styles.css".

3. From the Media pop-up men, choose **All**.

4. Click **OK**.

> **Attach External Style Sheet**   ×
>
> File/URL: ../styles.css ▼   Browse...   OK
>
> Add as: ⦿ Link   Preview
>   ○ Import   Cancel
>
> Media: all ▼
>
> You may also enter a comma-separated list of media types.
>
> Dreamweaver has sample style sheets to get you started.   Help

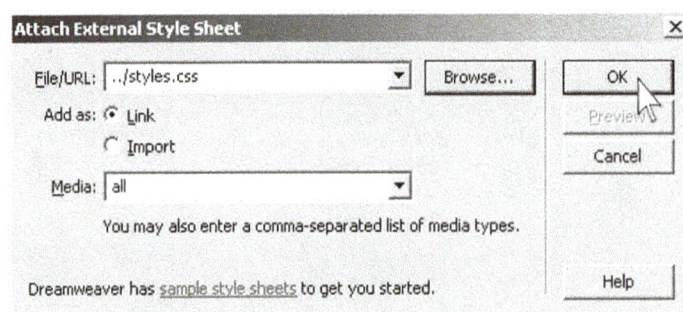

Step 9. Create and style template content

When building mini-sites like this one, fleshing out the template is the most important—and the most time-consuming—step. Basically, once you have completed your template and got it working, the rest should be plain sailing. One of the main tasks for completing our simple template will be the creation and styling of DIV elements.

Creating the locked content

The **\<body\>** of an HTML page is the overall container for all elements that will be displayed in the browser. Therefore, it is a good place to start styling our template content. Each HTML page you create in Dreamweaver already contains a **\<body\>** tag, so we can go straight to the step of creating a CSS rule to control its appearance.

Styling the \<body\> element

1. In the Tag Selector, in the bottom left of the document window, click on the **\<body\>** tag to select it.

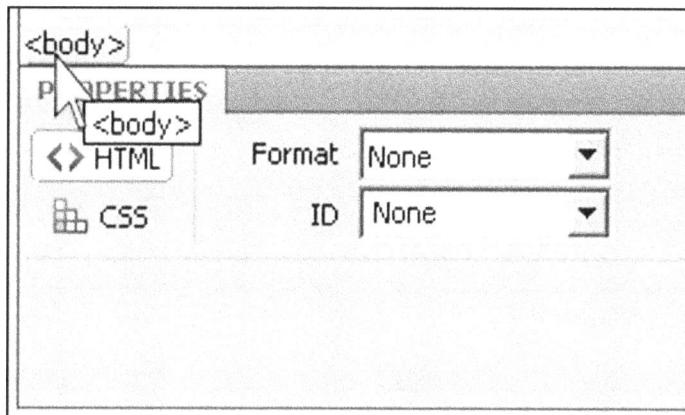

2. Choose **New** from the menu in the top right of the CSS Styles panel.

3. From the **Selector Type** drop-down menu, choose **Compound (based on your selection)**.

4. Since the **\<body\>** tag was selected, Dreamweaver automatically enters the name **body** into the **Selector Name** field.

5. Make sure that **styles.css** is selected in the **Rule Definition** section at the bottom of the dialog.

6. Click **OK** to diplay the CSS Rule Definition dialog.

7. In the **Type** category, choose **Arial, Helvetica, sans-serif** from the **Font-family** drop-down menu.

8. Click on the **Background** category and, in the **Background-color** field, enter the hexadecimal reference "#A7B8C9", a light blue colour which matches the banner we will be using in the header.

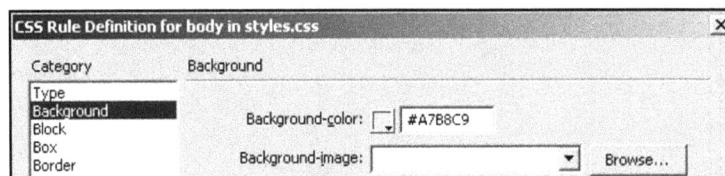

9. Click on the **Block** category and set the **Text-align** property to **center**. This will cause the wrapper DIV (which will hold all of the page content) to be centred on the page in older browsers. (As you will see shortly, in modern browsers, the wrapper DIV is centred by setting its left and right margins to **auto**.)

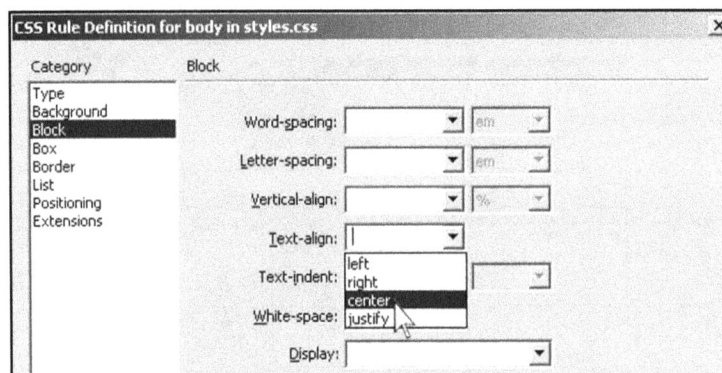

10. Click **OK** to close the CSS Rule Definition dialog.

Creating and styling the wrapper DIV

The wrapper DIV will hold all of the page content. In this example, we are creating a site with a fixed width of 760 pixels, suitable for a monitor resolution of 800 x 600, the smallest screen resolution still in common use.

1. From the main menu bar, choose **Insert > Layout Objects > Div Tag**.

2. In the **ID** field, enter the name **wrapper**.

3. Click **OK** to create the DIV element.

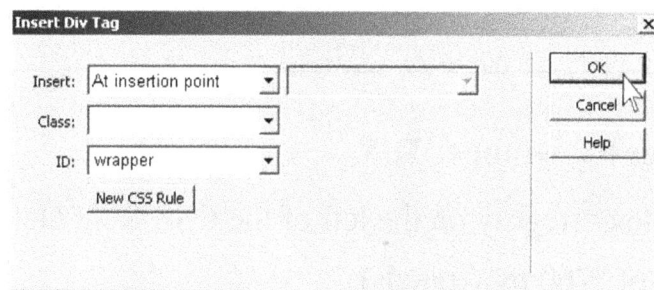

4. With the wrapper DIV still selected, choose **New** from the CSS Styles panel menu.

5. From the **Selector Type** drop-down menu, choose **Compound (Based on your selection)**.

6. Dreamweaver automatically enters **#wrapper** into the **Selector Name** field.

7. If necessary, choose **styles.css** (the css file you created earlier) from the **Rule Definition** drop-down menu at the bottom of the dialog.

8. Click **OK**.

Block category settings for wrapper DIV

9. In the **Block** category, set the **Text-align** property to "left". This is to countermand the **center** setting placed on the **<body>** element. Without this step, everything on the page would be centred.

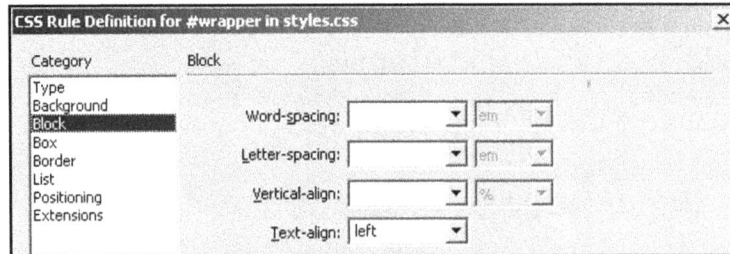

```
CSS Rule Definition for #wrapper in styles.css                        ×

Category          Block
 Type
 Background
 Block            Word-spacing: [            ] ▼  em  ▼
 Box
 Border           Letter-spacing: [           ] ▼  em  ▼
 List
 Positioning      Vertical-align: [           ] ▼  %   ▼
 Extensions
                    Text-align: | left         | ▼
```

Box category settings for wrapper DIV

10. Click on the **Box** category on the left of the CSS Rule Definition dialog.

11. Enter a **width** of "760 px" (pixels).

12. Set the **Padding** to zero all round.

13. In the **Margins** section, deactivate the **Same for all** checkbox then set the **Left** and **Right** margins to **Auto**. This will align the wrapper DIV to the centre of the browser window in modern browsers.

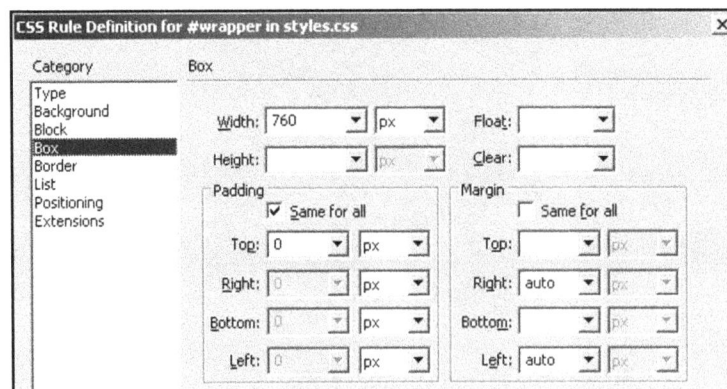

```
CSS Rule Definition for #wrapper in styles.css                        ×

Category          Box
 Type
 Background
 Block            Width: | 760 | ▼ px ▼      Float: [        ] ▼
 Box
 Border           Height: [     ] ▼ px ▼      Clear: [        ] ▼
 List
 Positioning     ┌Padding─────────────┐  ┌Margin──────────────┐
 Extensions      │  ☑ Same for all    │  │  ☐ Same for all    │
                 │ Top: | 0 | ▼ px ▼  │  │ Top: [   ] ▼ px ▼  │
                 │ Right: | 0 | ▼ px ▼│  │ Right: | auto | ▼ px ▼│
                 │ Bottom: | 0 | ▼ px ▼│  │ Bottom: [  ] ▼ px ▼ │
                 │ Left: | 0 | ▼ px ▼ │  │ Left: | auto | ▼ px ▼│
                 └────────────────────┘  └────────────────────┘
```

Border category settings for wrapper DIV

14. Click on the **Border** category. Set the **Style** property to **Solid**, the **Width** to "1 px" and the **Color** to "#000" (by choosing black from the palette).

15. Click **OK** to close the CSS Rule Definition dialog.

Creating and styling the header DIV

Our header DIV will consist of a background banner image. In this example, we will use a version of the background image which has the text "Rechelof Venture Capital" as part of the image. We could equally use a version of the image with no text and place the words "Rechelof Venture Capital" in the header as actual text.

1. Delete the placeholder text which Dreamweaver placed inside the wrapper DIV ('Content for id "wrapper" Goes Here').

2. Choose **Insert > Layout Objects > Div Tag**.

3. In the Insert section, choose **After start of tag** and **<div id="wrapper">** from the left and right drop-down menus, respectively.

4. In the **ID** field, enter the name **header**.

5. Click **OK** to create the DIV element.

6. In the Tag Selector, click **<div#header>** to select the **header** DIV you have just created.

7. Choose **New** from the CSS Styles panel menu.

8. From the **Selector Type** drop-down menu, choose **Compound (Based on your selection)**.

9. Dreamweaver will enter **#wrapper #header** in the **Selector Name** field. Click once on the **Less Specific** button to change the name to **#header**.

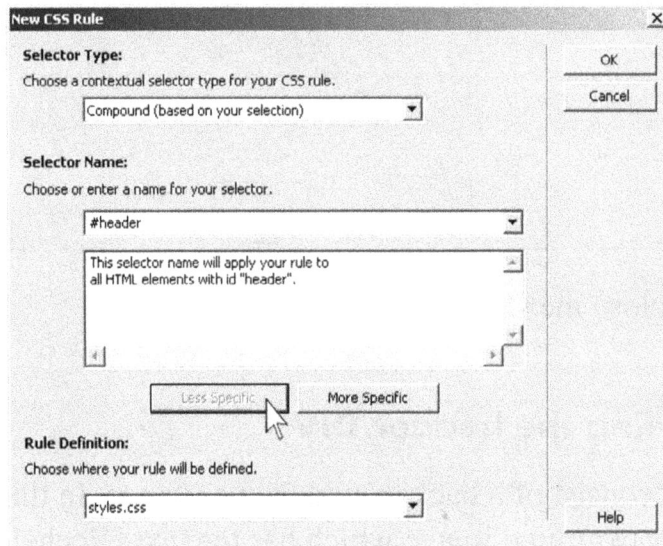

10. Make sure that the **Rule Definition** drop-down menu at the bottom of the dialog is set to **styles.css**.

11. Click **OK**.

Background category settings for header DIV

12. Click on the **Background** category on the left of the CSS Rule Definition dialog.

13. Click on the **Browse** button next to the **Background-image** field. Open the images folder and double-click the file called "banner.jpg" to select it.

14. Choose **No-repeat** from the **Background-repeat** drop-down menu.

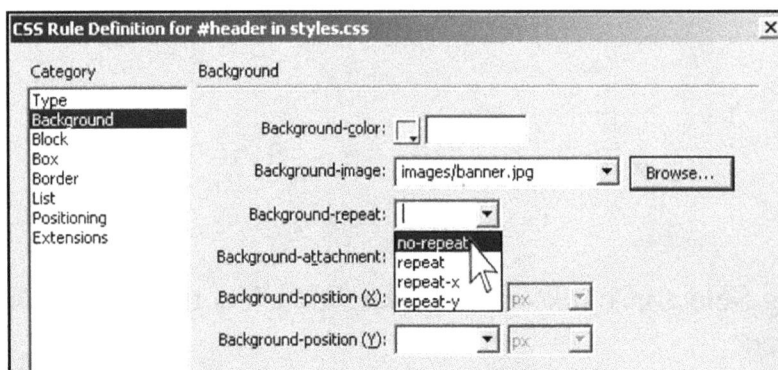

Box category settings for header DIV

15. Click on the **Box** category.

16. Enter a **height** of 180 pixels—to match the height of the banner.

17. Set the **Padding** and **Margin** to zero all round (leaving the **Same for all** box checked in each case).

18. Click the **Apply** button to preview the changes then click **OK**.

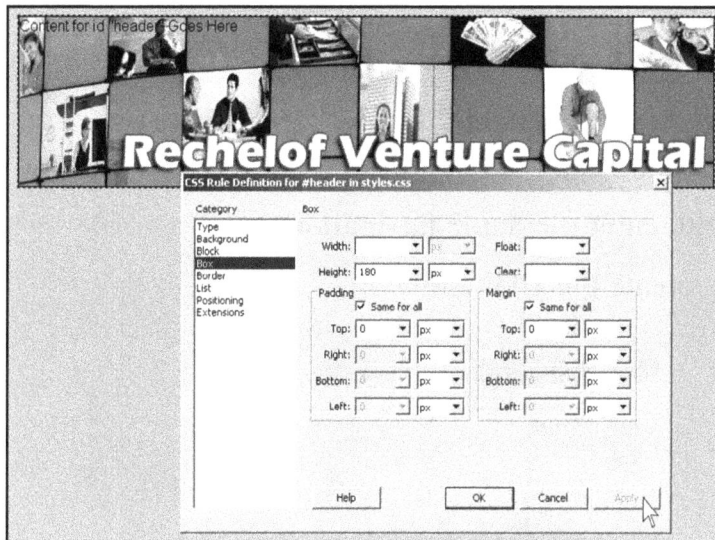

19. Delete the placeholder text 'Content for id "header" Goes Here'.

Creating and styling the navigation DIV

The navigation DIV will contain the 8 buttons to be used for navigating through the site. This will give us an opportunity to see how CSS can be used to completely transform the appearance of elements. We will enter the hyperlinks which will become the buttons in an unordered (bulleted) list, as shown below.

We will then create a CSS rule which will give them a fixed width, rearrange them in a row and make them look like buttons—like so.

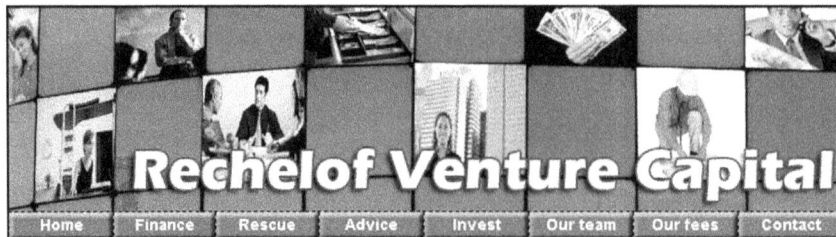

1. Choose **Insert > Layout Objects > Div Tag**.

2. Choose **After tag** and **<div id="header">** from the two drop-down menus at the top of the dialog.

3. In the **ID** field, enter the name **navigation**.

4. Click **OK** to create the DIV element.

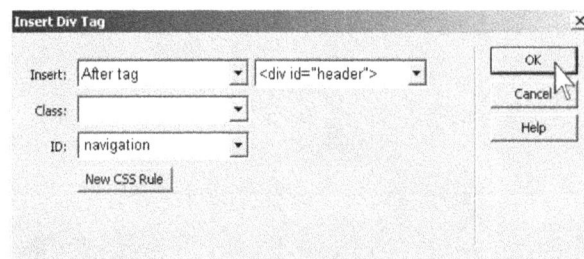

5. In the Tag Selector, click **<div#navigation>** to select the **navigation** DIV you have just created.

6. Choose **New** from the CSS Styles panel menu.

7. From the **Selector Type** drop-down menu, choose **Compound**.

8. Dreamweaver will enter **#wrapper #navigation** in the **Selector Name** field. Click once on the **Less Specific** button to change the name to **#navigation**.

9. Make sure that the **Rule Definition** drop-down menu at the bottom of the dialog is set to **styles.css**.

10. Click **OK**.

Box category settings for navigation DIV

11. Click on the **Box** category.

12. Set the **Padding** property to zero all round. (This will ensure that, when we calculate the width required for each button, there is no extra default space unaccounted for.)

13. Set the **Margin** property to "0 px", leaving the **Same for all** checkbox on.

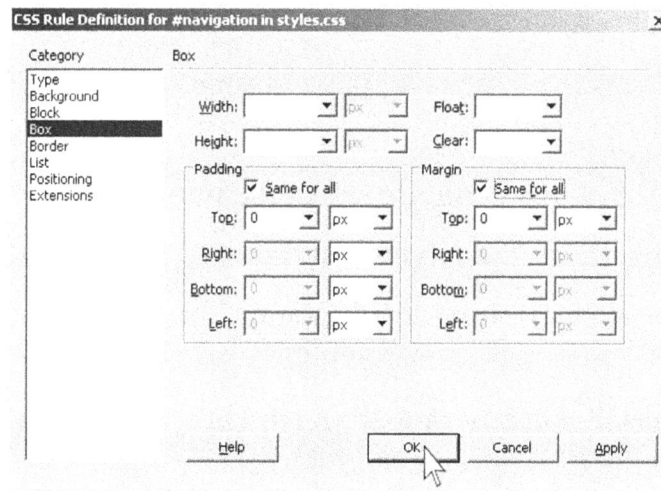

14. Click **OK** to close the CSS Definition dialog.

Creating and styling the unordered list

1. Highlight the placeholder text which Dreamweaver placed inside the navigation DIV ('Content for id "navigation" Goes Here.')

2. Click on the bullet icon in the HTML section of the Properties panel to convert the text into an unordered list (**<ul>**—a bulleted list).

3. Delete the placeholder text and the enter the button text for each page that we need to link to, pressing the Return key after each one—"Home", "Finance", "Rescue", "Advice", "Invest", "Our team", "Our fees", and "Contact".

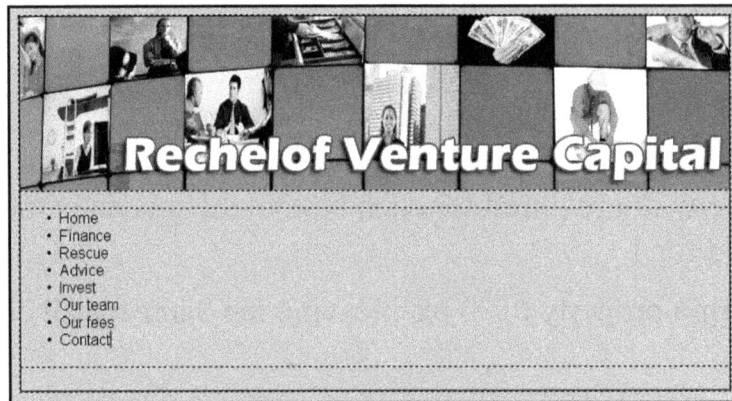

Since we do not want this list to behave like a normal list, we must now create a CSS rule which removes the list behaviour.

4. In the Tag Selector, click **<ul>** to select the unordered list.

5. Choose **New** from the CSS Styles panel menu.

6. From the **Selector Type** drop-down menu, choose **Compound (Based on your selection)**.

7. Dreamweaver will enter **#wrapper #navigation ul** in the **Selector Name** field. Click once on the **Less Specific** button to change the name to **#navigation ul**.

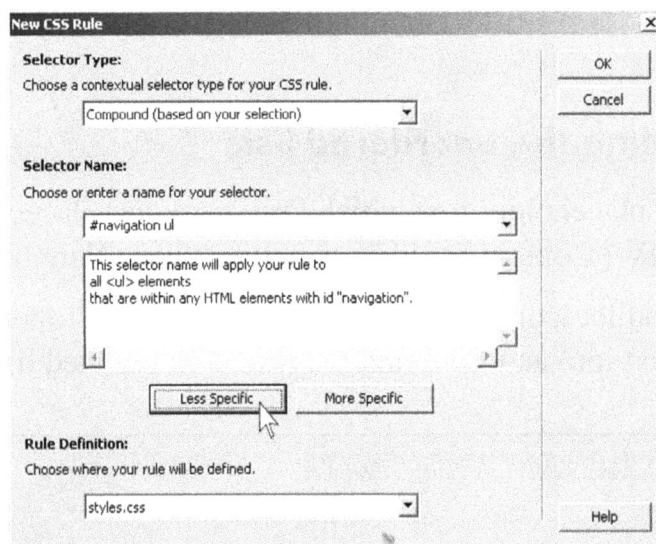

8. Make sure that the **Rule Definition** drop-down menu at the bottom of the dialog is set to **styles.css**.

9. Click **OK**.

Box category settings for navigation <ul>

10. Click on the **Box** category.

11. Set the **Padding** and **Margin** properties to zero all round. (This will ensure that, when we calculate the width required for each button, there is no extra default space unaccounted for.)

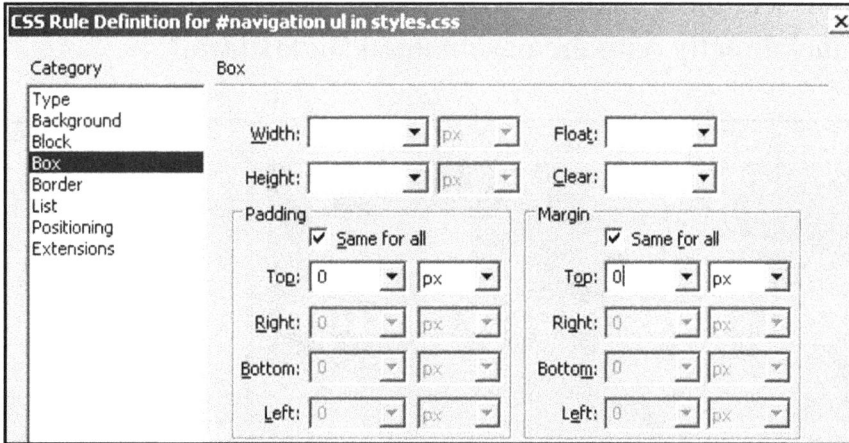

List category settings for navigation <ul>

12. Click on the **List** category.

13. Set the **list-style-type** property to **None**. (This will suppress the display of any bullets.)

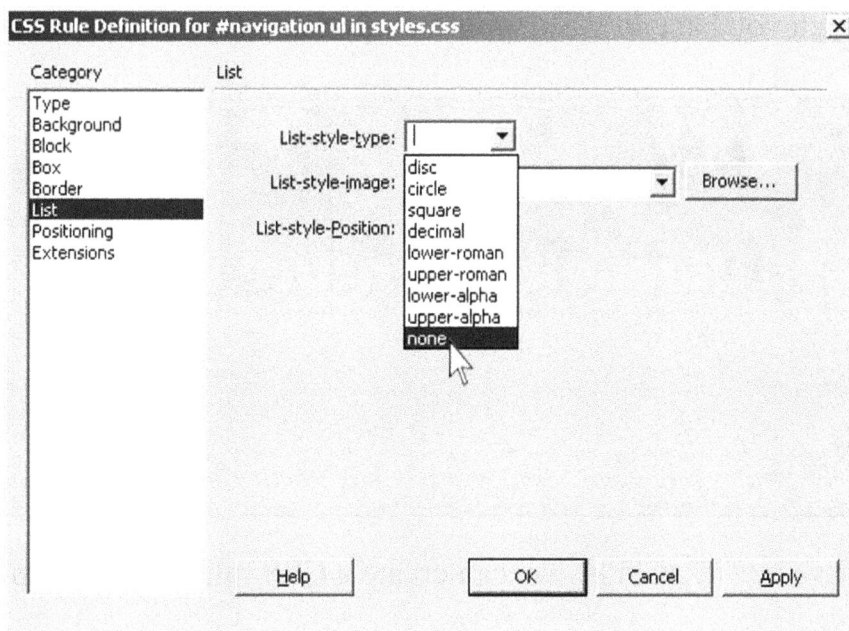

14. Click **OK** to close the CSS Rule Definition dialog.

Creating the navigation buttons

To create the navigation buttons, we first turn each item in our list into a hyperlink to the appropriate page. Next, we create a CSS rule which will format all links inside our unordered list to look like buttons.

1. Highlight the word "Home", the first item in our unordered list.

2. In the link section of the Properties panel, drag the **Point to file** button into the Files panel directly onto the page named "index.html".

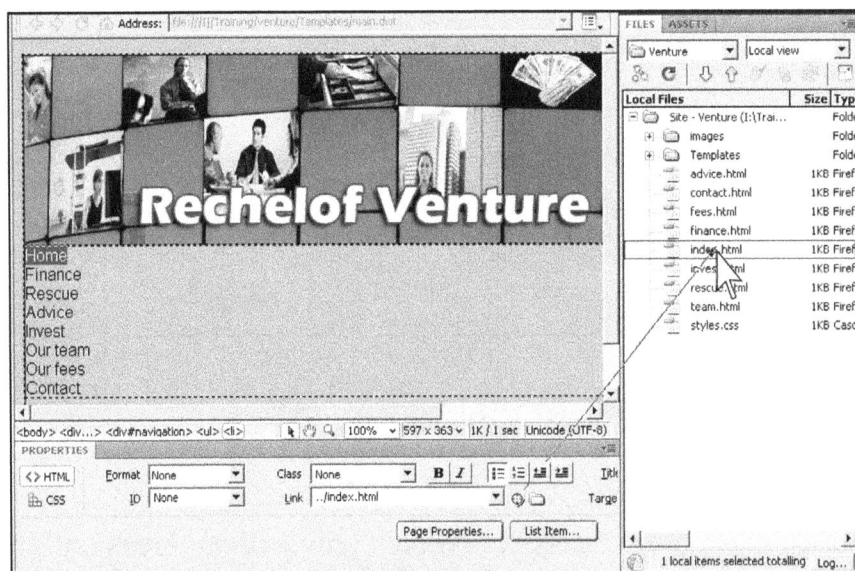

3. Using the same technique, create links to each of the remaining 7 pages in the site. When you have finished, your navigation DIV should look like this.

Now that we have our hyperlinks, we can create a CSS rule to transform them into buttons.

4. Highlight any one of the hyperlinks you have just created.

5. Choose **New** from the CSS Styles panel menu.

6. From the **Selector Type** drop-down menu, choose **Compound (Based on your selection)**.

7. Dreamweaver will enter **#wrapper #navigation ul li a** in the **Selector Name** field. Click once on the **Less Specific** button to shorten the name to **#navigation ul li a**.

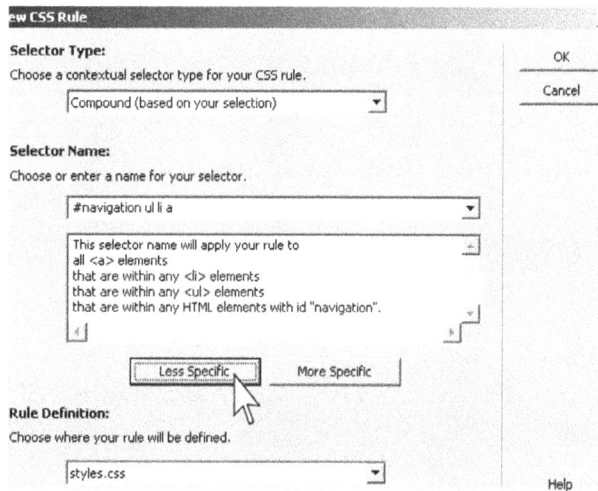

8. Make sure that the **Rule Definition** drop-down menu at the bottom of the dialog is set to **styles.css**.

9. Click **OK**.

Type category settings for navigation links

10. In the **Type** category of the CSS Rule Definition dialog, set the **Font-size** property to "0.9 em".

11. Set the **Font-weight** property to **Bold**.

12. Set the **Color** property to "#FFF" (by choosing white from the palette).

13. To remove the underline normally displayed with all hyperlinked text, set the **Text-decoration** property to **none**.

Background category settings for navigation links

To make our hyperlinks look like buttons, we will use a background image created in Adobe Photoshop. A second version of the same image—with a slightly different colour—will be used to create a CSS rollover effect.

14. Click on the **Background** category then click on the **Browse** button next to the **Background-image** field.

15. Open the images folder then double-click the file named "buttons1.jpg" to select it.

16. Set the **Background-repeat** property to **no-repeat**.

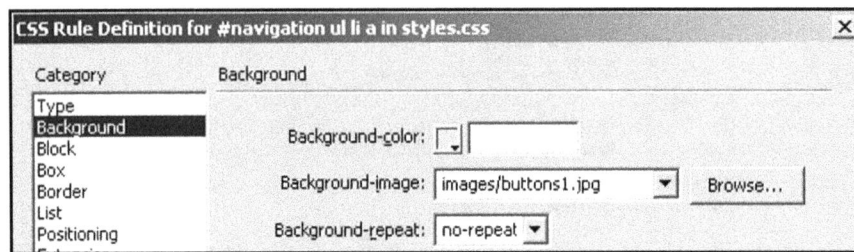

Block category settings for navigation links

We want our buttons to be a specific width and height. However, because **<a>** is an inline element, height and width settings cannot be applied to it. We must therefore override the normal inline display of this element and convert it to a block.

17. Click on the **Block** category.

18. Set the **Text-align** property to **center** to centre the text within the button.

19. Set the **Display** property to **Block** so that the **<a>** element will behave like a DIV and respond to values assigned to the width and height properties.

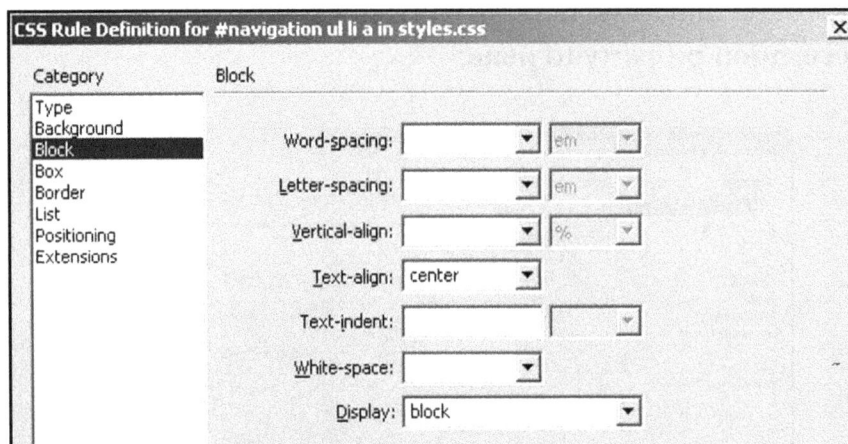

Box category settings for navigation links

20. Click on the **Box** category.

21. Set the **Width** property to "95 px". (The width of our main wrapper DIV is 760 pixels and we have 8 buttons. 760 divided by 8 gives us 95 pixels.)

22. Set the Height property to "25 px".

23. Set the **Top Padding** property to "3 px" and the zero on all other sides.

24. Click on the Apply button to see the effects of your CSS settings.

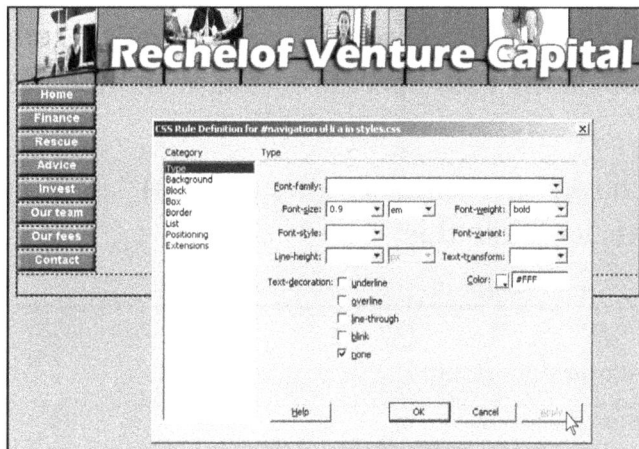

25. You will notice that, although the width and height settings are being adhered to, the buttons are arranged vertically. We need them to form a single horizontal navigation bar. To do this, we simply set the **Float** property to **Left**.

26. Click on the **Apply** button once more and, this time, the buttons should be arranged horizontally.

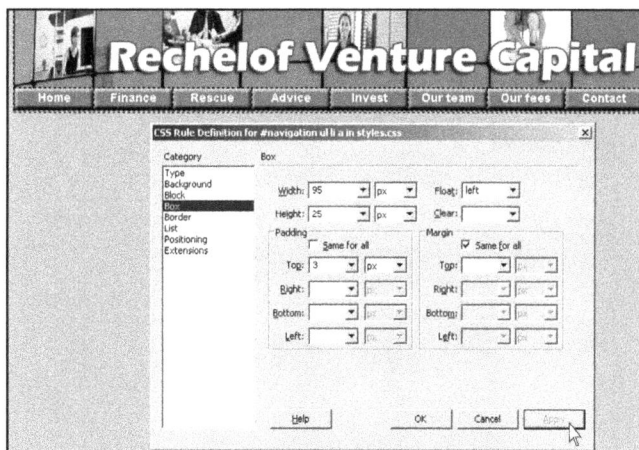

27. Click **OK** to close the CSS Rule Definition dialog.

Creating a CSS rollover effect

Using CSS, it is also possible to have the buttons change appearance when the mouse passes over them. To do this, we create another rule for the **<a>** element within our unordered list but, this time, add the keyword "hover".

1. Click on any of your navigation buttons.

2. Choose **New** from the CSS Styles panel menu.

3. From the **Selector Type** drop-down menu, choose **Compound (Based on your selection)**.

4. Dreamweaver will enter **#wrapper #navigation ul li a** in the **Selector Name** field. Click once on the **Less Specific** button to shorten the name to **#navigation ul li a**.

5. Add the text ":hover" immediately after the final "a". Your Selector Name field should now look like this.

Selector Name:

Choose or enter a name for your selector.

| #navigation ul li a:hover | ▼ |

6. Click **OK**.

Background category settings for a:hover

7. In the **Background** category of the CSS Rule Definition dialog, click on the **Browse** button next to the **Background-image** property; open the **images** folder and double click the file "buttons2.jpg" to select it.

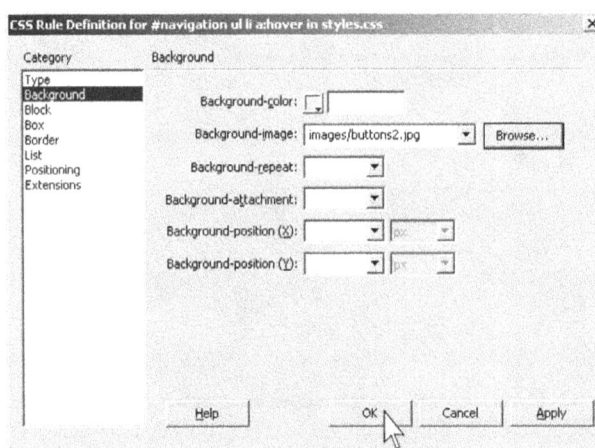

CSS Rule Definition for #navigation ul li a:hover in styles.css

Category   Background

Type
Background
Block
Box   Background-color: ☐
Border   Background-image: images/buttons2.jpg ▼ Browse...
List
Positioning   Background-repeat: ▼
Extensions
                 Background-attachment: ▼

                 Background-position (X): ▼ px ▼

                 Background-position (Y): ▼ px ▼

            Help   OK   Cancel   Apply

8. Click **OK** to close the CSS Rule Definition dialog.

Previewing the rollover effect

9. Choose **File > Save All** to save the changes to both the template and the linked CSS file.

10. Click on the **Live View** button at the top of the document window.

Now, when you position the cursor over any of the buttons, you should see the button change appearance—as the **background-image** property switches from "button1.jpg" to "button2.jpg".

11. Click on the **Live View** button once more to exit the live preview and return to **Design** mode.

Creating and styling the main DIV and elements within it

The main DIV will occupy the middle of the page and will contain the editable region of the template. As well as defining a CSS rule for the main DIV itself, we will need to create rules to control the appearance of headings and paragraphs within the DIV.

1. Choose **Insert > Layout Objects > Div Tag**.

2. Choose **After tag** and **<div id="navigation">** from the two drop-down menus at the top of the dialog.

3. In the **ID** field, enter the name **main**.

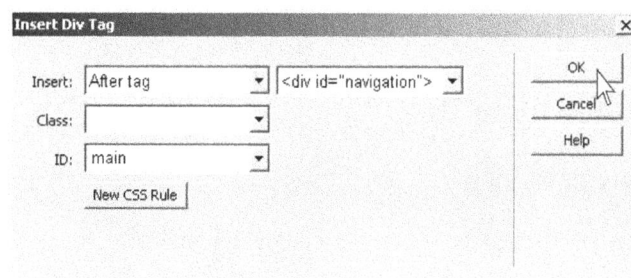

4. Click **OK** to create the DIV element.

Creating a rule for the main DIV

1. In the Tag Selector, click **<div#main>** to select the **main** DIV you have just created.

2. Choose **New** from the CSS Styles panel menu.

3. From the **Selector Type** drop-down menu, choose **Compound (Based on your selection)**.

4. Dreamweaver will enter **#wrapper #main** in the **Selector Name** field. Click once on the **Less Specific** button to change the name to **#main**.

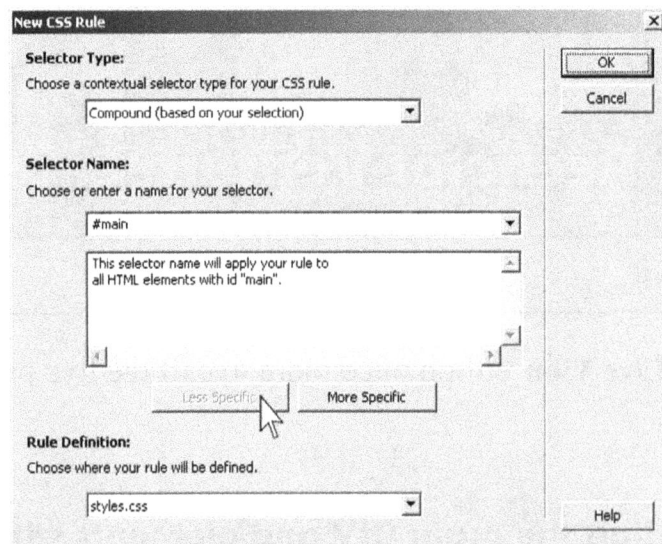

5. Make sure that the **Rule Definition** drop-down menu at the bottom of the dialog is set to **styles.css** then click **OK**.

All we really need to do for the main DIV itself is to create a small amount of padding to ensure that its contents are not too close to the edge of the containing wrapper DIV. We also need a white background.

Background category settings for main DIV

6. Click on the **Background** category.

7. Set the **Background-color** property to "#FFF" (white).

Box category settings for main DIV

8. Click on the **Box** category.

9. Set the **Padding** property to 10 pixels on all sides.

10. Click **OK** to close the CSS Rule Definition dialog.

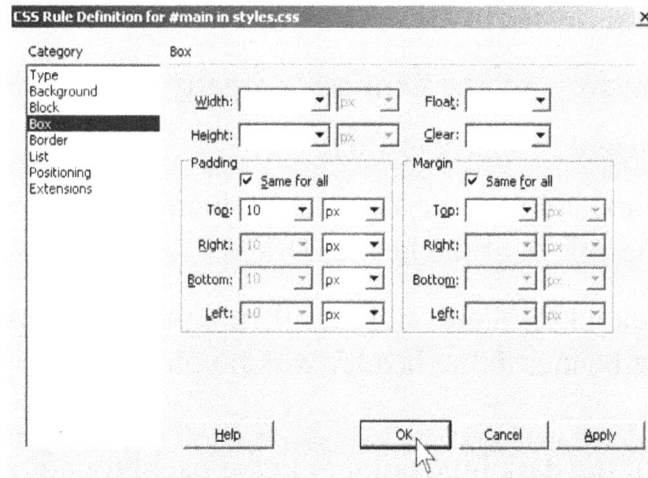

Creating rules for h1 and h2 headings within the main DIV

1. In the Tag Selector, click **<div#main>** to select the main DIV you have just created.

2. Choose **New** from the CSS Styles panel menu.

3. From the **Selector Type** drop-down menu, choose **Compound (Based on your selection)**.

4. Dreamweaver will enter **#wrapper #main** in the **Selector Name** field. Click once on the **Less Specific** button to change the name to **#main**.

5. Since we are specifically targeting headings within the main DIV, amend the selector name to read **#main h1**.

6. Make sure that the **Rule Definition** drop-down menu at the bottom of the dialog is set to **styles.css** then click **OK**.

Type category settings for main DIV h1 elements

7. In the **Type** category, set the **Font-size** property to "1.5 em".

8. Set the **Font-weight** property to **Bold**.

Let's now change the text color to the same dark blue found in the banner graphic we used as the background-image of the header DIV.

9. To do this, click on the **Color** pop-up; then, ignoring the palette, move the cursor over the banner in the header which you should be able to see behind the dialog.

10. Click on one of the dark blue colours in the background of the banner to sample it.

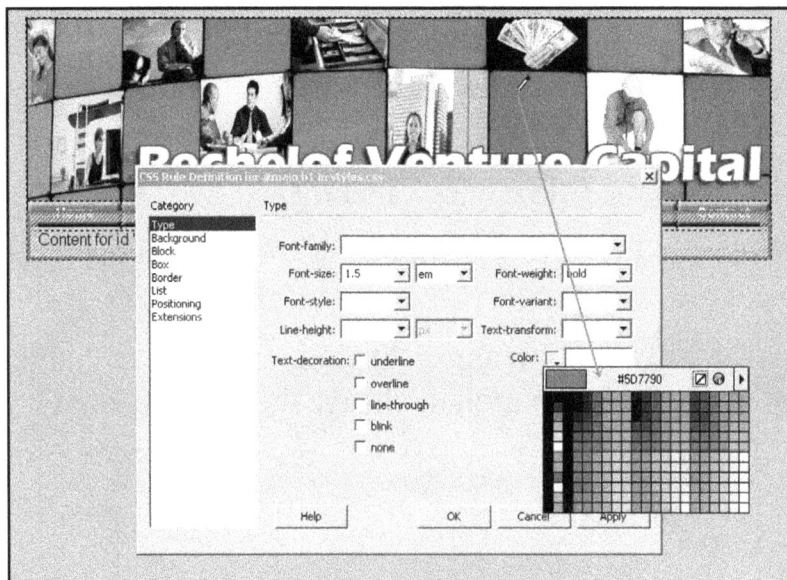

11. Click **OK** to close the CSS Rule Definition dialog.

Creating a rule for <h2> headings within the main DIV

Since the **<h2>** headings will basically be a smaller version of the **<h1>** headings, let us create this rule by duplicating the **<h1>** CSS definition we have just finished.

1. In the CSS Styles panel, right-click on **#main h1** and choose **Duplicate** from the context menu.

2. In the dialog which appears change the entry in the **Selector Name** field from **#main h1** to **#main h2**.

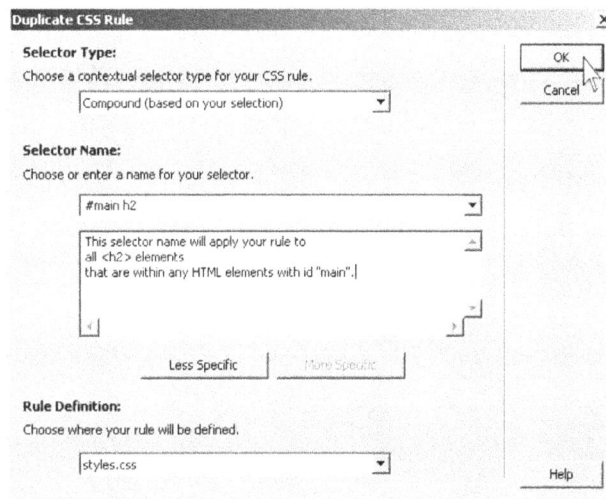

3. Click **OK**.

Type category settings for main DIV h2 elements

1. In the CSS Styles panel, right-click on **#main h2** and choose **Edit** from the context menu.

2. In the **Type** category, change the **Font-size** property to "1.25 em".

3. Click **OK** to close the CSS Rule Definition dialog.

Creating rules for paragraphs within the main DIV

Our third and final style definition for text within the main DIV will be for paragraphs—the **<p>** element. We will set the font size and line spacing.

1. In the Tag Selector, click **<div#main>** to select the **main** DIV you have just created.

2. Choose **New** from the CSS Styles panel menu.

3. From the **Selector Type** drop-down menu, choose **Compound (Based on your selection)**.

4. Dreamweaver will enter **#wrapper #main** in the **Selector Name** field. Click once on the **Less Specific** button to change the name to **#main**.

5. Since we are defining a rule for paragraphs within the main DIV, amend the Selector name to read **#main p**.

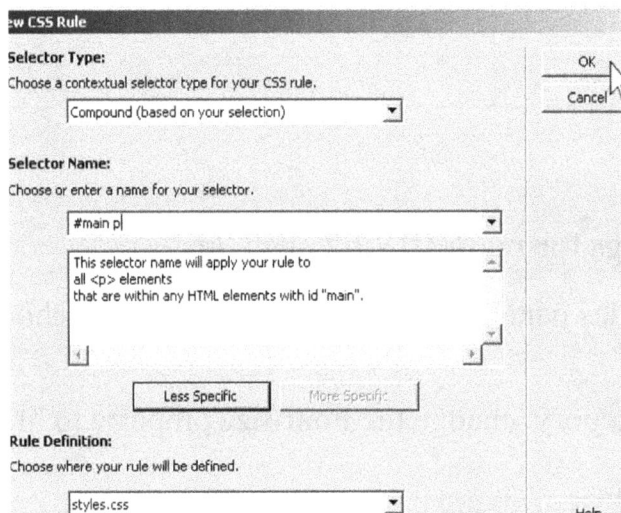

6. Click **OK**.

Type category settings for main DIV p elements

7. In the **Type** category, change the **Font-size** property to "0.9 em".

8. Set the **Line-spacing** property to "1.35 em"—equivalent to one and half line spacing (0.9 times 1.5 equals 1.35).

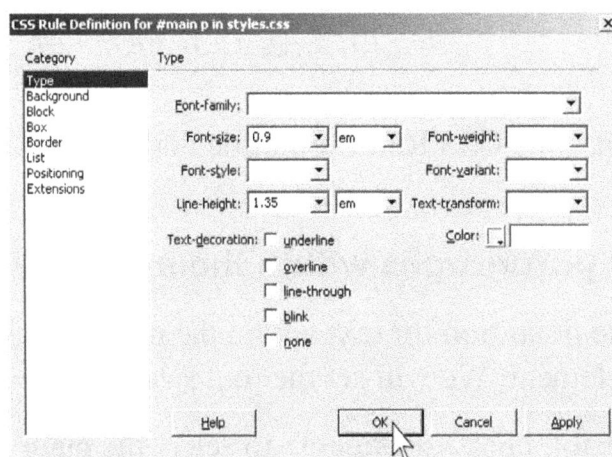

9. Click **OK** to close the CSS Rule Definition dialog.

Creating and styling the footer DIV

Our final layout component will be the footer DIV. This will contain a copyright notice and the company's logo.

1. Choose **Insert > Layout Objects > Div Tag**.

2. Choose **After tag** and **<div id="main">** from the two drop-down menus at the top of the dialog.

3. In the **ID** field, enter the name **footer**.

4. Click **OK** to create the DIV element.

5. In the Tag Selector, click **<div#footer>** to select the **footer** DIV you have just created.

6. Choose **New** from the CSS Styles panel menu.

7. From the **Selector Type** drop-down menu, choose **Compound (Based on your selection)**.

1. Dreamweaver will enter **#wrapper #footer** in the **Selector Name** field. Click once on the **Less Specific** button to change the name to **#footer**.

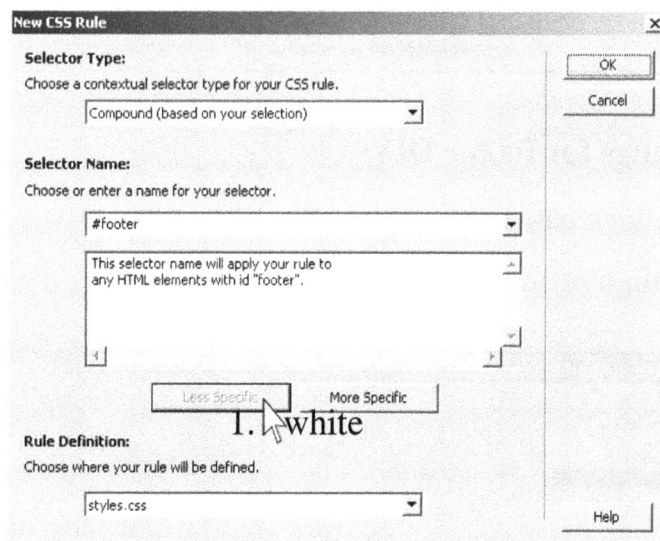

2. Click **OK**.

Type category settings for footer DIV

3. Set the **Font-size** property to "0.8 em".

4. Set the **Font-weight** property to "Bold".

5. Set the **Color** property to "#FFF" (white).

Background category settings for footer DIV

6. Click on the **Background** category.

7. Click on the **Browse** button next to the **Background-image** field. Open the **images** folder and double-click the file called "footer-back.jpg" to select it.

8. Choose **No-repeat** from the **Background-repeat** drop-down menu.

Block category settings for footer DIV

9. Click on the **Block** category.

10. Set the **Text-align** property to **right**.

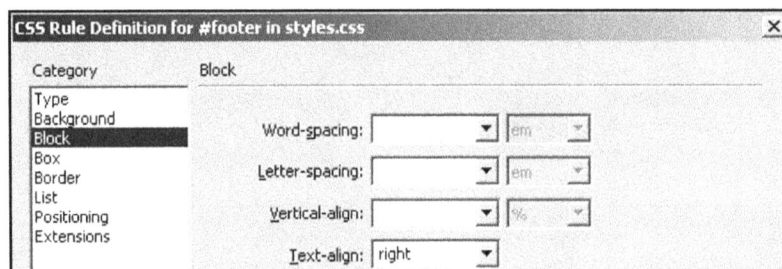

Box category settings

We will set the height of the footer DIV to 100 pixels to match the height of the background image we are using. The logo we will be importing has a height of 75 pixels which leaves a difference of 25 pixels. We will distribute this as a top padding of 13 pixels and a bottom of 12 pixels. (When measuring the overall height of a DIV, padding has to be included. Therefore, we will assign the DIV a height of 75 pixels.)

11. Click on the **Box** category.

12. Set the **Height** property to "75 pixels".

13. Set the **Top Padding** property to "13 px" and the other sides to "12 px".

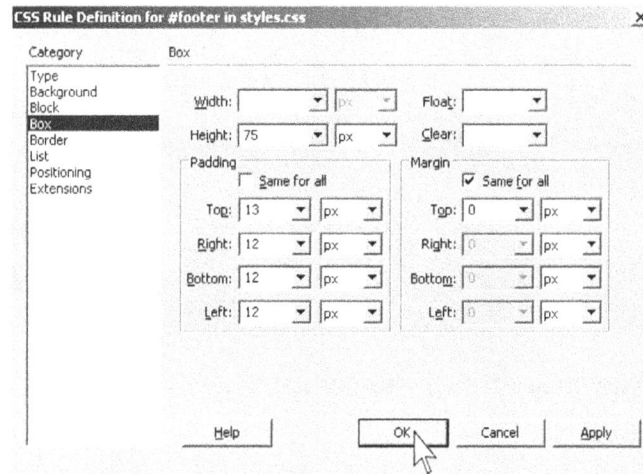

14. Click **OK**.

Adding content to the footer DIV

1. If you have not already done so, delete the placeholder text inside the footer DIV.

2. Choose **Insert > HTML > Special Characters > Copyright** to insert the copyright symbol ("©").

3. Type a space followed by the text "Copyright, Rechelof Venture Capital, 2010.".

4. Choose **Insert > HTML > Special Characters > Non-breaking space** twice or use the keyboard shortcut **Control-Shift-Space** (Mac, **Command-Shift-Space**).

5. Choose **Insert > Image**.

6. In the **images** folder (inside the **venture** folder), locate and double-click the file called "logo.gif".

7. In the **Alternate text** field, enter the text "Rechelof logo".

Your template should now look like this.

That completes the basic structure of our template. All we need to do is to define at least one editable region.

Defining an editable region

All the content that we have placed in our template so far is composed of locked regions. If we applied the template to a page, we would be unable to edit anything on that page. We need to tell Dreamweaver that the main DIV is an editable region where we can insert the content which will individualize each page.

1. Select the placeholder text inside the main DIV ('Content for id "main" Goes Here').

2. Choose **Insert > Template Objects > Editable Region**.

3. Enter the region name "mainContent" and click OK.

4. Dreamweaver creates the editable region and leaves the placeholder text inside it.

5. We can now delete the placeholder text, taking care not to delete the editable region itself in the process. If you do accidentally delete the editable region, just choose **Edit > Undo** and delete the placeholder text letter by letter. (We

left the placeholder text there simply because, without it, the main DIV would virtually disappear in Dreamweaver's Design View.)

That's it! Our template is finished. Choose **File > Save All** then **File > Close** to close the template.

Let's review our progress

Let's now take a step back for a moment to review just where we are in the Dreamweaver website creation cycle.

Steps completed so far

So far, we have completed the following steps.

1. Plan and design
2. Create Local Site Folder
3. Create Default Images Folder
4. Define Dreamweaver site
    a. Local information
    b. Server information (when available)
5. Create all files and folders
6. Create template
7. Create CSS file
8. Link CSS file to template
9. Add content to template
    a. Create locked content
    b. Define editable region(s)
    c. Create CSS rules

Steps left to be completed

And these are the steps we have left to be completed.

10. Apply template and add content to individual pages
11. Test site
12. Upload site to server and go live

Step 10. Add content to individual pages

Now, we need to open each of the pages in the site, apply the template to it and then add the necessary content.

Creating the Home page

Since "Home" is the first link on our navigation bar, let's begin with the home page, which has the file name "index.html". This is what the home page needs to look like.

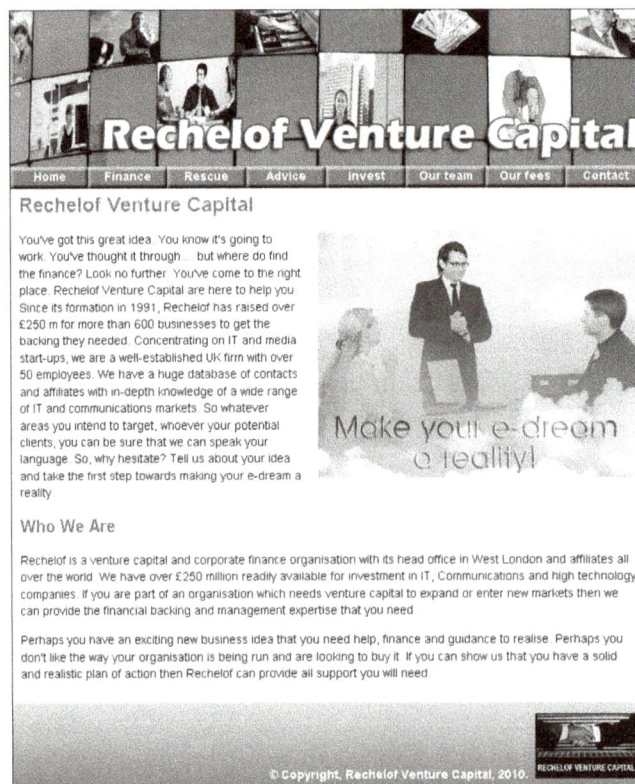

Applying the template to the home page

1. In the Files panel, double-click on the file named "index.html" to open it.

2. Choose **Modify > Templates > Apply Template to Page**.

3.   Highlight the only template listed in the dialog ("main"); then click **Select**.

Inserting the text for the Home page

All the text required for the pages in the site has been placed in a single text file named "venture.txt".

1.   Choose **File > Open**.

2.   Navigate to the root of the training folder and double-click the file called "venture.txt" to open it.

The text has been divided into sections; each section contains the text for one of the pages. Naturally, the text in the first section is for the home page.

3.   Select the text from the beginning of the document down to "Rechelof can provide all support you will need".

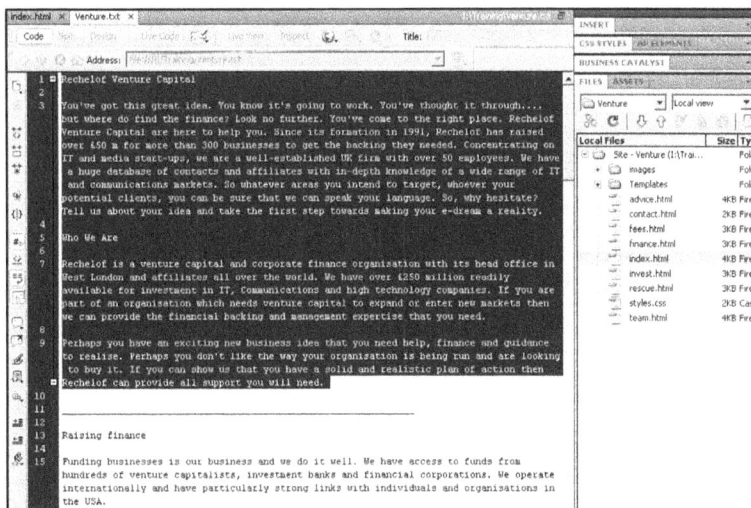

4.   Choose **Edit > Copy**.

5.   Click on the tab marked **index.html** to switch back to the home page.

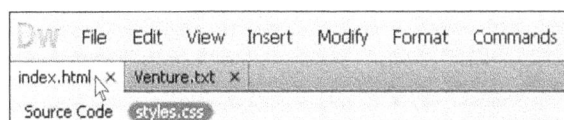

6. Click in the editable region.

7. Choose **Edit > Paste**.

Formatting the text

Whenever you paste text into a page in Design view, Dreamweaver automatically converts each paragraph into an HTML paragraph complete with **<p>** tags. This means that the text you have just pasted will follow the CSS rule you created earlier named **#main p**, since this controls all paragraphs in the main DIV.

Therefore, the only paragraphs we need to format are the two headings.

8. Highlight the heading "Rechelof Venture Capital".

9. Choose **Heading 1** from the **Format** pop-up menu in the **HTML** section of the Properties panel.

10. Highlight the sub-heading "Who We Are" and choose **Heading 2** from the **Format** pop-up menu.

Adding a floating image to the home page

The final element required on the home page is an image floating to the right with the text wrapping around it. To float the image, we will create a CSS class rule and then apply it to the image.

11. Click to position the cursor at the start of the first paragraph—in front of the text "You've got this great idea".

12. Choose **Insert > Image**.

13. Open the **images** folder and double-click on the file named "e-dream.jpg" to import it.

14. Choose **New** from the menu in the top right of the CSS Styles panel.

15. Set the **Selector type** to **Class**.

16. In the **Selector name** box, enter the class name **.imageRight**.

17. Click **OK**.

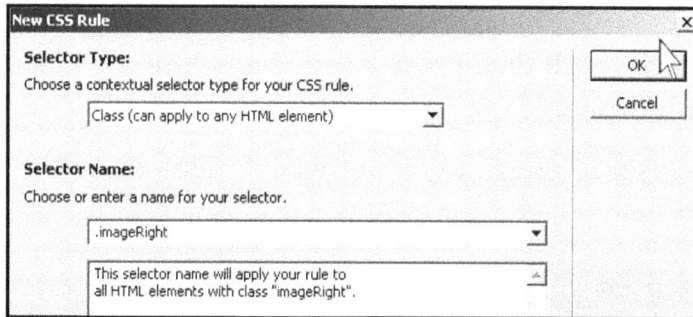

Box category settings for the .imageRight class

18. When the CSS Rule Definition dialog appears, click on the **Box** category.

19. Set the **Float** property to **right**. (This will cause the image to be positioned on the right of the main DIV with the text wrapping around it on the left.)

20. In the **Padding** section, deactivate the option **Same for all**; set the **Bottom** padding to "10 px" and the **Left** to "20 px". (This will prevent the text from getting too close to the image.)

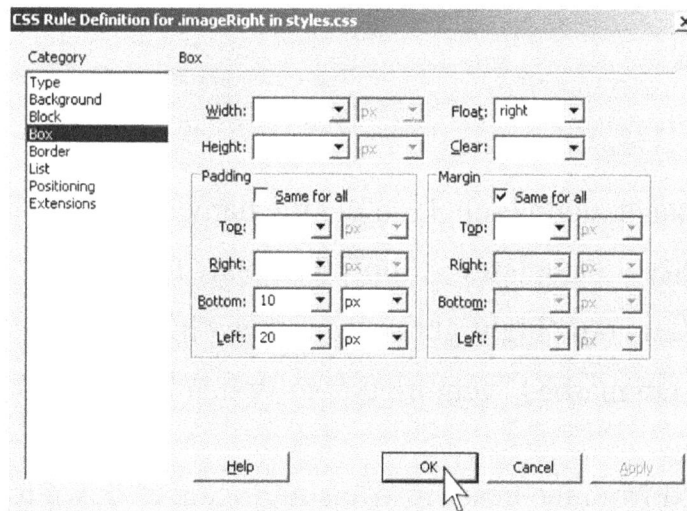

21. Click **OK**.

Since the CSS rule we have just defined is a class, it will not automatically affect any element on the page. We need to specify that the image belongs to our new "imageRight" class.

(Using a class gives us the flexibility of having some images in the main DIV floating on the right and others behaving differently. If we had given our CSS rule the name "#main img", it would have immediately affected all images in the main DIV.)

22. Click once on the image to highlight it.

23. Choose **imageRight** from the Class pop-up menu in the Properties panel.

And that's it for the **Home** page!

24. Choose **File > Save All** then press F12 (Mac: Option F12) to preview the page in your default browser.

25. Close the browser to return to Dreamweaver then close the index.html.

Creating the Finance page

Moving along the links on our navigation bar, our next page will be "finance.html". This page will contain just text and should only take a couple of minutes to complete.

1. In the Files panel, double-click on the file named "finance.html" to open it.

2. Choose **Modify > Templates > Apply Template to Page**.

3. In the **Templates** box, highlight **venture** then click **Select**.

4. Click on the tab marked "venture.txt" to switch back to the file containing the source text.

5. Select the text from the heading "Raising Finance" down to "all the necessary contracts".

6. Choose **Edit > Copy**.

7. Click on the tab marked "finance.html" to switch back to the **Finance** page.

8. Click in the editable region.

9. Choose **Edit > Paste**.

10. Highlight the heading "Raising Finance".

11. Choose **Heading1** from the **Format** pop-up menu in the Properties panel.

12. Choose **File > Save** then close the **Finance** page.

Creating the Rescue page

Next, we have "rescue.html", another basic page containing just text. However, we also have an email link at the bottom of the page.

1. In the Files panel, double-click on the file named "rescue.html" to open it.

2. Apply the template to the page using **Modify > Templates > Apply Template to Page**.

3. Click on the tab marked "venture.txt" to switch back to the file containing the source text.

4. Select the text from the heading "Business Rescue" down to the email address "rescue@rechelofventurecapital.com".

5. Choose **Edit > Copy**.

6. Click on the tab marked "rescue.html" to switch back to the **Rescue** page.

7. Click in the editable region.

8. Choose **Edit > Paste**.

9. Highlight the heading "Business rescue".

10. Choose **Heading1** from the **Format** pop-up menu in the Properties panel.

Creating an email link

When the text to be converted to an email link is the email address itself, Dreamweaver makes it easy to create the link.

11. Highlight the email address.

12. Choose **Insert > Email** link.

Dreamweaver automatically inserts the highlighted email address into both the **Text** and **Email** fields.

13. Click **OK** to create the hyperlink.

14. Press F12 (Mac: Option F12) to test the page in the default browser.

15. If you have an email client loaded on your machine, such as Outlook, click on the email link to test it.

16. Close the browser window to return to Dreamweaver.

17. Choose **File > Save** then close the **Rescue** page.

Creating the Advice page

The **Advice** page also has a link; but, this time, it is a "Back to top" link to a named anchor on the page itself. (If you need to refresh your memory on how named anchors work, have a look at page 82, in Chapter 7: Creating Hyperlinks.)

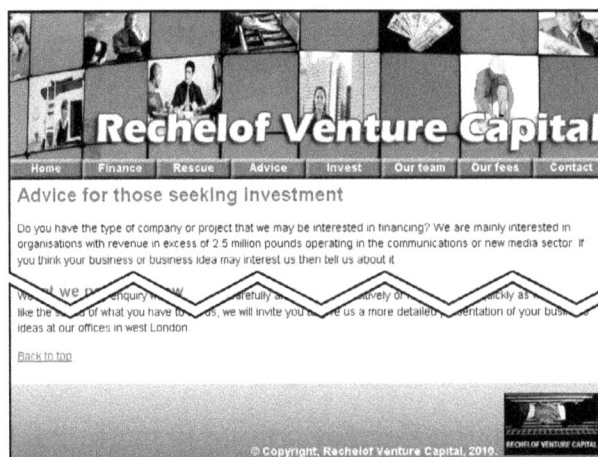

1. In the Files panel, open "advice.html".

2. Apply the template to the page.

3. Click on the tab marked "venture.txt" to switch back to the file containing the source text.

4. Select the text from the heading "Advice for those seeking investment" down to "Back to top".

5. Choose **Edit > Copy** (**Control-C**).

6. Switch back to "advice.html".

7. Click in the editable region.

8. Choose **Edit > Paste** (**Control-V**).

9. Highlight the heading "Advice for those seeking investment".

10. Choose **Heading1** from the **Format** pop-up menu in the Properties panel.

Creating a link to a named anchor

To create a "Back to top" link, you need to insert a named anchor at the very top of the page and then create a hyperlink to it. However, all our pages are based on the template and the top of the page is in a locked region. This means that we must return to the template to be able to insert the named anchor.

11. In the Files panel, open the **Templates** folder and then double-click on the template ("main.dwt") to open it.

When you open an HTML page in Design View, the cursor is positioned at the start of the page, exactly where we need it. However—just so you know—let's look at the technique for positioning the cursor at the start of a page at other times.

12. In the Tag Selector, click on the **<body>** tag to select it. Since the **<body>** contains the entire page contents, this is an effective way of selecting everything on the page.

13. Now, press the Left cursor key (<--) on your keyboard to move to the start of the document.

14. Choose **Insert > Named Anchor**.

15. Enter the name "top".

16. Click **OK**.

17. Choose **File > Save** and, since you have just made changes to a template file, Dreamweaver will display the following dialog.

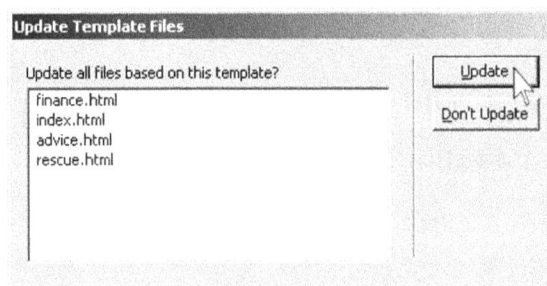

18. Click the **Update** button to update the four pages to which you have applied the template then click the **Close** button.

19. Close the template and return to "advice.html".

20. Highlight the text "Back to top".

21. Choose **Insert > Hyperlink**.

22. Choose **#top** from the drop-down menu next to the Link box then click **OK**.

Since the named anchor ("top") was placed on the template, all pages based on the template now contain that same named anchor; so, we will be able to create a "Back to top" link on any page in the site. Alternatively, we could simply copy the link we have just created onto any other page.

23. Save the changes to the **Advice** page then close it.

Creating the Invest page

Our next page "invest.html" is a basic text-only page containing an email link.

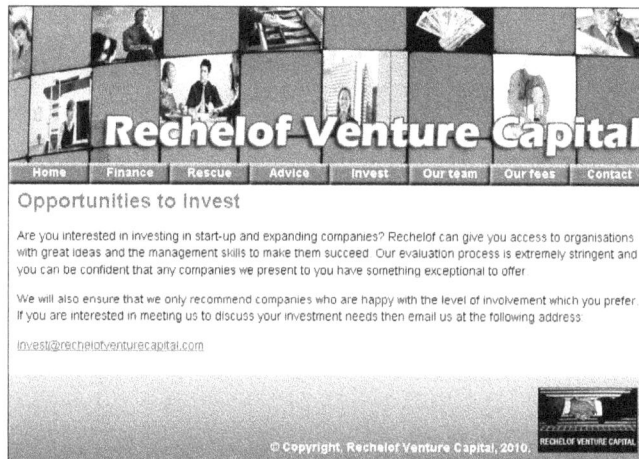

1. Open "invest.html".

2. Apply the template to the page.

3. Copy in the appropriate text from "venture.txt".

4. Highlight the heading "Opportunities to invest".

5. Choose **Heading1** from the **Format** pop-up menu in the Properties panel.

6. Highlight the email address at the bottom of the page.

7. Choose **Insert > Email** link.

8. Click **OK** to create the hyperlink.

9. Choose **File > Save**.

10. Close "invest.html".

Creating the Team page

The Team page has a two-column layout and will give us a chance to practice controlling DIVs with a class style. So far, all of the CSS rules we have created for DIVs have targeted a specific DIV element on the page.

When creating pages that have repeating elements, you will normally identify the DIV with a class rather than an ID, since IDs must be unique within the page while many elements on one page can have the same class.

1. Open "team.html" and apply the template to the page.

2. Click on the tab marked "venture.txt" to switch back to the file containing the source text.

3. Select the text from the heading "Meet the heads of our team" down to the end of the first paragraph only—ending "Harold Johnson, Matthew Straker and Rebecca Fletcher".

4. Copy the selected text.

5. Switch back to "team.html" and paste the text into the editable region of the page.

6. Highlight the heading "Meet the heads of our team".

7. Choose **Heading1** from the **Format** pop-up menu in the Properties panel.

To create our two column layout, we will first of all place each item in our list of staff profiles in a separate DIV. Inside this DIV, we will them insert an image and apply a CSS class to it to float to the left.

After the image, we will place a paragraph of text and—to prevent the text from wrapping underneath the image and maintain our two column structure, we will assign the paragraph a left margin 20 pixels wider than the width of the image.

Creating and styling the listing DIV

8. Select the menu option **Insert > Layout Objects > DIV** tag.

9. In the **Class** field, enter the name "listing" and click **OK**.

10. Choose **New** from the CSS Styles panel menu.

11. From the **Selector Type** drop-down menu, choose **Class**.

12. Enter the name **.listing** and click OK.

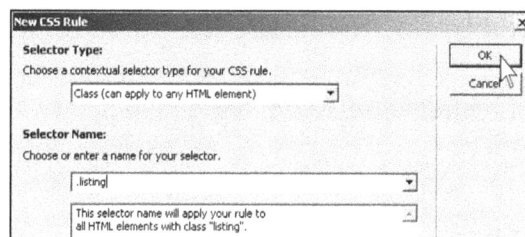

13. In the CSS Rule Definition dialog, click on the **Box** category.

14. In the **Margin** section, deactivate the option **Same for all**.

15. Set the **Bottom Margin** to "40 px" to put some space between the three **listing** DIVs we will create.

16. Click **OK**.

Styling the listing text

Now we need to create a style for the paragraph of text next to the image.

17. Switch across to the source text ("venture.txt") and, in the "Meet the members of our team" section, copy the paragraph profiling Harold Johnson, including his email address.

18. Switch back to "team.html"; delete the placeholder text inside the **listing** DIV ('Content for class "listing" Goes Here') and Paste in Harold's profile.

19. When you Paste text inside an empty DIV, Dreamweaver will not turn it into an HTML paragraph; so, select the text and choose **Paragraph** from the **Format** pop-up menu in the Properties panel.

20. With the cursor still in the paragraph, choose **New** from the CSS Styles panel menu.

21. From the **Selector Type** drop-down menu, choose **Compound (Based on your selection)**.

22. Dreamweaver will enter **#wrapper #main .listing** in the **Selector Name** field. Click twice on the **Less Specific** button to change the name to **.listing**. Finally, add a space followed by "p" to change the name to **.listing p**.

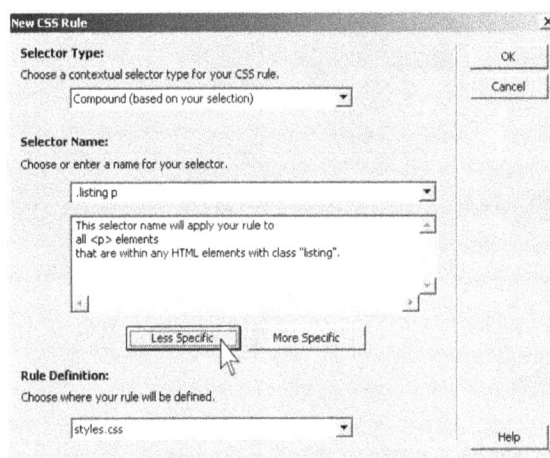

23. Click **OK**.

24. In the CSS Rules Definition dialog, click on the **Box** category.

25. In the margin section, deactivate the option **Same for all** and enter a **Left** margin setting of "170 px". (The width of each profile image is 150 pixels; plus 20 pixels of white space, gives us 170 pixels.)

26. Click **OK**.

Inserting and floating an image

Now we need to insert our photograph of Harold Johnson and float it to the left. The photograph needs to be inserted in front of the paragraph, not inside it.

27. Highlight the paragraph of text inside the listing DIV then press the left cursor key on your keyboard to move the cursor to a position immediately before the paragraph.

28. Choose **Insert > Image**, and double-click on the file named "harold.jpg", inside the **images** folder, to import it.

29. When the Accessibility dialog appears, enter the name "Harold Johnson" in the **Alternate Text** field then click **OK**.

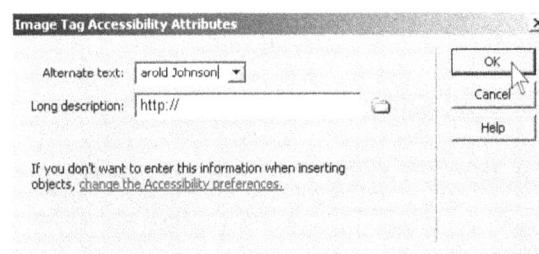

There are two ways of floating an image. Firstly, you can use CSS as we saw when creating the "imageRight" class on page 167. The benefit of this is that you can then add further attributes to the class, such as padding or borders.

However, if floating the image is all you want to do, then you can use a simple HTML attribute: align. Let's use this second method here.

30. Click on the image to highlight it.

31. On the bottom row of the Properties panel, set the **Align** property to **Left**.

The image should now float to the left with the text wrapping around it with a gap of 20 pixels as specified by our CSS rule.

Duplicating the listing DIV

To complete the layout, we will simply copy the DIV and then change the contents of the copies.

32. Click anywhere inside the listing DIV, then click on **<div.listing>**, in the Tag Selector in the bottom left of the document window, to highlight the DIV.

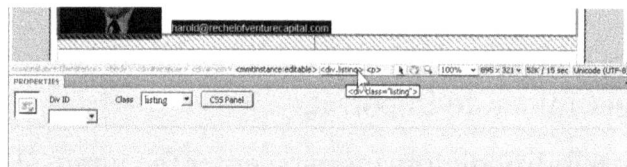

33. Choose **Edit > Copy**.

34. Press the right cursor key on your keyboard to position the cursor after the **listing** DIV.

35. Choose **Edit > Paste** twice to create two copies of the listing DIV.

You should now have three copies of Harold Johnson's photo and profile, as shown below.

Replacing the copied photos

36. Delete the second photo and choose **Insert > Image**.

37. Double-click on the file named "rebecca.jpg", inside the **images** folder to import it.

38. When the Accessibility dialog appears, enter the name "Rebecca Fletcher" in the **Alternate Text** field then click **OK**.

39. With the image still selected, choose **Left** from the **Align** pop-up menu in the bottom right of the Properties panel.

40. Delete the third photo and choose **Insert > Image**.

41. Double-click on the file named "matt.jpg", inside the **images** folder.

42. Enter the name "Matthew Straker" in the **Alternate Text** field of the Accessibility dialog then click **OK**.

Now, we need to replace the profiles.

Replacing the profile text

43. Switch over to "venture.txt" and copy Rebecca Fletcher's profile and email address.

44. Switch back to "team.html", delete the text next to Rebecca's picture and replace it with the text you have just copied.

45. Repeat this procedure to update Matthew Straker's profile.

Creating email hyperlinks

The final tasks on this page are to turn the three email addresses into hyperlinks and add a "Back to top" link.

46. Highlight Harold Johnson's email address.

47. Choose **Insert > Email** link.

Dreamweaver automatically inserts the highlighted email address into both the **Text** and **Email** fields.

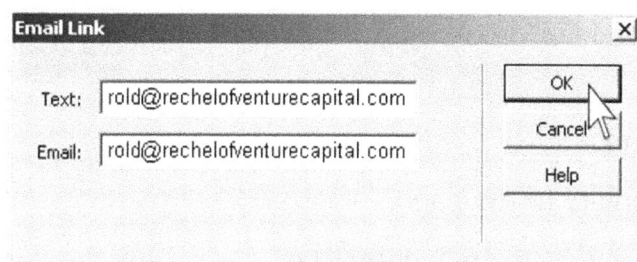

48. Click **OK**.

49. Repeat the above procedure to turn the email addresses of Rebecca and Matt into hyperlinks.

50. Click after Matt's email address, press Enter and type the text "Back to top".

51. Highlight the text "Back to top".

52. Choose **Insert > Hyperlink**.

53. Choose **#top** from the drop-down menu next to the **Link** box then click **OK**.

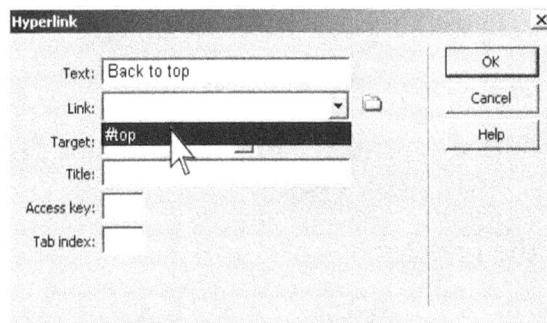

54. Press F12 (Mac: Option F12) to preview the page in your browser then close the browser window to return to Dreamweaver.

55. Save and close the **Team** page.

Creating the Fees page

The penultimate page, "fees.html" is a basic text only page.

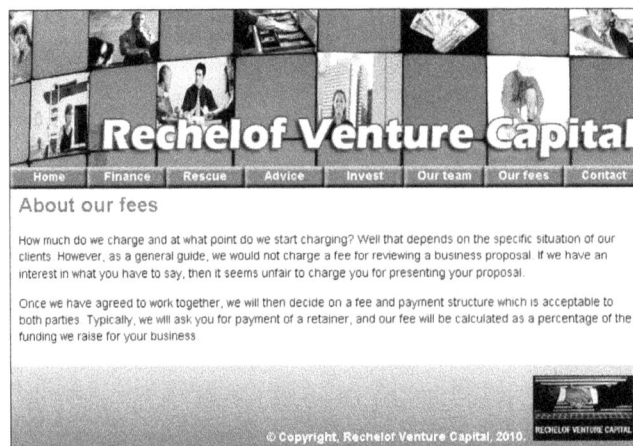

1. Open "fees.html".

2. Apply the template to the page.

3. Copy in the fees text from "venture.txt".

4. Highlight the heading "About our fees".

5. Choose **Heading1** from the **Format** pop-up menu in the Properties panel.

6. Choose **File > Save**.

7. Close "fees.html".

Creating the Contact page

The contact page requires a form. However, since we won't be discussing forms until the next chapter, we will return to finish the contact page later. For the moment, let's just bring in the text.

1. Open "contact.html".

2. Apply the template to the page.

3. Copy in the contact text from "venture.txt".

4. Highlight the heading "Contacting us".

5. Choose **Heading1** from the **Format** pop-up menu in the Properties panel.

6. Choose **File > Save**.

7. Close "contact.html".

Only two more steps to go in our website creation cycle

That completes step 10, adding content to individual pages (apart from the Contact page that is). We have just two more steps to go.

11. Test site

12. Upload site and go live

We will return to the Dreamweaver website creation cycle and finish these last two steps at the end of chapter 13—after we have discussed techniques for maintaining and testing your site.

12. Forms

Web forms are an essential component on pretty much every website which allow site owners to interact with site visitors. Everyone who has been using the web for any length of time will have encountered many forms. For a start, the first page that most people go to when they access the internet is a search engine; and what do they see? A form. It may only have one field, namely the search box; but it's still a form.

Figure 12-1: A search engine form has just one field and a submit (search) button

The type of interaction permitted by forms is wide and varied. Here are some typical examples.

- Search forms for locating products, services and information
- Check-out forms for making purchases
- Sign up forms for becoming a member of a site
- Subscription to a mailing list (often a big mistake!)
- Online application forms

Elements of a web form

A web form consists of several elements which work together to permit website visitors to send information to the owners of the site. The key components of a form are as follows.

- Input fields (for entering information)
- Labels (for clarification and guidance in filling out the form)
- Layout and formatting elements (to make the form look clear and attractive)
- A submit button (to initiate the process of transmitting the data entered by the user)

The key phases of a web form

Whenever web surfers navigate to a page containing a form, they are witnessing what one might call the front end of the form. If they choose to interact with the form then they will initiate other processes, some of which take place in their own browser and some behind the scenes, on the server. This whole cycle can be divided into the following five phases.

1. **Display**—The form is displayed in the user's browser.

2. **Submission**—The user presses the Submit button.

3. **Validation**—A script checks the data entered by the user and either displays an error message and blocks the form submission or sends the data to be processed on the server.

4. **Processing**—The data is received by a script on the server which processes it and decides what to do with it. This typically involves writing to and reading from databases and sending emails to the relevant people.

5. **Feedback**—Relevant information is sent back to the user. If the form requested information matching certain criteria, then the relevant data is displayed in the user's browser. If the user has made a purchase, they will be sent a confirmation of payment and a promise of delivery; and so forth.

Creating a form in Dreamweaver

To create a form in Dreamweaver, you can either use the **Forms** section of the Insert panel (**Window > Insert**) or use the **Insert > Form** sub-menu.

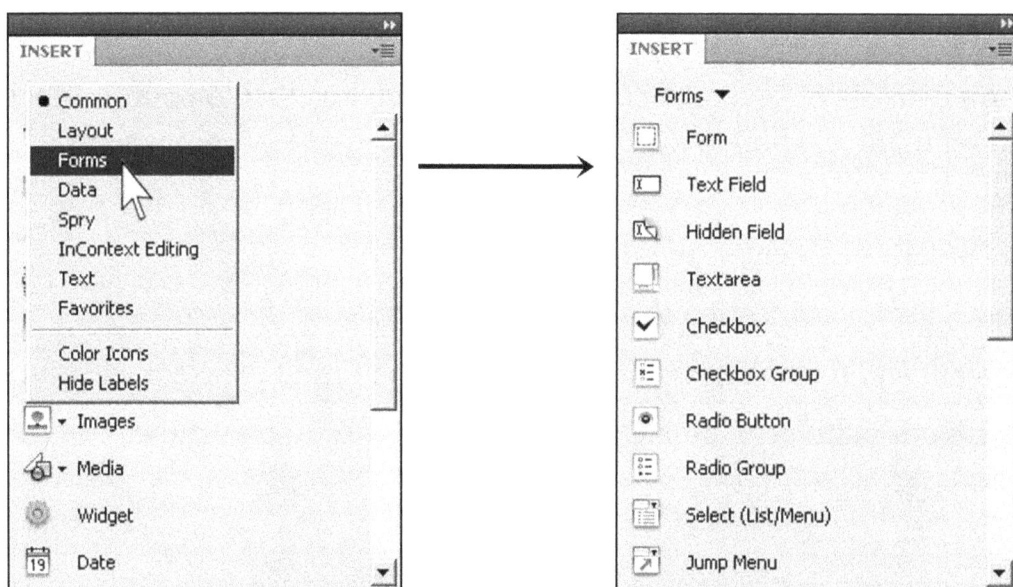

Figure 12-2: Displaying the Forms section of the Insert panel

To display the Insert panel, choose **Window > Insert**. The Insert panel provides a method of using Dreamweaver commands by clicking on buttons which are equivalent to various menu commands. It is divided into sections; so you may need to choose **Forms** from the pop-up menu at the top of the Insert panel, as shown in figure 12-2, on page 184.

The various commands displayed in the **Forms** section of the Insert panel can also be accessed in the main menu bar. Choose **Insert > Form** and the sub-menu displayed shows all the same commands as the **Forms** section of the Insert panel—albeit without the icons.

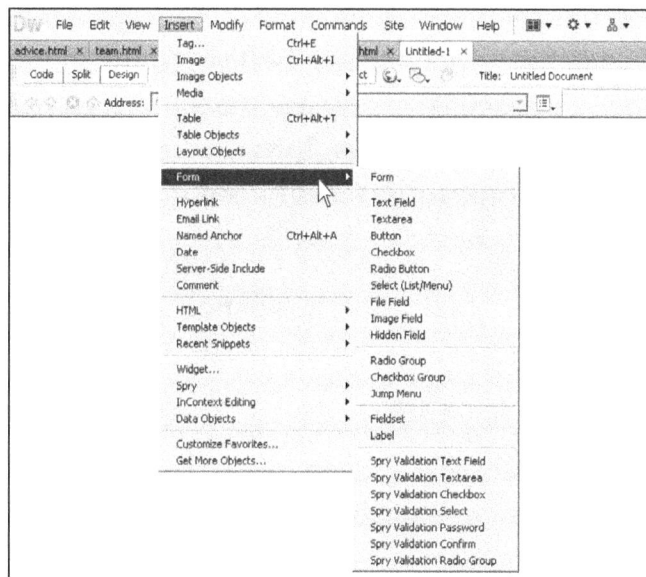

Figure 12-3: The Insert > Form sub-menu

Either of these two methods can be used to build forms in Dreamweaver. In this chapter, we will be using the **Insert > Form** approach; but feel free to use the Insert panel if you prefer.

Creating the form itself

When building a form, the first thing you need to insert is the form itself. You must then ensure that all of the controls relating to the form are placed inside it. This may sound rather obvious but, when working visually and building forms for the first time, it is easy to build forms that don't work properly.

To create a form in Dreamweaver, just choose **Insert > Form > Form**. Dreamweaver creates the form and, in Design View, displays it as a red rectangle. Anytime you are placing elements in the form, make sure that your cursor is somewhere within that red rectangle.

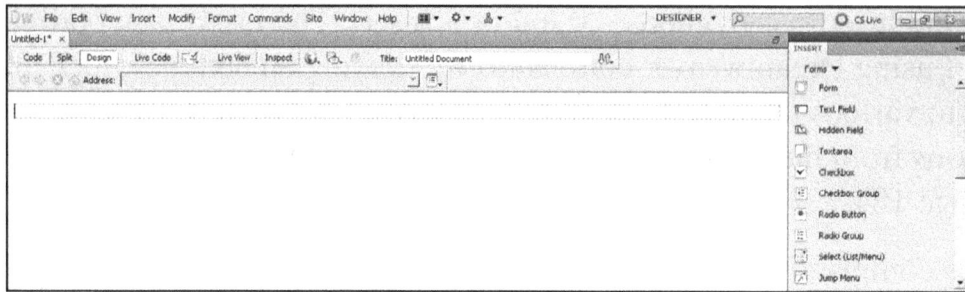

Figure 12-4: In Design View, Dreamweaver displays a form as a red rectangle

Naming a form

It is a good idea give each form that you create a name which reflects its function; for example "Enquiry". This is for reasons of scalability; for example, if you later decide to add some JavaScript to the page, you can use the name to target elements in the form. Also, since it is possible to have more than one form on the same HTML page, naming each one enables you to distinguish between them.

To name a form, click inside the red rectangle representing the form and enter a name in the **Form ID** box on the left of the Properties panel (as shown in figure 12-5).

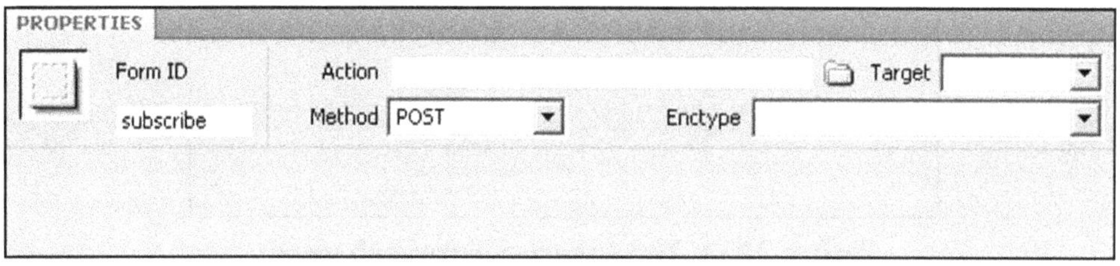

Figure 12-5: Naming a form

Using a table for form layout

There are two main tools for arranging and formatting the elements within a form: CSS and tables. Since most forms have a tabular structure, it is possible to use a table to lay out the elements in a form. When doing so, make sure that the form is the first element to be created and that the table then goes inside the form.

- Click inside the red rectangle representing the form.

- Choose **Insert > Table**.

- Enter the number of rows and columns required to layout your form.

- To make the table more accessible to screen readers, enter a short description of the function of the table in the **Summary** field; for example, " Table for entering a general enquiry".

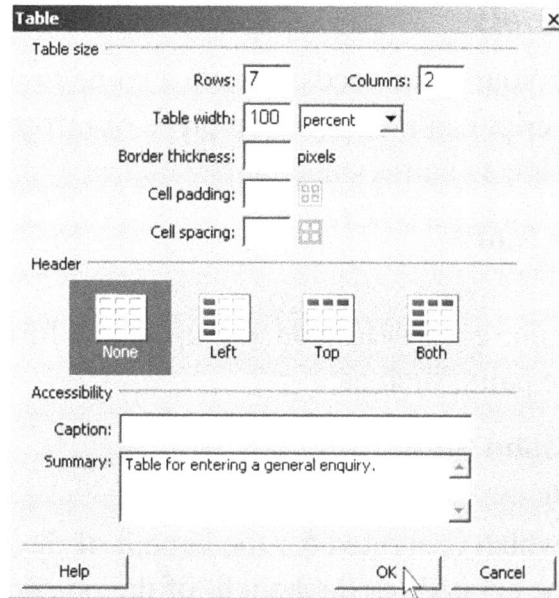

Figure 12-6: Creating a table for form layout

It is also perfectly feasible to use only CSS for the layout of your forms and dispense with tables altogether.

Using Dreamweaver's form accessibility features

Dreamweaver's accessibility features will make it easier for you to create forms which are accessible to all visitors to your website, including those using assistive technologies such as screen readers. (These features are activated by default.)

- Choose **Edit > Preferences** (or **Dreamweaver > Preferences** on a Mac).

- Click on the **Accessibility** category on the left of the Preferences dialog.

- Activate the **Form objects** checkbox.

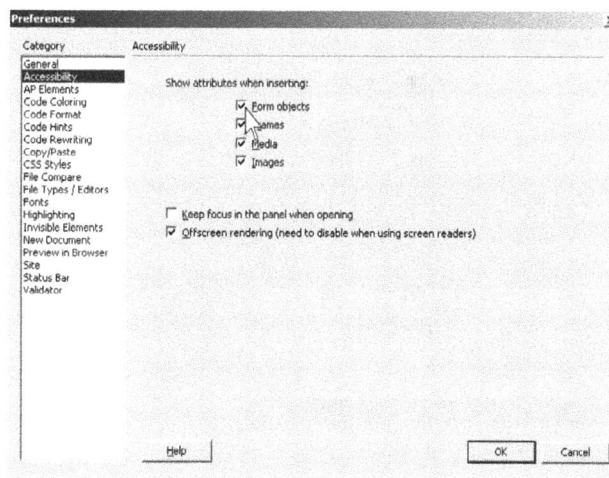

Figure 12-7: Activating Dreamweaver's form accessibility options

Fields, names and labels

Each field that you add to your form needs to have a name to identify it so that, when the form is submitted, a script can identify each piece of information. The script needs to receive information as name/value pairs, such as:

> **Name = "John Smith"**
>
> **Age = 39**

If you do not explicitly name each field, you end up with a form which generates unidentifiable name/value pairs, such as:

> **Textfield1 = "John Smith"**
>
> **Textfield2 = 39**

In addition to the name, which is created for the benefit of the script that will process the form, a label should be created for the benefit of the person completing the form. The label is normally displayed either in the same table cell as the form field that it relates to or in an adjacent cell.

Dreamweaver's form accessibility dialog makes the creation of correctly named and labelled form fields easy.

- Position the cursor where you would like the label for the control to be placed. For example, in a typical two-column layout using a table, you would position the cursor in the left column of your table.

- Choose **Insert > Form** followed by the appropriate control (e.g. **TextField**).

- If the **Form objects** accessibility options are active, Dreamweaver will then display the **Input Tag Accessibility Attributes** dialog.

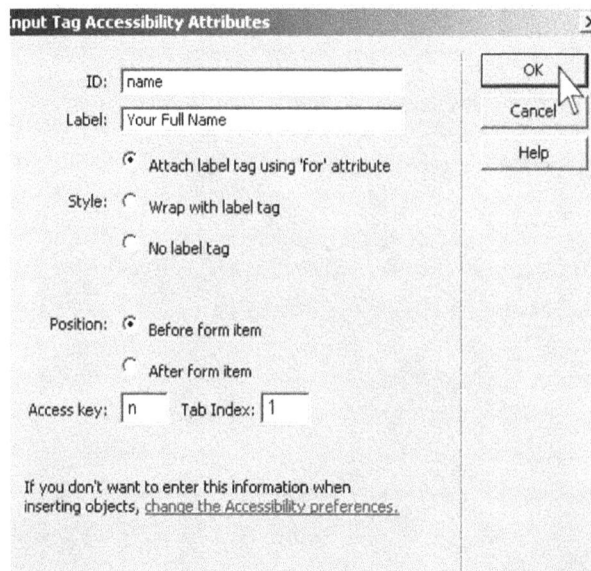

Figure 12-8: Dreamweaver's Input Tag Accessibility Attributes dialog

ID (and name)

The value entered in the ID field will be used both for the **name** and **ID** attributes of the field. It should not contain any spaces or special characters. The **name** attribute will be used by the script processing the form. The **ID** attribute can be used to control the appearance of the field using CSS. For example, if you create a field and give it an **ID** of "name", you could later create a CSS rule called "#name" to control its position and appearance.

The Label

By contrast, the value you enter in the Label box of the dialog will appear on the page and is for the benefit of the user. Thus, while the ID can be cryptic and script-friendly, the label should always be clear and user-friendly.

The label also needs to be associated with the control to which it refers. Dreamweaver offers two options: **Attach label tag using "for" attribute** and **Wrap with label tag**.

Attach label tag using "for" attribute

If you are placing the label in one cell of a table and the control in another, choosing this option will add a for attribute to the label in the HTML code to clarify which form field it relates to. For example:

> **<label for = "name">Your Full Name:</label>**

Wrap with label tag

If you are placing the label and control in the same cell of a table, choosing this option will include the form field tag inside the label tag. For example:

> **<label>Your Full Name:**
>
> **<input type = "text" name ="name" id="name" />**
>
> **</label>**

No label tag

There is a third option: **no label tag**. This should be used for controls which do not require a label, such as a submit button. The general rule is that only controls which are used to enter data need to be given both a label and an ID. Since buttons are used to submit (or reset) the form and not for inputting data, they do not need a label—unless you wanted a label next to your submit button saying something like "Complete all fields then click the submit button".

Position: before/after form item

This option allows you to specify where the label is placed relative to the form field. Before item is usually the more user-friendly and accessible choice.

Access key

The **Access key** option allows you to specify a keyboard shortcut for activating the field. Thus, if you specify that "n" is the access key for the Name field, the user will be able to access the field by pressing **Alt-n** (Internet Explorer) or **Alt-Shift-n** (Firefox for Windows) or **Control-n** (Safari and Firefox for Mac).

If you use this feature, you must accept that it will only be implemented by a small proportion of users. The **Tab index** feature (See below.) provides a more standardized and predictable method of adding keyboard accessibility to your forms.

Tab index

The **Tab index** attribute is used to pre-determine the order in which users can navigate through the form fields using the Tab key on their keyboard. To use this feature, each form field is simply assigned a number which will determine its place in the tab order. When creating forms, it is often the case that fields will be inserted after the initial design. It is therefore useful to leave gaps between the **Tab index** numbers assigned to form fields. This saves you having to reassign new numbers to every field each time you insert a new field between two existing ones.

Separating the label and form field

Regardless of which label options you choose, Dreamweaver always places the label and form field in the same cell of the table—if you are using a table to lay out your form. If you want to have normal form arrangement of labels in the left column and form fields in the right, each time you insert a field, you will need to drag it into the right-hand column after inserting it.

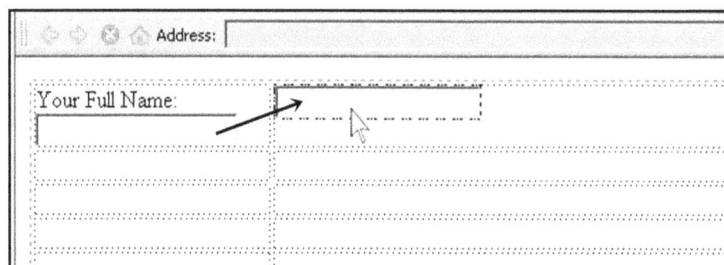

Figure 12-9: Separating a form field from its label

Remember also that, when you plan to place the label in a separate cell to the control, you should always choose the option **Attach label tag using "for" attribute**; so that association between the two items can be recognized by screen readers.

Creating text fields

Text fields are the most common type of control encountered in online forms. They are used to allow the user to enter information by typing or pasting it into the field. This field type is used to allow the input of data that you have no way of anticipating, such as a person's postal code or their preferred user name.

To create a text field, choose **Insert > Form > Text Field** and complete the Input Tag Accessibility Attributes, as discussed in the previous section.

Having created the text field and moved it to the adjacent cell in the table (if necessary), click on the field to select it and look at the options in the Properties panel. You will notice that Dreamweaver allows you to choose between three different types of text field: **Single line**, **Multiline** and **Password**.

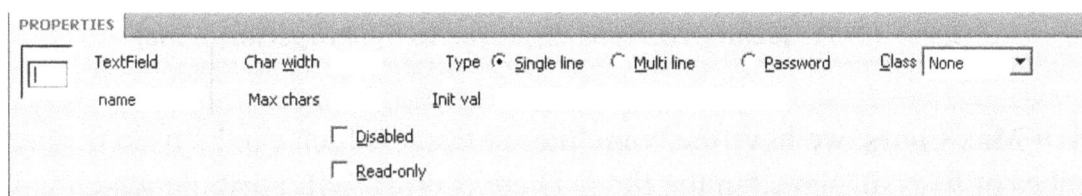

Figure 12-10: Text field attributes displayed in the Properties panel

The **Single line** option is perhaps the most frequently used and allows the user to input one line of text. **Password** is identical but causes the browser to mask the data being entered by the user and display bullets or asterisks instead.

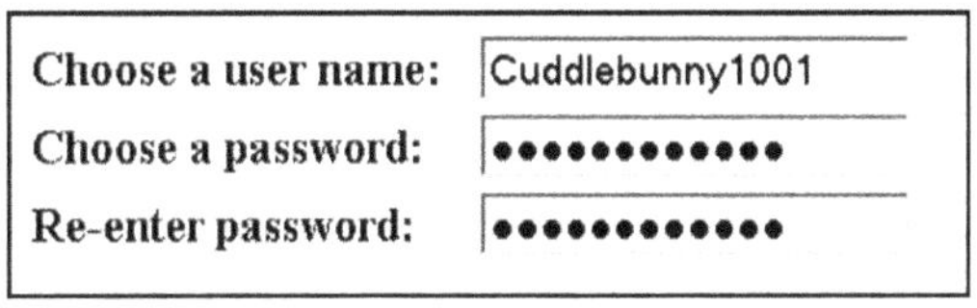

Figure 12-11 : Text entered into a password field is masked by the browser

Both of these options relate to the HTML **<input>** element.

> **<input type = "text"... />**

> **<input type = "password"... />**

In addition to the Type property, the Properties panel also allows you to set the **Char width** or number of characters which the text field can display. This is not the same as specifying the width of the text field in the browser: to do this, you would need to create a CSS rule.

The **Max Chars** property allows you to limit the number of characters which the field will accept; while **Init value** can be used to set a default value which will appear in the field when the form first loads.

Setting the **Type** attribute to **Multiline** converts a text field from an **<input>** to a **<textarea>** element. The normal way of creating this element is to choose **Insert > Form > Textarea**; but both techniques produce the same result. When a **textarea** field is highlighted, the Properties panel displays the options shown in figure 12-12, below.

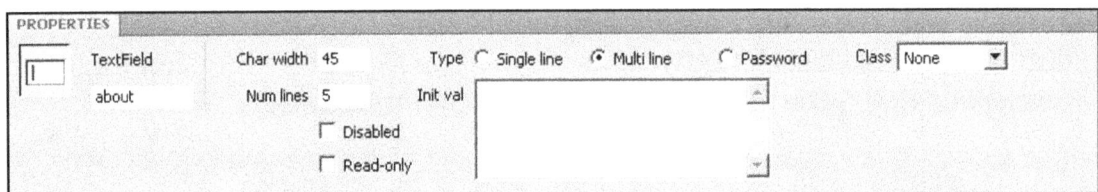

Figure 12-12: Textarea options displayed in the Properties panel

Instead of **Max Chars**, we have the **Num lines** attribute which can be used to specify the number of lines displayed in the field. There is no HTML attribute which will limit the number of characters which can be input into a **textarea** field.

Textarea controls are useful for allowing users to enter a significant amount of information into a single field and are used for fields with labels like "Please give details:", "Bio:" or "Home Address:". When the number of lines displayed in the field is exceeded, a scrollbar appears automatically to enable the user to scroll up and down to reveal any line of text.

The Select control

When the data you are capturing from the user is not open-ended but can be limited to a finite number of choices, HTML forms offer a number of controls for displaying those choices. One of the most widely-used is the **select** control which creates a drop-down menu with a series of options.

To create a **select** control, choose **Insert > Form > Select (List/Menu)**. After creating the control, you can use the Properties panel to specify the options which will displayed in the drop-down menu and which option will be selected by default when the form first loads.

- Highlight the select control.

- In the Properties panel, click on the button marked **List values**.

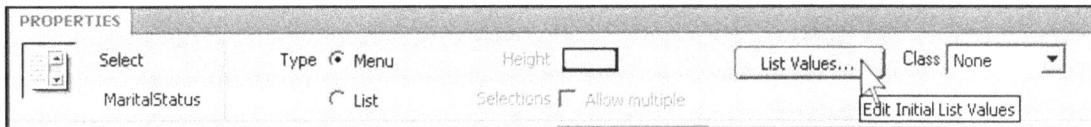

Figure 12-13: The List Values button in the Properties panel

This displays the **List Values** dialog box which allows you to enter and edit the text that you want to appear in the drop-down menu.

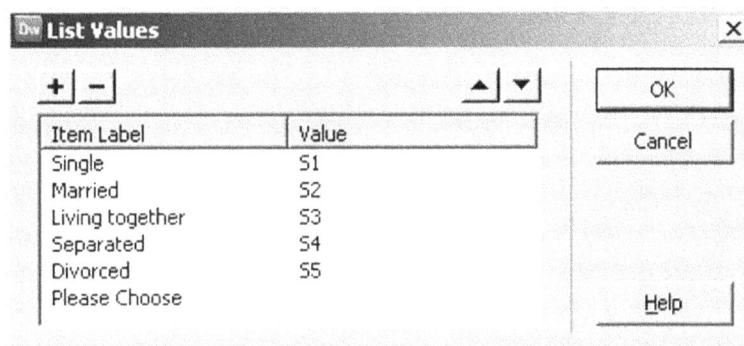

Figure 12-14: Editing list values for a select control

Item Label and Value columns

The List Values dialog has two columns headed **Item Label** and **Value**. The **Item Label** column should contain the values you want displayed in the drop-down menu. This is the only column that you must complete. The second column is optional and should be used when there is an identifier relating to the item which it would more useful to submit to the script handling the form.

Thus, if you are editing values for a select field called "MaritalStatus" and, in your database, people with a marital status of "Single" have a special code of "S1", you would enter "Single" in the **Item Label** column and "S1" in the **Value** column, as shown in figure 12-14, above.

Adding items

To enter items, click on the plus sign (+) in the top left of the dialog, then make an entry in the **Item Label** and **Value** columns, as necessary. You can also use the Tab key on your keyboard both to move from field to field and to add new items—simply by pressing Tab repeatedly.

Reordering items

To change the order of items, click on any item in the list and use the arrow buttons in the top left of the dialog to move the item up or down.

Setting a default value

Having clicked **OK** to close the Value List dialog, you can use the Properties panel to set the default item which will be displayed in the drop-down menu when the form first loads.

With the **select** field still highlighted, in the Properties panel, click on any item in the list marked **Initially selected**. (You may need to scroll down to make the appropriate value visible.)

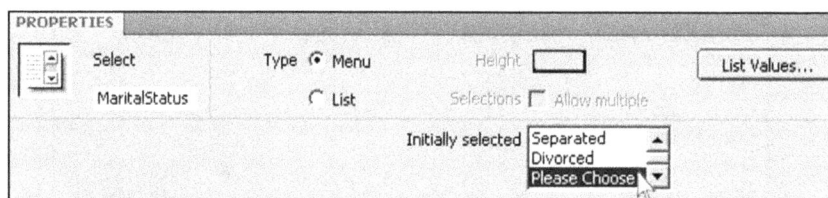

Figure 12-15: Setting the default value for a Select control

The first candidate for default value is usually the most popular or likely choice (such as setting the default of a "Country" field to "UK" or "USA"). However, a better choice is to have as the default a prompt or reminder to choose a value; for example, "Please choose" or "Unspecified". Without using such an option as the default, you can never be certain whether the user has actually made a choice or simply left the default value in place.

Displaying a list instead of a menu

The select control can also display a list instead of a drop-down menu. This is useful when there are relatively few items in the list and offers two main advantages over the menu style. Firstly, the items in the list remain permanently visible and, secondly, it is possible for users to select more than one item.

To have a **select** control display a list rather than a menu, highlight the control and, in the **Type** section of the Properties panel, switch from **Menu** to **List**. Next, in the height field, enter the number of items you want to display. Ideally, this will be the same as the number of items in your list. Finally, optionally, activate the **Selections > Allow multiple** checkbox, as shown in figure 12-16, on page 195.

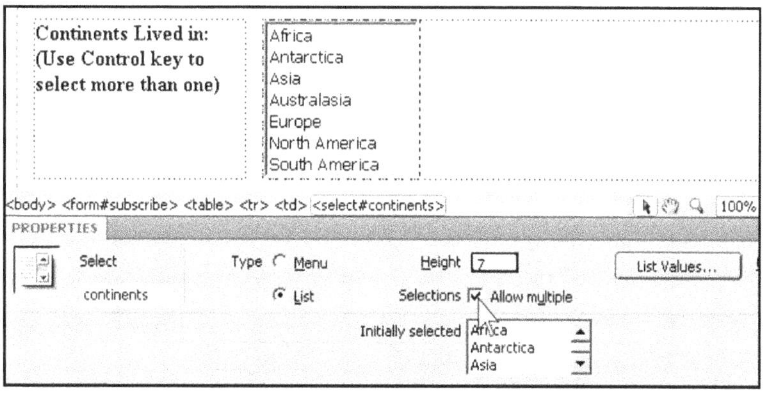

Figure 12-16: Converting a select control from a Menu to a multiple selection List

The ability to select more than one item and the technique for doing so may not be obvious to all your users. It is therefore useful to add an explanatory note to the form, such as "Use Control key to select more than one".

As so often in computing, the Shift key can be used to make contiguous selections and the Control key to make discontiguous ones.

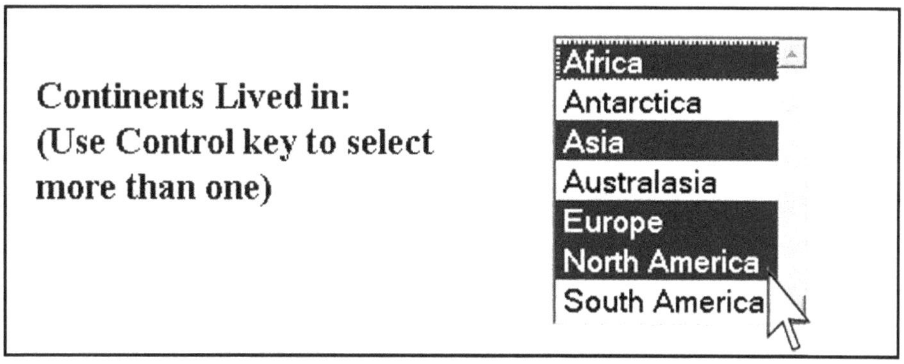

Figure 12-17: Selecting multiple items in a list

Creating radio buttons

Radio buttons are circular controls which work as a mutually exclusive group—when you activate one member of the group, all other members are automatically switched off. Although it is possible to create a single radio button in Dreamweaver using **Insert > Form > Radio Button** , it is more useful to insert a whole group of radio buttons in one operation.

To do this, choose **Insert > Form > Radio Group**. You will notice that Dreamweaver displays the Radio Group dialog (See figure 12-18 on page 196.) instead of the usual Input Tag Accessibility Options dialog. However, the program will still automatically insert label tags for each radio button in the group.

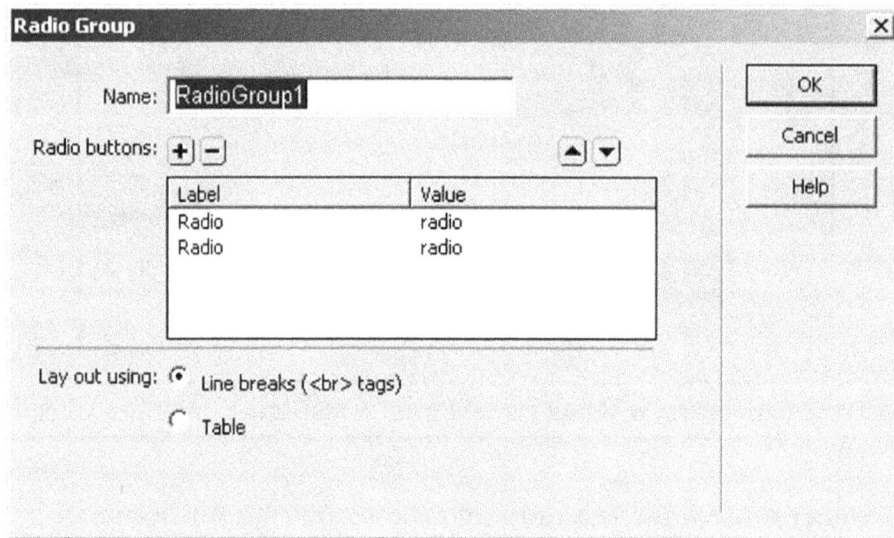

Figure 12-18: The Radio Group dialog with Dreamweaver's default labels

The Radio Group dialog is similar to the List Values dialog we saw earlier when discussing **select** controls. At the top of the dialog, you should enter the common name for all the radio buttons in the group. (It is this common name that makes them function as a group.)

Dreamweaver initially places two items in the list (the minimum number required to form a group). So, you normally start by modifying the label and values to suit your requirements. If you require any more items, click on the plus sign in the top left of the dialog. The dialog also features buttons for deleting and reordering items.

As with **select** controls, it is often a good idea to include a default value in your **radio group** which explicitly reminds the user that they have not yet made a choice; for example "Unspecified".

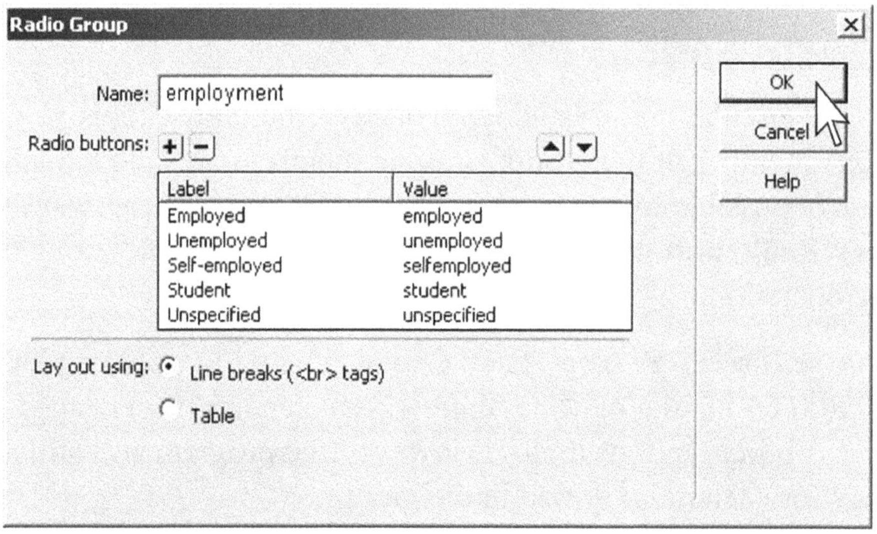

Figure 12-19: It is useful for a radio group to include a default item such as "Unspecified"

Having clicked **OK** to close the Radio Group dialog, you can use the Properties panel to set the default value. Simply click on the radio button which you want to make the default and change the **Initial state** property from **Unchecked** to **Checked**.

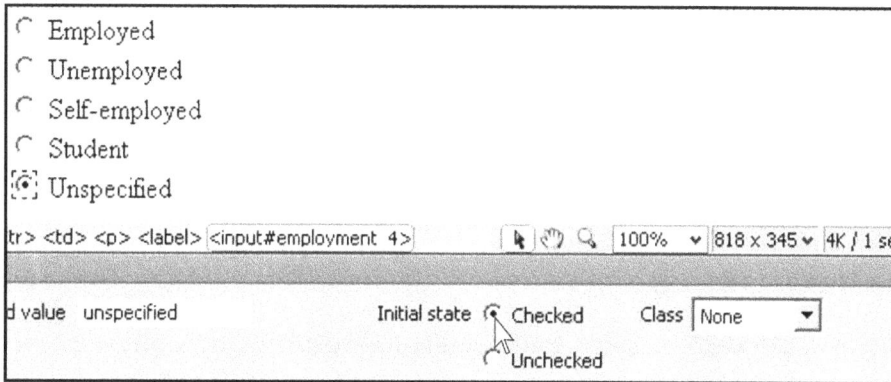

Figure 12-20: Specifying a default radio button

The fieldset control

The **fieldset** element is used on forms as a container for related form controls. A **radio group** is one example of a series of related controls which can be placed inside a **fieldset.**

To place a group of radio buttons inside a **fieldset**, simply highlight all of them then choose **Insert > Form > Fieldset**. The fieldset dialog appears. (See figure 12-21, below.) It contains a single field for entering the legend which will appear as a heading within the fieldset.

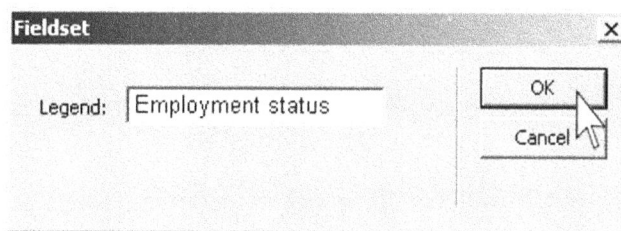

Figure 12-21: The Fieldset dialog

In most browsers, the fieldset is normally displayed as a frame around the items it contains. However, naturally, its appearance and behaviour can be customized using CSS rules.

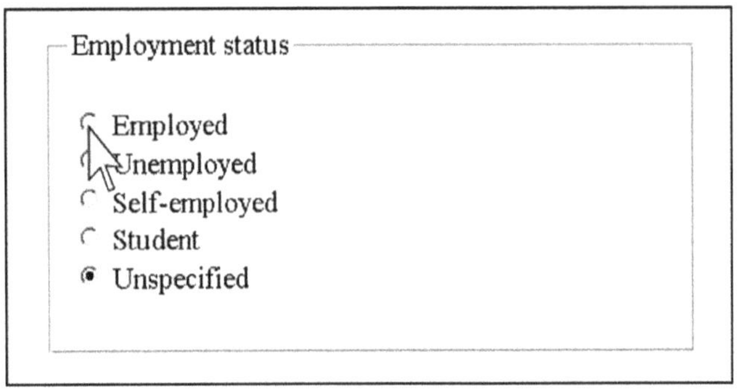

Figure 12-22: A Fieldset as it appears in a browser

Creating checkboxes

Like radio buttons, checkboxes are usually arranged in groups but are not mutually exclusive. The user can activate and deactivate each checkbox independently of the others. Dreamweaver treats checkboxes in much the same way as radio buttons, allowing you to create them individually (using **Insert > Form > Checkbox**) or as a group (using **Insert > Form > Checkbox Group**).

The Checkbox Group dialog box is practically identical to the Radio Group dialog and everything functions in the same way.

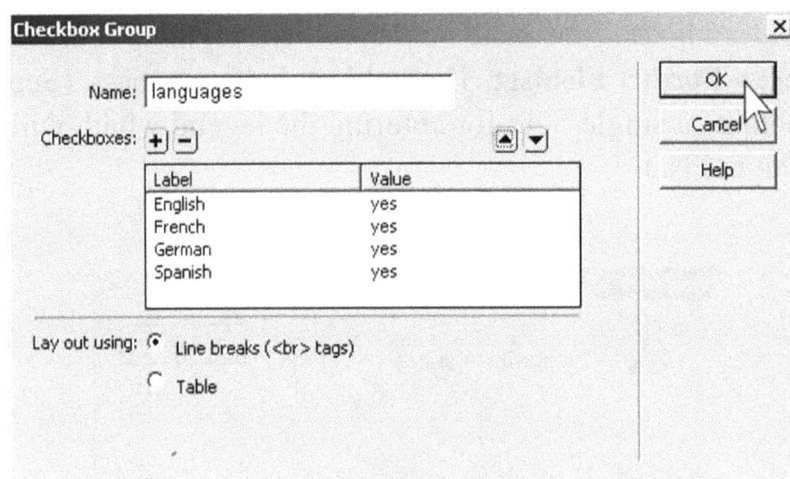

Figure 12-23: The Checkbox Group dialog is almost identical to the Radio Group dialog

Since checkbox groups are not mutually exclusive, it is not possible to create an item to act as a default for the group. Instead, you can specify the default state for each button individually. Highlight each checkbox that you would like to be already activated when the page loads and change the **Initial state** property from "Unchecked" to "Checked".

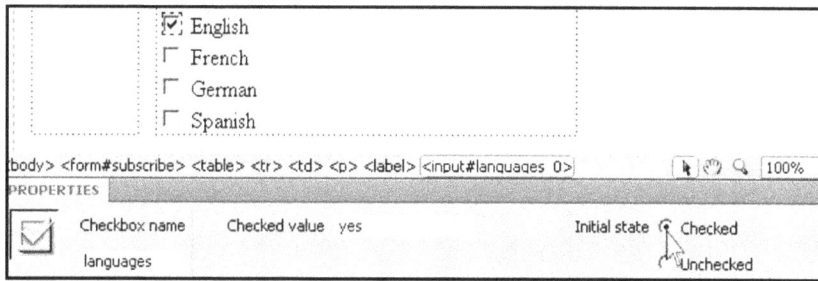

Figure 12-24: Setting default state for checkboxes

For clarity and to create an accessible label which is linked to a checkbox group, you can place them in a fieldset element. Highlight the group then choose **Insert > Form > Fieldset** and enter the legend you would like to appear above the checkboxes.

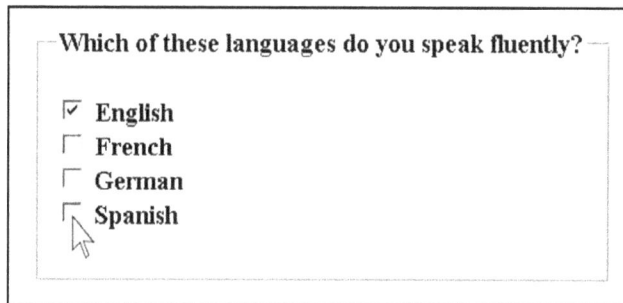

Figure 12-25: A checkbox group in a fieldset headed by a legend

Creating buttons

As well as the controls which enable users to enter information, every form requires a submit button to instigate the transmission of the user's information to the server.

- To add a button to a form, choose **Insert > Form > Button**.
- Enter a unique ID for the button.
- Choose the option **Do not Create Label**, since only fields which are used for data input require a label.
- Click **OK**.

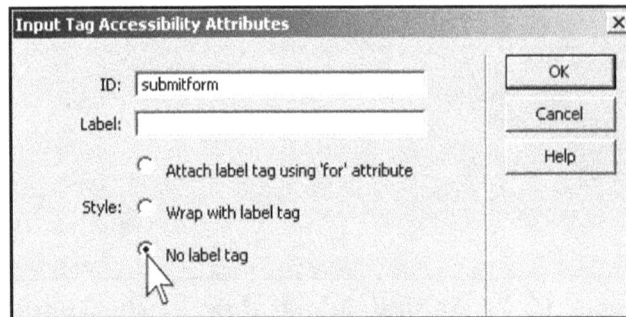

Figure 12-26: Buttons are not used for data input and so do not require a label

Reset and submit buttons

The default behaviour of buttons inserted in this way is to submit the form and the text value displayed on the button is "Submit". Both of these attributes can be changed in the Properties panel.

If you want to create a button which resets the form rather than submitting it, insert the button as described above; then in the Properties panel, click on the **Action > Reset Form** radio button.

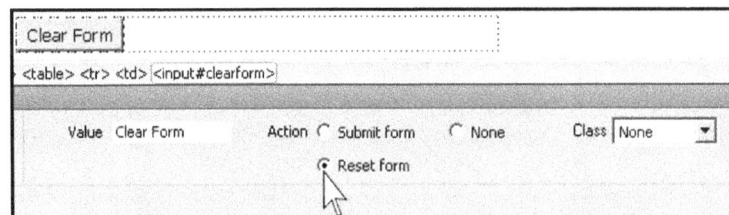

Figure 12-27: Creating a Reset button

To change the text displayed on a button (both the **Submit** and **Reset** varieties), change the text in the **Value** box in the Properties panel.

Setting the form action

The submit button provides a method of submitting a form; but what actually happens when the user submits the form? Well, this is determined by an attribute of the form itself: the **action** attribute.

To set the **action** attribute, you must first select the form. Click anywhere inside the form then, in The Tag Selector, click on the **<form>** tag to highlight it. Next, enter a value in the **Action** field of the Properties panel or click on the Browse button (the folder icon) and locate the file.

```
<body> <form#subscribe>
PROPERTIES

   Form ID        Action   subscribe.aspx              Target
   subscribe      Method  POST         ▼      Enctype
```

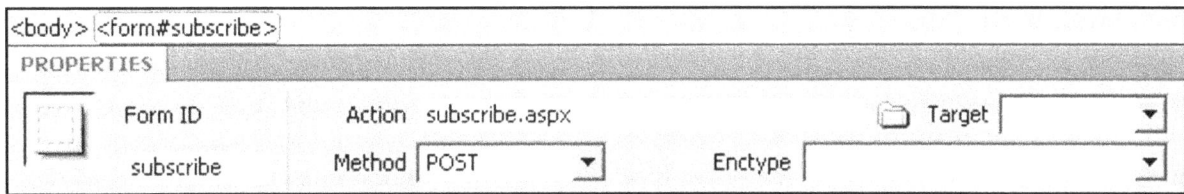

Figure 12-28: Specifying the action attribute of a form

The file referenced in the action attribute of the form has to be a server-side file containing a script which will process the information sent via the form. (For a brief description of server-side pages, see Chapter 1: Getting started, page 4.) It will therefore not have a ".html" file extension but, rather, one which is used by a server-side scripting language—such as ".php", ".pl", ".asp" or ".aspx".

Writing these scripts requires experience of a server-side programming language. However, it is possible to acquire simple form-processing scripts which will email the information entered into a form to a specified email address in a neat and readable format.

You will first need to find out from your web hosting company which scripting languages are supported on your server. If PHP is the default scripting language on your server, you could do a search for "free PHP form handling scripts" in your favourite search engine. Once you find a script, simply download it and follow the instructions for personalizing it.

Another source of free form-handling scripts will often be the company hosting your website. Log into your control panel and search for free scripts or send them an email asking if they offer such scripts.

Specifying the form method

The other key form attribute, the **Method**, specifies how the form data is transferred from the client to the server. This can be set to one of two possible values: **Get** or **Post**.

The Get method

The **Get** method is typically used for search forms and causes the data in the form to be transmitted along with the URL. Thus, for example, if you do a search in Google for "cheap car insurance" then look at the address in the URL, it will be something like:

http://www.google.com/#q=cheap+car+insurance

Following the hash (#) sign are several parameters, the key one being "q", while the others are automatically gleaned by Google from your computer environment. To do another search, you can even change the text displayed after "q=" and press Enter.

The fact that the Get method uses the URL to transmit data makes it unsuitable for forms which include sensitive data or information which can be very lengthy.

The Post method

The Post method should be used for all forms that request personal information. It sends the information directly to the server rather than adding it to the URL and offers a bit more security. It is also more suitable for transmitting large amounts of data.

In addition to using the Post method, forms which transmit sensitive data should be placed on a secure server. Secure server pages use the HTTPS (HyperText Transfer Protocol with Secure Sockets Layer) standard, as opposed to just HTTP. All data transmitted via HTTPS is encrypted while data sent using HTTP is sent as plain text.

To host secure pages on your web server, you will need to purchase an SSL (Secure Sockets Layer) certificate from a certificate authority such as Thawte (www.thawte. com) then ask your hosting company to install it on your server. This normally costs a few hundred dollars a year.

Let's end this chapter by getting some practice on building a form from scratch. In the last chapter, we left the Contact page of our website unfinished. We can now go back and complete that page by adding the enquiry form shown below.

Dreamweaver allows you to create and work on as many sites as you want; and to switch back and forth between sites. Let's begin therefore by making sure that we are working on the **Venture** site created in the last chapter.

1. If necessary, choose **Window > Files** to display the Files panel.

2. If the **Venture** site is not your current site, then choose **Venture** from drop-down menu in the top left of the Files panel to switch back to that site.

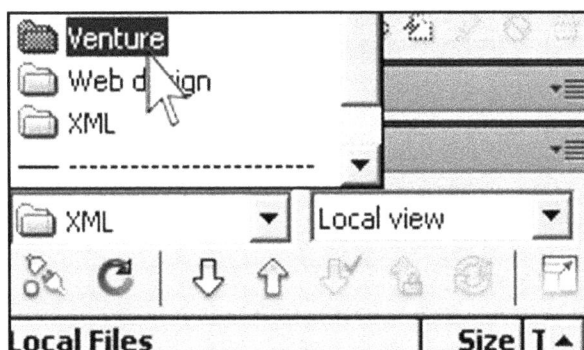

Creating the form itself

1. In the Files panel, double-click on "contact.html" to open it.

2. Position the cursor at the end of the text in the editable region.

3. Choose **Insert > Form > Form**.

Dreamweaver displays the form as a dotted red rectangle partially obscured by the editable region.

Naming the form

4. With the cursor still in the form, enter the name "Enquiry" in the **ID** field of the Properties panel.

Creating a CSS rule for the form

5. With the form still selected, choose **New** from the CSS Styles panel.

6. From the **Selector Type** drop-down menu, choose **Compound (Based on your selection)**.

7. Dreamweaver will enter **#wrapper #main #Enquiry** in the **Selector Name** field. Click twice on the **Less Specific** button to change the name to **#Enquiry**.

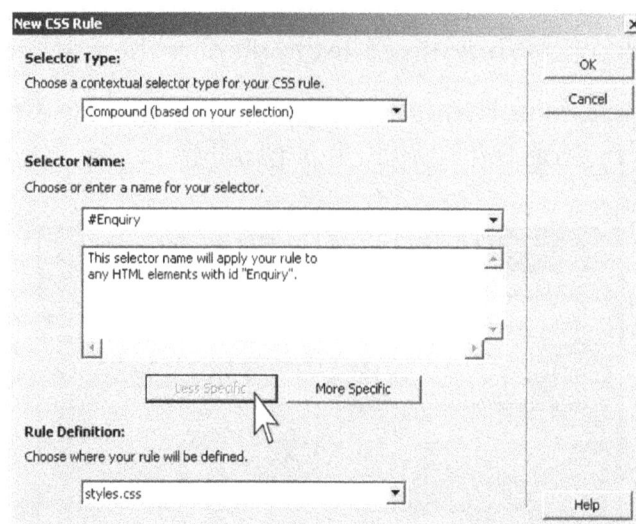

8. Click **OK**.

We will set the set the background of the form to light blue, give it a 1 pixel black border and a fixed width of 500 pixels.

Background category settings of Enquiry form

9. Click on the **Background** category on the left of the CSS Rule Definition dialog.

10. Enter the hexadecimal code " #BDC9D9" in the **Background-color** field.

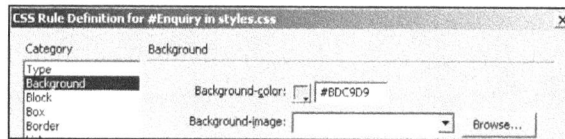

Box category settings of Enquiry form

11. Click on the **Box** category.

12. Set the **Width** property to "500 px".

13. Set the **Padding** to "10 px" on all sides.

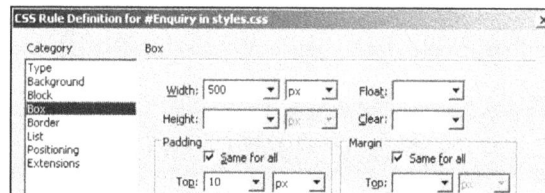

Border category settings of Enquiry form

14. Click on the **Border** category.

15. Set the **Style** to **Solid**, the **Width** to "1 px" and the **Color** to "#000" (black).

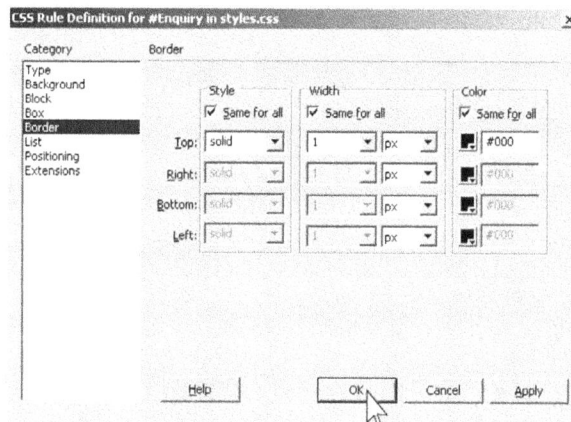

16. Click **OK** to close the CSS Rule Definition dialog.

Adding a fieldset to contain the whole form

To help organise the form, we shall place all of the controls in a **fieldset**. The **<legend>** element which Dreamweaver places inside the **fieldset** will act as a caption or heading for the form as a whole.

1. Click to position the cursor anywhere within the form.

2. Choose **Insert > Form > Fieldset**.

3. Enter the text "Enquiry Form" in the Legend field and click OK.

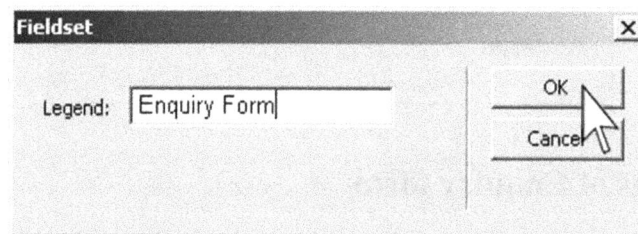

```
┌─────────────────────────────────────────────────┐
│ Fieldset                                      ×  │
│                                                   │
│                                        ┌───────┐  │
│                                        │  OK   │  │
│  Legend:  │Enquiry Form│               ├───────┤  │
│                                        │ Cancel│  │
│                                        └───────┘  │
│                                                   │
└─────────────────────────────────────────────────┘
```

Creating a CSS rule for fieldsets

We will be using two further **fieldset** elements nested inside this one and we want all three to be invisible; since the reason for creating them is to add structure and accessibility to the form, rather than formatting. We can therefore create a CSS rule which targets all **fieldsets** on the page.

4. Choose **New** from the CSS Styles panel menu.

5. From the **Selector Type** drop-down menu, choose **Tag (redefines an HTML element)**.

6. Choose **fieldset** from the **Selector Name** drop-down menu or just type it in.

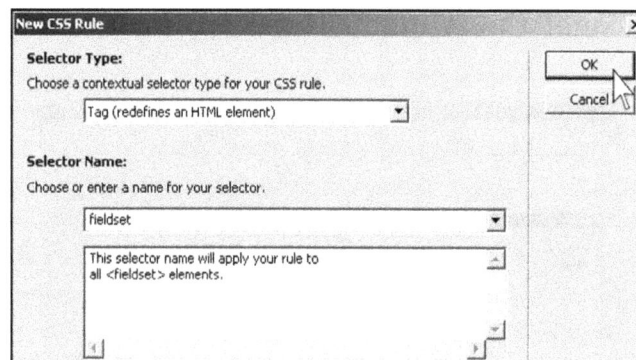

```
┌─────────────────────────────────────────────────┐
│ New CSS Rule                                   ×  │
│                                                   │
│  Selector Type:                        ┌───────┐  │
│  Choose a contextual selector type for │  OK   │  │
│  your CSS rule.                        └───────┘  │
│     │Tag (redefines an HTML element) ▼│ ┌───────┐ │
│                                        │ Cancel│  │
│  Selector Name:                        └───────┘  │
│  Choose or enter a name for your selector.        │
│     │fieldset                        ▼│          │
│     ┌───────────────────────────────────┐        │
│     │This selector name will apply your │        │
│     │rule to all <fieldset> elements.   │        │
│     │                                   │        │
│     └───────────────────────────────────┘        │
└─────────────────────────────────────────────────┘
```

7. Click **OK**.

All we need to do here is to ensure that we set the **border style** attribute to **None**.

Border category settings for fieldset element

8. Click on the **Border** category on the left of the CSS Rule Definition dialog.

9. Set the **Style** property to **None**.

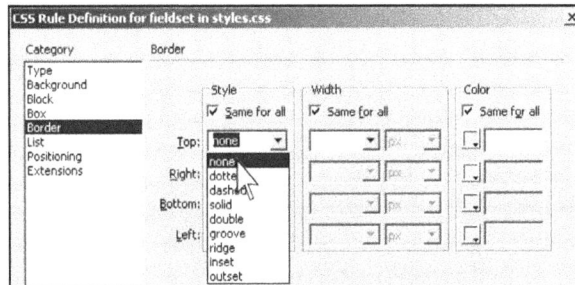

10. Click **OK** to close the CSS Rule Definition dialog.

Creating the Name field

1. Click to position the cursor within the fieldset—but after the legend "Enquiry Form"—as shown below.

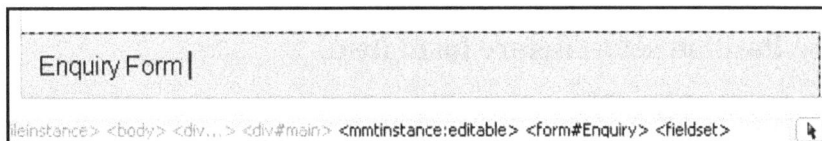

A good way to gauge the current location of your cursor is to look at the last tag on the Tag Selector. If it says **<fieldset>**, that indicates that your cursor is in the fieldset. If it says **<legend>**, just click a bit more to the right; not so close to the legend text.

2. **Choose Insert > Form > Text Field.**

3. Enter "name" in the **ID** box.

4. Enter "Name:" in the **Label** box.

5. Activate the option **Attach label using 'for' attribute**.

6. Leave the **Position** set to **Before form item**.

7. Enter "n" in the **Access key** box.

8. Enter the number "5" in the **Tab Index** box. Although this is the first item in the form, numbering items in steps of 5 will make it easier to insert other items.

9. Click **OK** to create the field.

Creating the Email Address field

1. Click after the **Name** field and press Enter to create a new paragraph.

2. **Choose Insert > Form > Text Field.**

3. Enter "email" in the **ID** box.

4. Enter "Email Address:" in the **Label** box.

5. Activate the option **Attach label using 'for' attribute**.

6. Leave the **Position** set to **Before form item**.

7. Enter "e" in the **Access key** box.

8. Enter "10" in the **Tab Index** box.

9. Click **OK** to create the field.

Creating the Telephone field

1. Click after the **Email Address** field and press Enter to create a new paragraph.

2. **Choose Insert > Form > Text Field.**

3. Enter "telephone" in the **ID** box.

4. Enter "Telephone:" in the **Label** box.

5. Activate the option **Attach label using 'for' attribute**.

6. Leave the **Position** set to **Before form item**.

7. Enter "t" in the **Access key** box.

8. Enter "15" in the **Tab Index** box.

9. Click **OK** to create the field.

Creating the Your Enquiry field

The **Your Enquiry** field needs to accommodate several lines of text; so we will insert a **Textarea** control, rather than a **Text Field**.

1. Click after the **Telephone** field and press Enter to create a new paragraph.
2. Choose **Insert > Form > Textarea**.
3. Enter "enquiry" in the **ID** box.
4. Enter "Your Enquiry:" in the **Label** box.
5. Activate the option **Attach label using 'for' attribute**.
6. Leave the **Position** set to **Before form item**.
7. Enter "q" in the **Access key** box.
8. Enter "20" in the **Tab Index** box.
9. Click **OK** to create the field.

That's it for the text fields. Your form should now look like this.

We can now turn our attention to the layout of the form. We are aiming for a two column layout with labels aligned in the left column and the controls aligned in the right column.

Creating a CSS rule for paragraphs within the form

By pressing Return after creating each text field, you will have ensured that each label and text field pair is housed inside a separate paragraph. We can now create a CSS rule which will target these paragraphs to help us with the layout of the form.

1. Click on the **Your Enquiry** field to select it.
2. Look at the tags in the Tag Selector. It should contain the tags shown in the following screen shot.

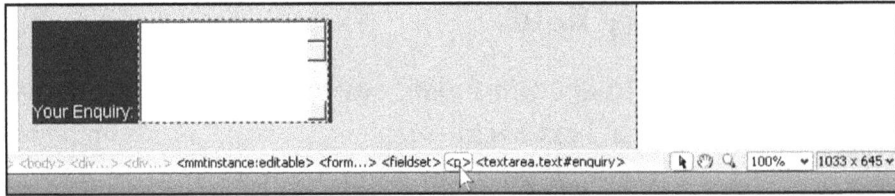

3. Click on the **<p>** tag to select the paragraph containing the **Your Enquiry** field.

4. Choose **New** from the CSS Styles panel menu.

5. From the **Selector Type** drop-down menu, choose **Compound (based on your selection)**.

6. Dreamweaver enters the Selector name **#wrapper #main #Enquiry fieldset p**. Click twice on the **Less Specific** button to change the name to **#Enquiry fieldset p**.

Since our form has an **ID** of **Enquiry**, starting the names of all CSS rules relating to the form with **#Enquiry** will be enough to identify them.

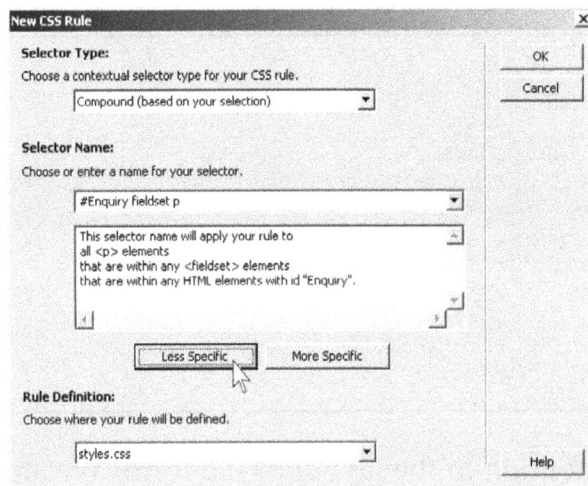

7. Click **OK**.

The purpose of this style will be to indent the paragraphs slightly from the left edge of the form and to control the vertical space between paragraphs.

Box category settings for #Enquiry fieldset p

8. Click on the **Box** category in the CSS Rule Definition dialog.

9. In the **Margin** section, switch off the option **Same for all**.

10. Set the **Top** margin to "10 px", the **Right** to "0 px", the **Bottom** to "0 px" and the **Left** to "50 px".

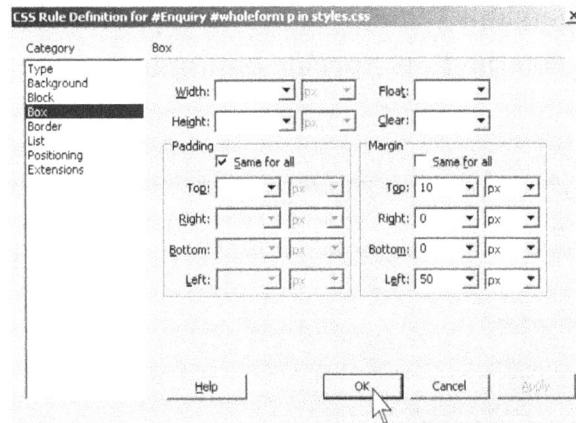

11. Click **OK** to close the CSS Rule Definition dialog.

Creating a CSS rule for labels

We now want the labels inside each paragraph to have a fixed width, so that the left edges of the text fields next to them will be aligned. However, the **<label>** element is an inline element and inline elements cannot have a **width** property.

We encountered a similar situation when we were styling the navigation buttons in the previous chapter (See page 150.) The solution to this problem is to set the **Display** property of the labels to **Block**. They will then behave like block rather than inline elements and respond to the **width** property.

Block elements are paragraphs and cannot have elements next to them. So, we must also set the **Float** property of the label rule to **Left**. However, floating an element causes whatever follows it on the page to move into the space next to it. This applies not only to the element immediately following it, but to everything that follows.

This worked fine in the last chapter because it gave us a horizontal navigation bar. However, here, we do not want the labels to move up to the previous line; so, the final property we will need to set is **Clear**. The **Clear** property stops an element from moving up into the space next to a floating item. It can be set to **Left**, **Right** or **Both**, depending on the **Float** which precedes it. In this case, we need to set the **Clear** property to **Left**, since we want to avoid our labels being affected by a **Left Float**.

1. Click on the "Name:" label to highlight it.

2. Choose **New** from the CSS Styles panel menu.

3. From the **Selector Type** drop-down menu, choose **Compound (based on your selection)**.

4. Dreamweaver enters the Selector name **#wrapper #main #Enquiry fieldset p label**. Click twice on the **Less Specific** button to change the name to **#Enquiry fieldset p label**.

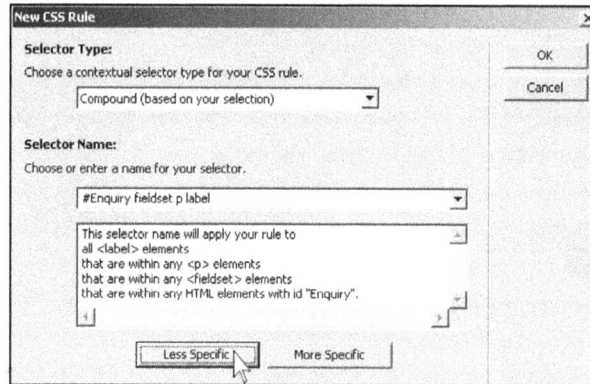

5. Click **OK**.

To illustrate the difference between inline and block elements, let's begin by attempting to set the width of the label.

6. Click on the **Box** category of the CSS Rule Definition dialog.

7. Set the **Width** property to "125 px".

8. Click the **Apply** button.

You will notice that, because **<label>** is an inline element, the **width** has no effect.

Now let's see what happens when we make it behave like a block element.

9. Click on the **Block** category.

10. Set the **Display** property to **Block**.

11. Click the **Apply** button once more.

The **width** property has now caused each of the labels to have a fixed width. However, because they are now being displayed as block elements, they are behaving like paragraphs and each text field has been pushed onto the next line.

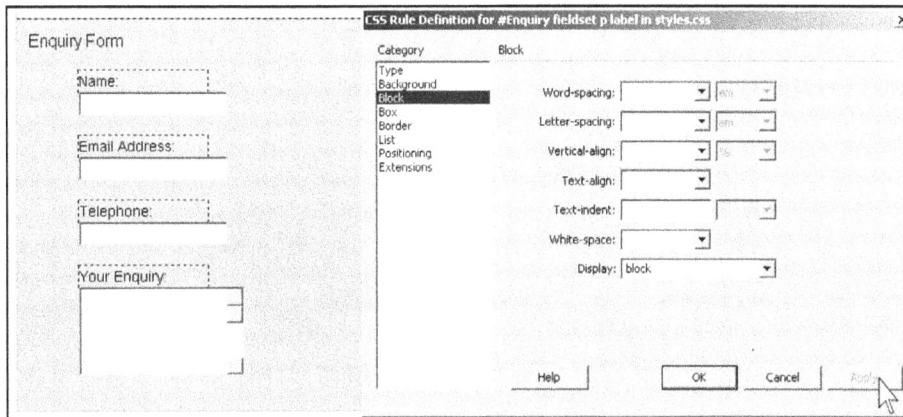

12. Click on the **Box** category once more.

13. Set the **Float** property to **Left**.

14. Set the **Clear** property to **Left**.

15. Click **OK**.

You should now have four labels with text fields next to them, as shown below.

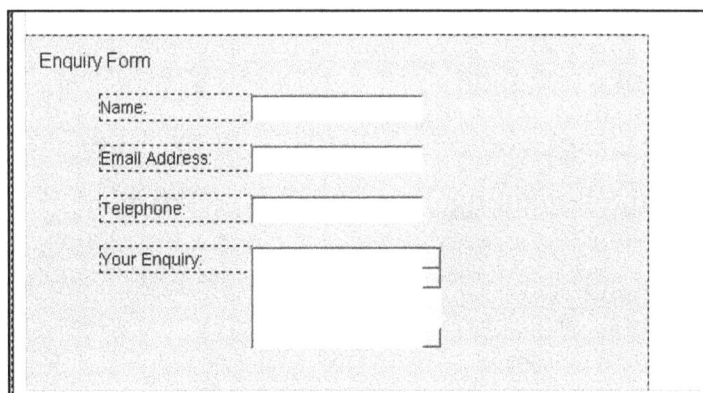

Creating a CSS rule for text fields

Let's now create a CSS rule to make the text fields a bit wider and also to ensure that the **textarea** control is the same width as the single text fields. To do this, we will create a class which can be applied to both **<input>** (single line text fields) and **<textarea>** elements.

1. Choose **New** from the CSS Styles panel menu.

2. From the **Selector Type** drop-down menu, choose **Compound (based on your selection)**.

3. Replace the name entered by Dreamweaver with **input.textfields, textarea. textfields**.

This syntax means that our CSS rule will apply to both **<input>** and **<textarea>** elements of the **textfields** class.

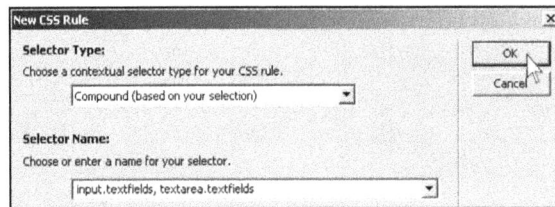

4. Click **OK**.

5. Click on the **Box** category on the left of the CSS Rule Definition dialog.

6. Set the **Width** property to "250 px".

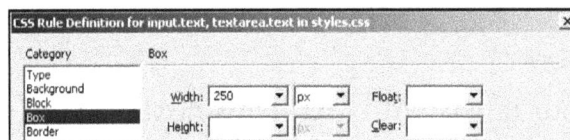

7. Click **OK**.

8. Highlight the **Name** text field.

9. In the Properties panel, choose **textfields** from the **Class** drop-down menu.

10. Set the class of the remaining 3 text fields to **textfields**.

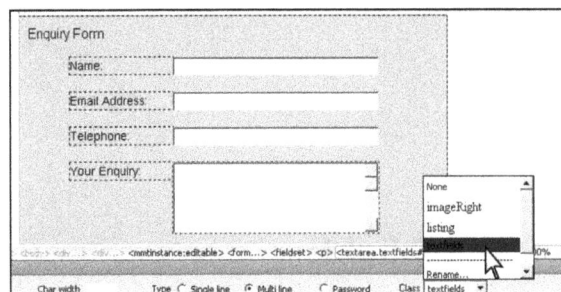

Creating the Gender radio buttons

Gender is a typical example of where we might use a mutually exclusive radio button group. Each radio button will have its own label and, in addition, we will place both radio buttons inside a fieldset containing a legend which will act as a heading for the group.

1. Click after the **Enquiry textarea** field and press Enter.

2. Choose **Insert > Form > Fieldset**.

3. Enter "Gender:" in the **Legend** box and click OK.

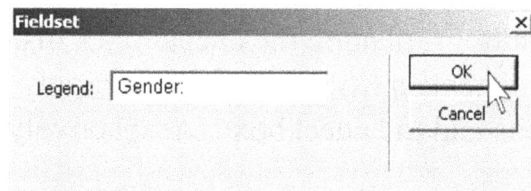

4. Click to the right of the text "Gender:" to position the cursor inside the fieldset you have just created but not inside the legend.

5. Choose **Insert > Form > Radio Group**.

6. In the Radio Group dialog, complete the fields as shown below.

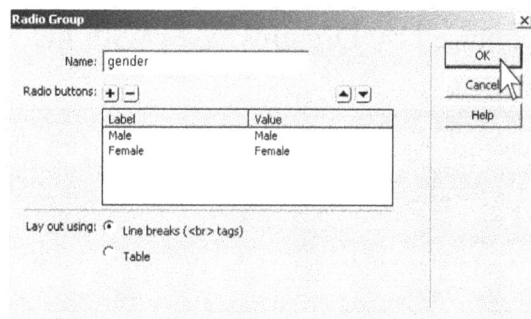

7. Click **OK**.

Creating a class for the Gender and Subscribe fieldsets

We now need the legend "Gender" to be indented by 50 pixels, so that it aligns with "Name", "Your Email", "Telephone" and "Your Enquiry".

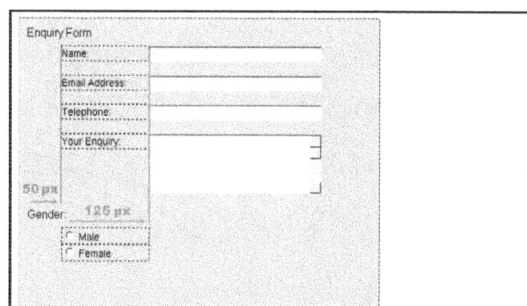

Since, from the user point of view, the word "Gender" serves the same purpose as these four labels, it should be aligned with them and have the same appearance. Similarly, the radio buttons should align with the text fields. To achieve this, we will create a second class to indent the radio buttons by 125 pixels, the same width that we assigned to the text field labels.

We will also be creating a group of checkboxes to allow user to subscribe to the company's email bulletins; and we will be formatting them in exactly the same way as the Gender radio buttons, placing the checkboxes inside a **fieldset** element. It therefore makes sense to create a CSS class rule and apply it to the two fieldsets containing the radio buttons and the checkboxes, respectively.

Because this is going to be a class, the main fieldset that contains all the form elements will not be affected by the new rule.

1. Choose **New** from the CSS Styles panel menu.

2. From the **Selector Type** drop-down menu, choose **Compound (based on your selection)**. Although we are creating a class style, we will prefix class name with "fieldset"; this makes it a **compound**.

3. Replace the name entered by Dreamweaver with **fieldset.options**.

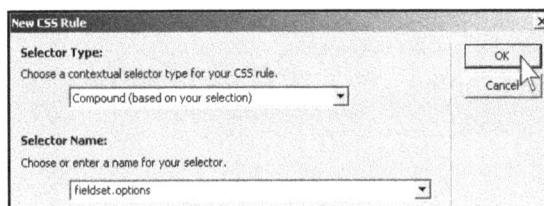

4. Click **OK**.

5. Click on the **Box** category on the left of the CSS Rule Definition dialog.

6. In the **Margin** section, deactivate **Same for all** and set the **Left Margin** to "50 px".

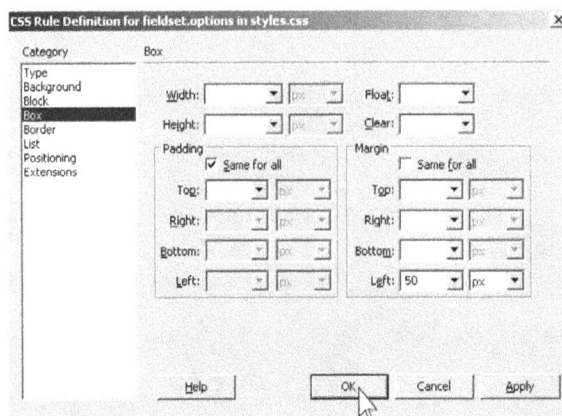

7.   Click **OK**.

Now we need to apply the new class rule to the fieldset. We have used the Tag
Selector many times before. Let's use it now to apply the class to the fieldset
containing the Gender radio buttons.

8.   Click on one of the radio buttons.

9.   In the Tag Selector, right-click on the second **<fieldset>** tag and choose
     Set Class > options from the context menu.

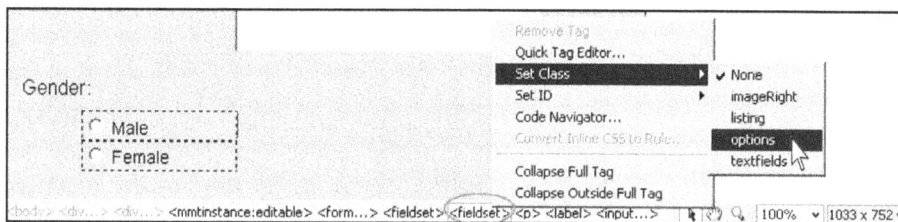

Creating a class for the radio button labels

1.   Highlight one of the radio button labels (either the word "Male" or "Female").

2.   Choose New from the CSS Styles panel menu.

3.   From the **Selector Type** drop-down menu, choose **Compound (based on your
     selection)**.

4.   Dreamweaver enters the Selector name **#wrapper #main #Enquiry fieldset.
     options p label**. Click twice on the **Less Specific** button to change the name to
     #Enquiry fieldset.options p label.

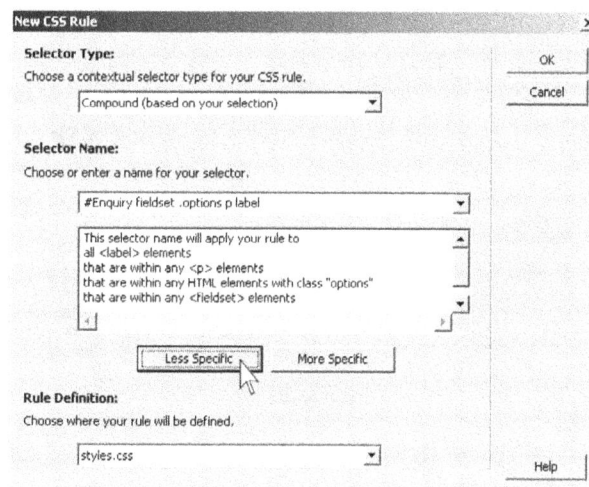

5.   Click **OK**.

6.   Click on the **Box** category on the left of the CSS Rule Definition dialog.

7. In the **Margin** section, deactivate **Same for all** and set the **Left** margin to "75 px".

Why 75 pixels? Well, since the labels are inside paragraphs, they are being affected by the rule we created earlier called **#Enquiry fieldset p** which contains a left margin indent of "50 px". 75 plus 50 gives us 125 which marries up with the width of the text field labels above.

8. Set the **Width** property to "250 px". The rule we are creating will also apply to the checkbox labels we will create next and will accommodate slightly more text than the value of 125 pixels which will otherwise be inherited from the CSS rule we created earlier called **#Enquiry fieldset p label**.

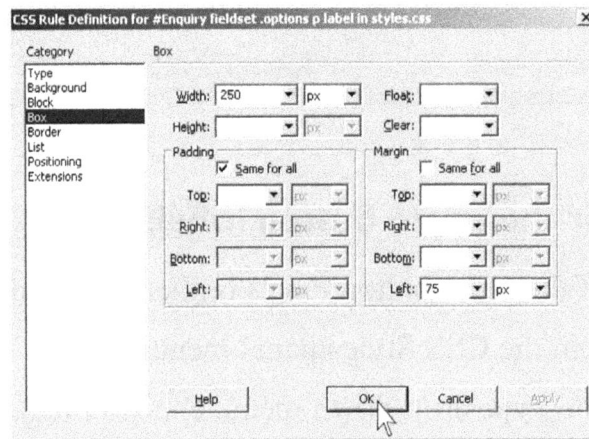

9. Click **OK**.

Creating the "Subscribe to" checkboxes

1. Click after your second radio button label.

2. Choose **Insert > Form > Fieldset**.

3. Enter "Subscribe to:" in the **Legend** box and click OK.

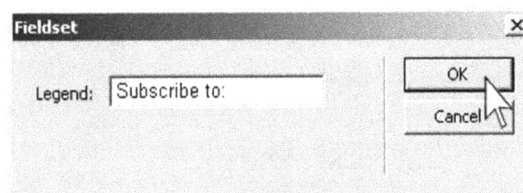

4. Click to the right of the text "Subscribe to:", positioning the cursor inside the fieldset you have just created but not inside the legend.

5. Choose **Insert > Form > Checkbox Group**.

6. In the Checkbox Group dialog, complete the fields as shown below. (Click the + sign to get a new item when you need it.)

7. Click **OK**.

Renaming the checkboxes

As with the Radio Group, the Checkbox Group dialog asks you to enter common name for the whole group. However, unlike radio buttons, checkboxes need to have a unique name. So let's give the three checkboxes names which reflect their function.

8. Click on the first checkbox—next to the label "Rechelof Newsletter".

9. In the Properties panel, change the **Checkbox name** to "newsletter".

10. Change the name of the second checkbox to "bulletin".

11. Rename the third checkbox "opportunities".

Setting the default state of the checkboxes

Let's also set the initial state of the checkboxes to checked so that, when the form loads, all three checkboxes will be already activated.

12. Click on the "Rechelof Newsletter" checkbox.

13. In the Properties panel, set the **Initial state** property to **Checked**.

14. Do the same for the other two checkboxes.

Now we need to apply the CSS class rule called **.options** to the fieldset so that the checkboxes align with the radio buttons.

> 15. Click on one of the checkboxes.

> 16. In the Tag Selector, right-click on the second **<fieldset>** tag and choose **Set Class > options** from the context menu.

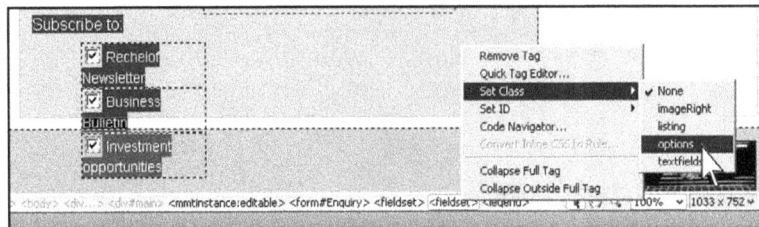

Creating a style for the legends

Most of the text in the form is inside a paragraph and, since we earlier created a CSS rule to handle all paragraphs inside our **main** DIV, our form text follows this rule. The only form text not inside a paragraph is the legend text. So that the form text blends in with the rest of the text on the page, let's make the legend inside the fieldset that contains all the form elements identical to our heading 2 rule (**#main h2**) and the legends inside the "Gender" and "Subscribe to" fieldset the same as our paragraphs (**#main p**).

We can do this by assigning a different class to the two types of legend.

Setting the "Enquiry Form" legend style

> 1. In the CSS Styles panel, right-click on the style named **#main h2** and choose **Edit Selector** from the context menu.

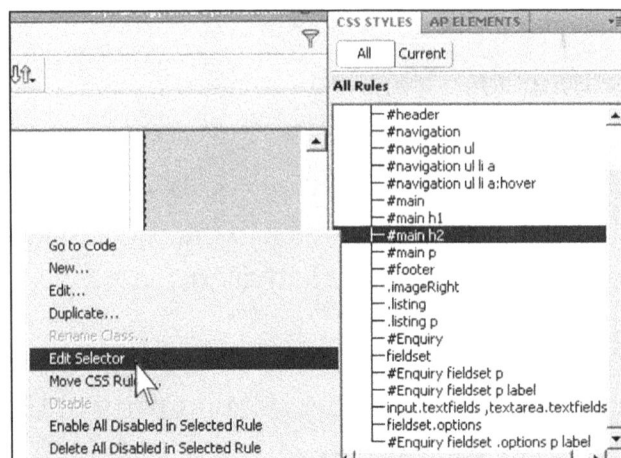

2. Modify the name so that it reads **#main h2, legend.h2-style** then press Enter.

Using the comma in this way allows us to assign the same set of attributes to different styles. Now we need to assign the **h2-style** class, that we have just defined, to the main fieldset.

3. Highlight the legend "Enquiry Form".

4. In the Properties panel, choose **h2-style** from the **Class** drop-down menu.

Setting the "Gender" legend style

5. In the CSS Styles panel, right-click on the style named **#main p** and choose **Edit Selector** from the context menu.

6. Modify the name so that it reads **#main p, legend.p-style**.

7. Highlight the legend "Gender:".

8. In the Properties panel, choose **p-style** from the **Class** drop-down menu.

Setting the "Subscribe to" legend style

9. Finally, highlight the legend "Subscribe to:".

10. In the Properties panel, choose **p-style** from the **Class** drop-down menu.

Creating a submit button

The last control required by the form is the submit button. Let's begin by positioning the cursor after the "Gender" fieldset.

1. Click on one of the checkboxes.

2. In the Tag Selector, click on the **<fieldset.options>** tag to select that element on the page.

3. Press the right cursor key on your keyboard (-->) to move the cursor one place forward. (You are now outside the fieldset.)

4. Press Enter to create a new paragraph.

5. Choose **Insert > Form > Button.**

6. In the **ID** field, enter the name "submit".

7. Leave the **Label** field blank and, in the **Style** section, choose the option **No Label.**

Styling the Submit button

Let us create a CSS rule to position and format the button in the form.

8. Click on the button to select it.

9. Choose **New** from the CSS Styles panel menu.

10. From the **Selector Type** drop-down menu, choose **Compound**.

11. Dreamweaver enters the Selector name **#wrapper #main #Enquiry .wholeform p #submit**. Click twice on the **Less Specific** button to change the name to **#Enquiry .wholeform p #submit**.

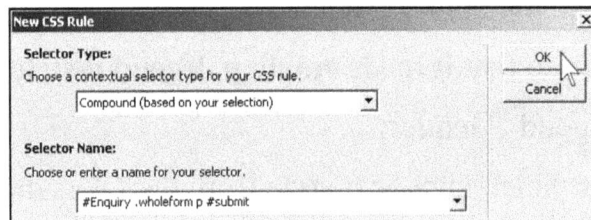

12. Click **OK**.

13. Set the **Font-size** property to "0.9 em".

14. In the **Type** category of the CSS Rule Definition dialog, set the **Color** property either to "#5D7695" or to the same as dark blue colour as your headings.

15. Set the **Font-weight** property to **Bold**.

16. Click on the **Box** category.

17. Set the **Width** property to "80 px".

18. In the **Margin** section switch off **Same for all**, set the **Top** margin to "20 px"and set the **Left** margin to "160 px".

19. Click **OK**.

The completed form

That completes our form—or, to be more precise, that completes the front-end of our form. We will get some practice on submitting a form to a script in Chapter 13: Site management and checking. We shall also be looking at form validation in Chapter 14: An Introduction to JavaScript and Spry.

Enquiry Form

Name:

Email Address:

Telephone:

Your Enquiry:

Gender:

  ○ Male
  ○ Female

Subscribe to:

  ☑ Rechelof Newsletter
  ☑ Business Bulletin
  ☑ Investment opportunities

Submit

13. Site Management and Checking

In this chapter we will look at the key tools available in Dreamweaver for verifying that your site is working correctly. When developing a site, thoroughly testing that everything works should be an ongoing task that you perform regularly. Once the site is up and running, you should continue to use Dreamweaver's site management tools to ensure that no errors have crept in since your last check.

Here is a summary of the site management features that we shall be examining in this chapter.

- Find and Replace
- Spell-checking
- Preview in Browser
- Browser compatibility checking
- Link checking
- Site reports
- Document validation

The Results panel

Dreamweaver's site management tools consist of a series of reporting tools which display results in the Results panel, in one of a series of tabs. You can interact with the results displayed; for example you can right-click to open a file which has been flagged as containing a broken link.

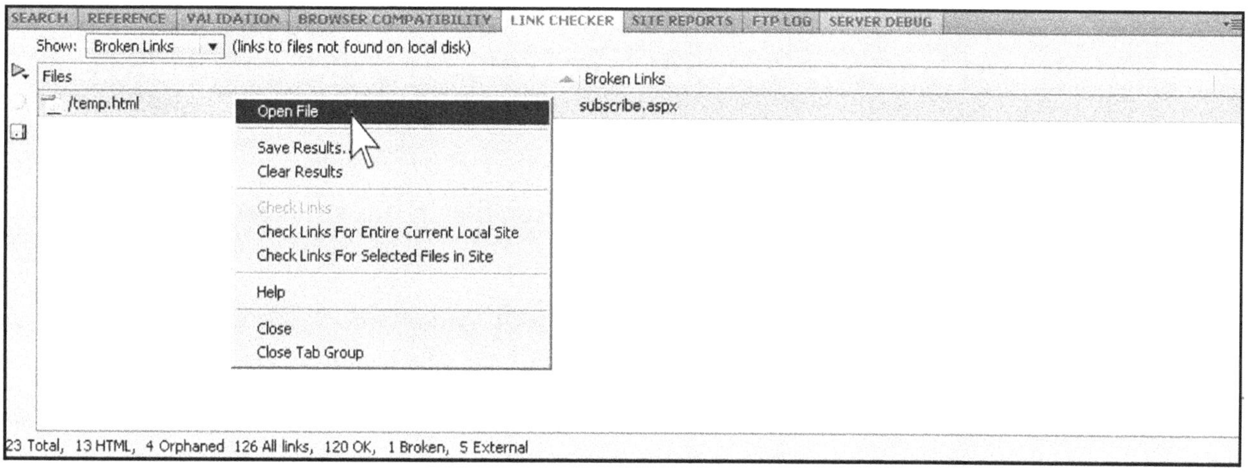

Figure 13-1: Dreamweaver's Results panel allows interaction with the results displayed

Find and Replace

On the face of it, Dreamweaver's **Edit > Find and Replace** command resembles similar commands found in many text-handling programs. However, since it is tailored to the business of updating web pages, it has a few distinctive features.

Firstly, you can specify the scope of your search—which pages in a site you want to be included. This is done by choosing one of the options in the **Find in** drop-down menu.

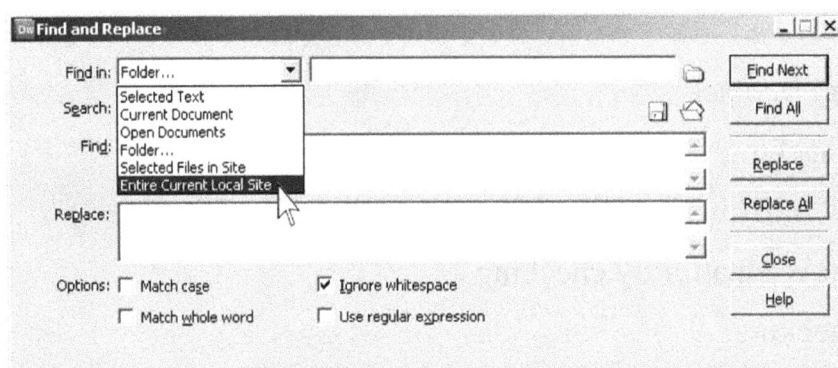

Figure 13-2: Specifying the scope of a search in Dreamweaver's Find and Replace dialog

The options are:

- **Current document**—The document you are currently working on.

- **Open documents**—All documents you currently have open.

- **Folder**—When you choose this option, a Browse button appears which allows you to select a folder using the file system.

- **Selected files in site**—All files which are currently selected in the Files panel. (You can use the Shift key to make contiguous selections and Control (or Command on a Mac) to make non-contiguous selections.

- **Entire Current Local Site**—Examines every file in the site you are currently working on.

Next, you can specify which aspect of the document you want to search in. The two key options are **Source Code** which looks in the HTML code and **Text** which is like searching in Design view.

Then we have the Find and Replace boxes where you can enter copious amounts of text or code, if necessary. And, finally we have the **Options** checkboxes.

- **Match Case**—Distinguishes between upper and lower case occurrences.

- **Match whole word**—When active, Dreamweaver will not change the text being searched for when it forms part of another string.

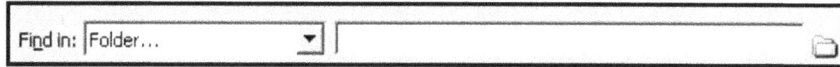

- **Ignore white space**—contracts all white space down to a single space (e.g. treats "and   how" as the same as "and how".

- **Use regular expression**—Allows you to include regular expressions in the search box.

Try it for yourself!

Find and Replace in action

Let's see the Find and Replace feature in action using the site that we built in the last two chapters. Let's say that we want the name of the company to stand out whenever it occurs; so we decide to make it bold. If the site contained a lot of pages, it would be very tiresome to look for every occurrence manually. This is the kind of situation where the Find and Replace command is of real benefit.

1. If necessary, choose **Window > Files** to display the Files panel.

2. If the **Venture** site is not your current site, then choose **Venture** from drop-down menu in the top left of the Files panel to switch back to that site.

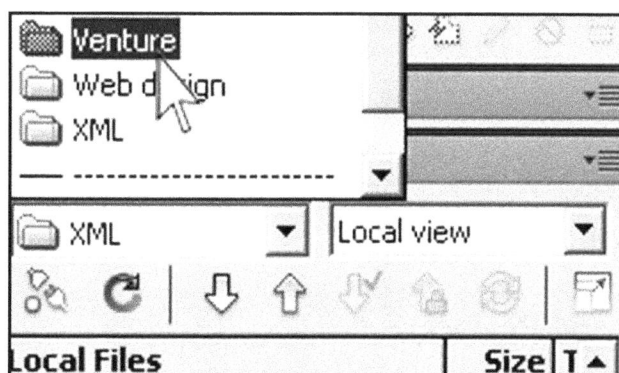

Copying the HTML source code

The Bold button in Dreamweaver's Properties panel surrounds the highlighted text with the **\<strong\>** tag, which is normally rendered by the browser as bold. So to make the company name "Rechelof" bold, we need to search the source code of the pages rather then the text.

3. In the Files panel, double-click on "index.html" to open it.

4. Highlight the words "Rechelof Venture Capital" anywhere on the page.

5. Click on the Bold button (the "B" icon) in the HTML section of the Properties panel.

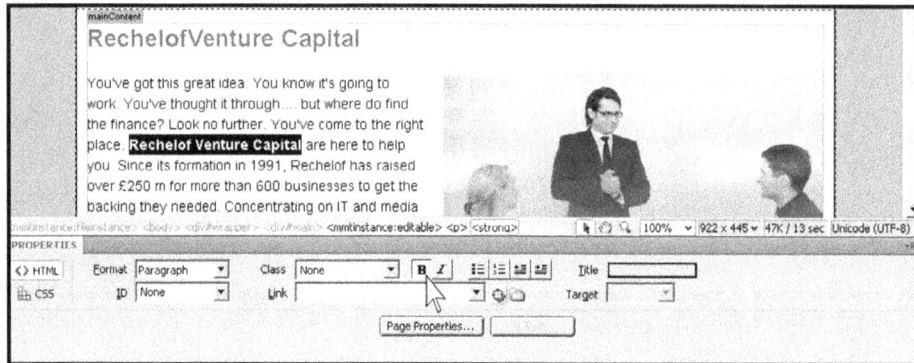

6. With the word still highlighted, click on the **<strong>** tag in the Tag Selector to select it.

7. Click on the Code button in the top left of the document window.

8. Right-click on the selected text and choose **Copy** from the context menu.

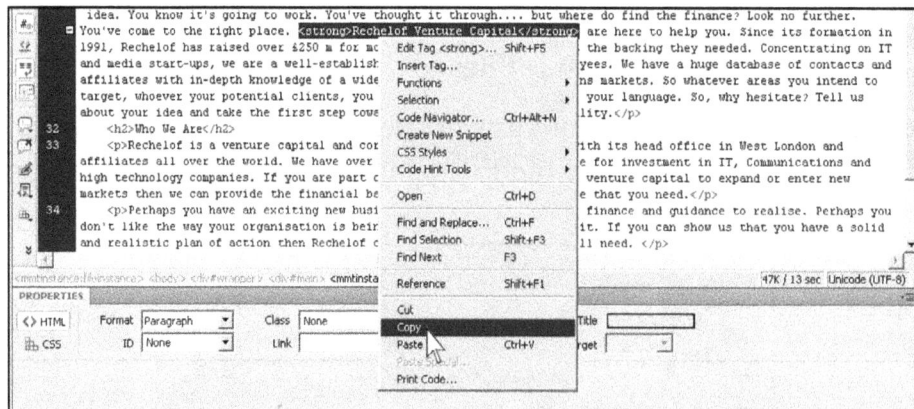

9. Close the file without saving it.

Performing the Find and Replace

10. Choose **Edit > Find and Replace**.

11. Choose **Entire Current Local Site** from the **Find in** drop-down menu.

12. Choose **Source Code** from the **Search** drop-down menu.

13. Type "Rechelof Venture Capital" in the **Find** box.

14. Paste the HTML code that you copied into the **Replace** box.

15. Click the **Replace All** button.

16. Click **Yes** when Dreamweaver display the following warning dialog.

Dreamweaver displays the Results panel showing a list of the files where the search string was found and replaced.

Spell checking

The spell-check facility in Dreamweaver is fairly basic; but it is obviously a vital step in making a site ready for deployment.

Dictionary preferences

Before you perform a spell-check, it is important to ensure that you have the correct dictionary selected. Choose **Edit > Preferences** (Windows) or **Dreamweaver > Preferences** (Mac) and, if necessary, click on the **General** category on the left of the Preferences dialog. At the bottom of the dialog, click on the **Spelling dictionary** pop-up menu and choose the appropriate language.

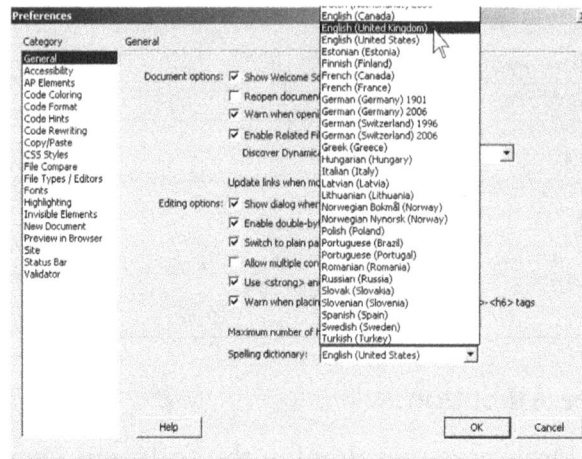

Figure 13-3: Setting the dictionary to be used for spell-checking

Unfortunately, it is not possible to perform a spell-check on the entire site or even on multiple pages; the **Check Spelling** command will only check the currently active document. The best compromise is usually to open all the pages you want to check, perform a check on each one, save any changes then close the document and move on to the next one. Also, don't forget to perform a spell-check on template pages as well as document pages.

To open several documents at once, in the Files panel, hold down the Control key (Command on Mac) and click on each file to be selected. Using this technique, you can also select files in different folders. Next, right-click on any of the selected files and choose **Open** from the context menu.

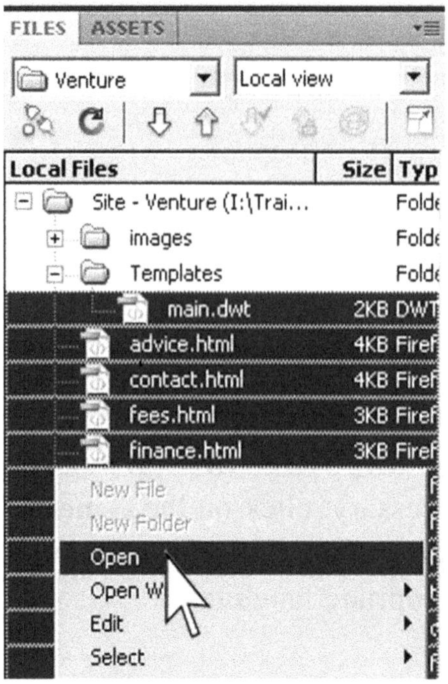

Figure 13-4: Hold down the Control (Mac, Command) key to select multiple files

Performing a spell-check

To perform the spell-check, choose **Command > Check Spelling**. Whenever Dreamweaver finds what a word that is not in the dictionary, it will pause and offer you a series of suggestions as to what the correct spelling should be.

If this is a genuine error, either click on the correct spelling or—if none of the suggestions is correct, enter the correct spelling and click the **Change** button. You can also click **Change All** to change this spelling wherever it occurs within the document.

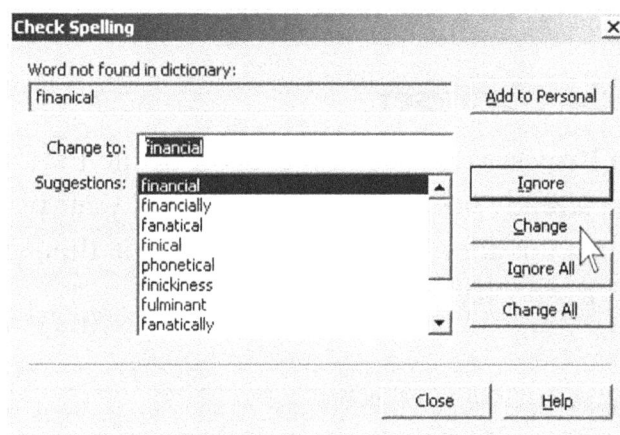

Figure 13-5: Use the Change and Change All buttons to correct genuine spelling mistakes

If Dreamweaver flags a word which you know is not actually a spelling mistake, such as a proper noun, you can click **Ignore** or **Ignore All** to move on to the next error. However, if the word is encountered in future spell-checks, it will continue to be flagged as an error. Alternatively, click on the **Add to Personal** button to add it to the personal dictionary, a supplementary user dictionary which is included in all spelling checks. If the word is encountered in the future, it will then be regarded as being in the dictionary and will not be flagged as an error.

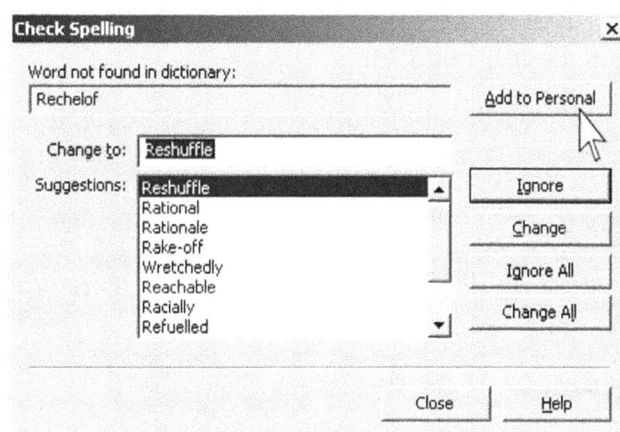

Figure 13-6: Use the Add to Personal button to add words to the user dictionary

Customizing Dreamweaver's Preview In Browser Feature

As we have seen, when working on your web pages in Adobe Dreamweaver, you can preview them in a web browser at any time by pressing F12 (Mac: Option F12). Additionally, Dreamweaver allows you to configure multiple browsers to be used for previewing. Having specified a primary, or preferred, browser, you can then choose a secondary browser and as many additional browsers as you like.

Naturally, the first step in this procedure is to ensure that all the necessary browser software has been downloaded and is installed on your computer. Next, on Windows, choose **Edit > Preferences** or, on a Macintosh, **Dreamweaver > Preferences**.

Primary and secondary browser

Click on the **Preview in Browser** category on the left of the Preferences dialog window. You may have already configured a browser as your primary browser and possibly another as your secondary. If you wish to change this, simply click on the appropriate checkboxes to specify which is which.

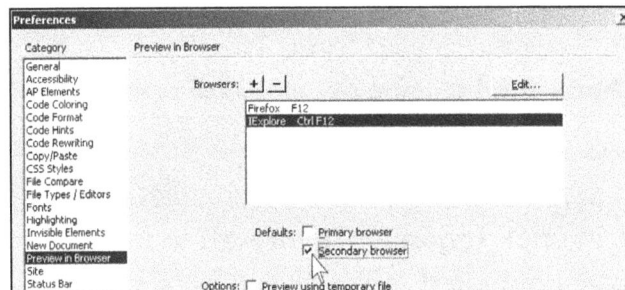

Figure 13-7 Specifying a primary and secondary browser

Adding browsers

To add other browsers, just click on the plus sign (+); enter a name for the browser; navigate to the browser software and double-click to open it. You can repeat this procedure as many times as you need to.

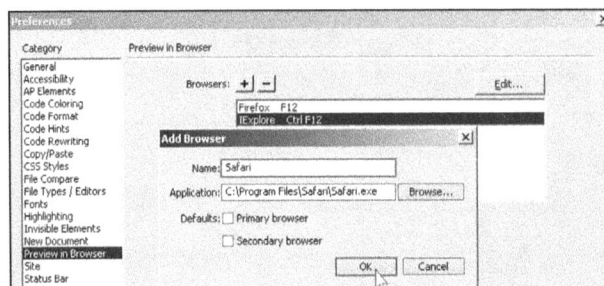

Figure 13-8 Adding a new item to the Browsers list

To preview a page using one of your configured browsers, click on the Preview in Browser button (the globe) located on the Document toolbar which is normally displayed at the top of the document window. From the drop-down menu, choose the browser that you'd like to use. You can also use the keyboard shortcuts: to preview using your primary browser, press F12 on Windows or Option-F12 on a Macintosh; to preview in the secondary browser, press Control-F12 on Windows or Command-F12 on a Macintosh. Alternatively, simply choose the name of any other browser from the pop-up list.

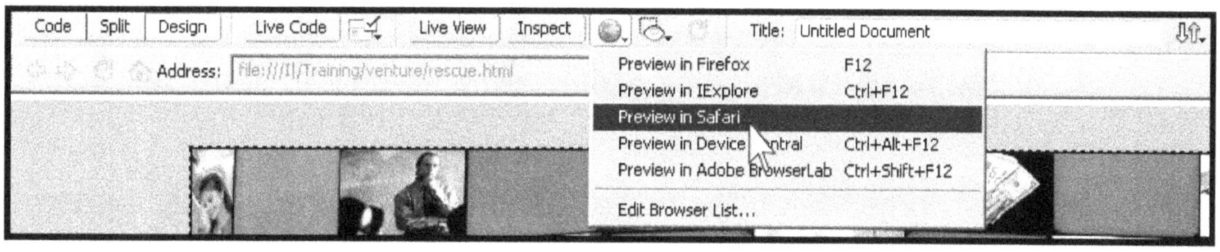

Figure 13-9 Use the Preview in Browser button to preview in a particular browser

Having looked at the preview, to return to Dreamweaver, simply close the browser window.

Preview using temporary file

There may also be times when you'd like to preview a page but don't want to save the changes you've made to your document. Dreamweaver offers you this possibility but, before we get to that, let's examine what happens when we preview a file that has been modified.

Dreamweaver shows us a dialogue box asking us if we'd like to save the changes. If we click **No**, we are given a preview of the last version that was saved rather than the version that we're currently working on. If we click **Yes**, Dreamweaver will save our changes before previewing the file.

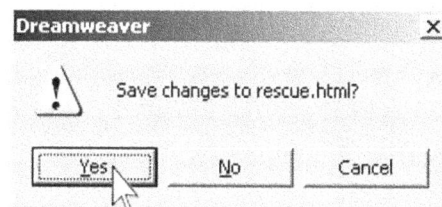

Figure 13-10 When you preview a page, Dreamweaver asks whether you want to save it

This behaviour can sometimes be inconvenient, since you may not be ready to save your changes.

If you'd like to preview files at any time without saving your changes, return to the **Browser Preview** section of Dreamweaver's Preferences and activate the option **Preview using temporary file**.

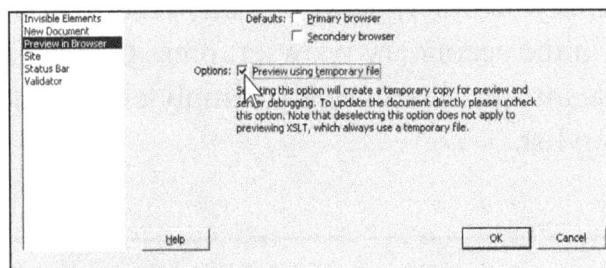

Figure 13-11 Activating Preview using temporary file

When this option is switched on, Dreamweaver will always create a temporary file containing the latest version of your document and then show you a preview of it. When the browser window opens, look at the name of the file being previewed. It will be a temporary file name generated by Dreamweaver and not the name of document you are working on.

Checking browser compatibility

In addition to previewing in individual browsers, Dreamweaver can also check whether your pages are compatible with a particular browser. The advantage of this feature is that you do not have to install the browser in question for it to work.

To begin, click on the **Browser Compatibility** tab of the Results window or choose **Window > Results > Browser Compatibility**.

Setting target browsers

You can run the browser compatibility check on several browsers simultaneously and also specify which version of each browser you wish to target. Click on the green **Check Browser Compatibility** button in the top left of the panel and choose **Settings** from the pop-up menu.

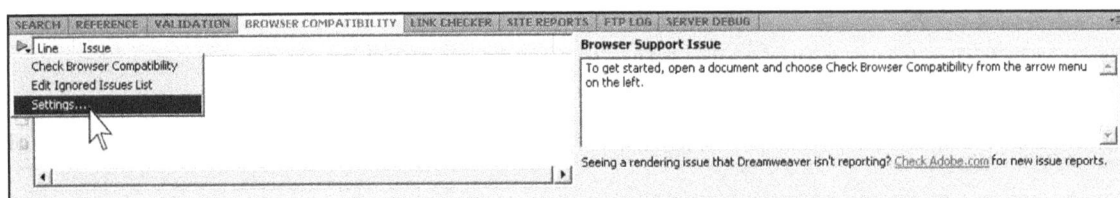

Figure 13-12: Accessing the target browser settings

The Target Browsers dialog appears.

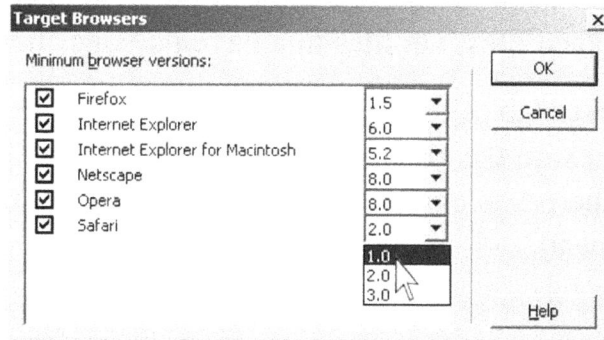

Figure 13-13 The Target Browsers dialog

Use the checkboxes on the left of the browsers listed to specify which browsers should be included in the compatibility check. Click on the drop-down menus on the right to specify the oldest version of each browser that you want to include in the check. Thus, for example, if you choose version "1.0" for Safari, Dreamweaver will include version 1.0, 2.0 and 3.0.

Performing the check

To actually run the check, open the document that you wish to check; then click on the green button in the top left of the panel and choose **Check Browser Compatibility**.

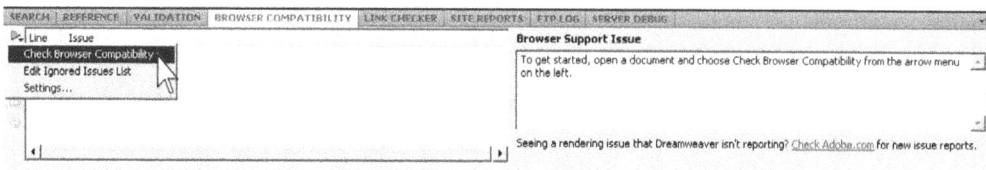

Figure 13-14: Running a browser compatibility check

Link Checking

Broken hyperlinks and broken links to images are annoying and confusing for website visitors and should be avoided at all costs. One rule of thumb that helps reduce the risk of such errors creeping in is that you should never create a local link to a page that does not yet exist. This is why it is a good idea to create all of the files and folders which will constitute your site before you start adding content to templates or pages. That way, whenever you create a link to a page, the page already exists and you can use Dreamweaver's excellent **Point to file** button to automatically generate the link.

The options in Dreamweaver's Link Checker panel will search for such broken links and produce an interactive list of results which makes it easy to repair each broken link. As well as finding broken links, the Link Checker can also be used to identify external links and orphaned files; i.e. files that have no pages linking to them.

Click on the **Link Checker** tab of the Results window or choose **Window > Results > Link Checker**. Next, click on the green **Check Links** button in the top left of the **Link Checker** window and choose an option, such as **Check Links for Entire Current Local Site**, from the pop-up menu.

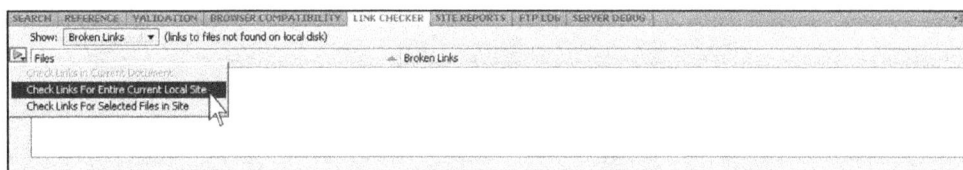

Figure 13-15: Launching a link checker report

Dreamweaver runs the report and displays a list of results in the Link Checker panel. You can then specify which type of result you want to display from the **Show** pop-up menu: **Broken Links**, **External Links** or **Orphaned Files**.

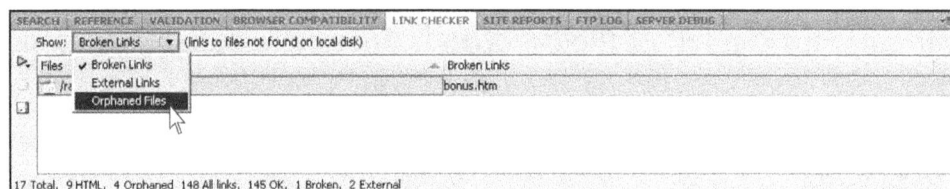

Figure 13-16: Choosing which result type should be shown in the Link Checker panel

Fixing broken links

As well as listing all files containing broken links and listing the broken links, the Link Checker panel allows you to fix broken links, either by opening the file and making the correction there or by making corrections to erroneous filenames. To open a file listed as containing broken links: either right-click on the file name and choose **Open** from the context menu; or simply double-click on the file name.

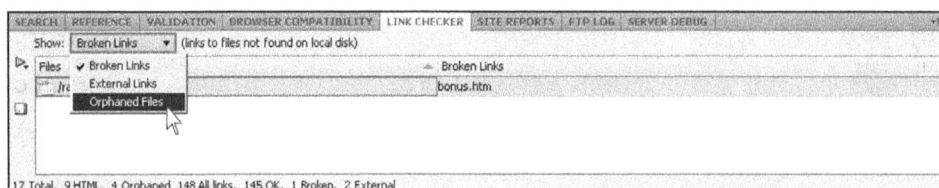

Figure 13-17: Opening a file containing a broken link in the Link Checker panel

If you can see that the broken link is the result of simple error in the file path used in the link, you can simply click on the broken link, correct it and press the Enter key. If the change you made has corrected the problem, the file will immediately disappear from the list of errors.

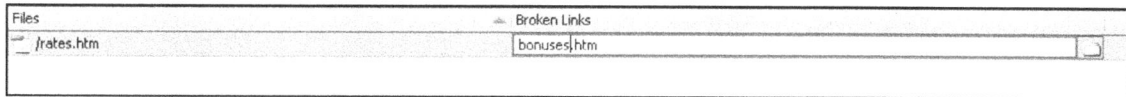

Figure 13-18: Fixing a broken link by editing the file path in the Link Checker panel

Alternatively, you can click on the folder icon, browse for the correct file and double click to create a link to it. Again, once the problem is corrected, the file disappears from the list.

Orphaned files

Fixing broken links will often also fix an orphaned file problem. (The link may have been broken because it did not link to the right file which, in turn, became orphaned.) Occasionally, you may also create a file which is designed to be displayed in a pop-up window and therefore is not linked to in the normal way and ends up being flagged as orphaned.

Orphaned files are very often images that have not been used (or have yet to be used) on your site. If they are obsolete, they can be deleted using the Files panel. If they will be required at some point in the future, then you can simply ignore that particular entry in the Link Checker error results.

External links

The fact that external links are listed in the Link Checker results does not imply that they are broken, since Dreamweaver does not actually test them. It simply lists all external links for you convenience. It is up to you to manually test them.

To test an external link after running a Check Links report in the Link Checker panel, double-click the name of the file containing the external link to open it. Press F12 (Mac: Option F12) to launch the page in your primary browser and click on the link to make sure that it still works.

Running site reports

Dreamweaver's site reports feature can be used to scan the entire page to pick up errors in the code. The two most important errors it will highlight are missing alt tags and untitled documents. To use this feature, choose **Site > Reports** to display the following dialog. Activate the problems you would like to search for and click the **Run** button.

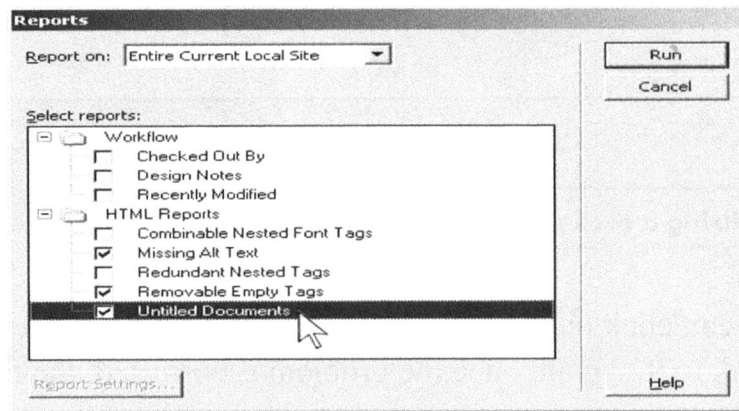

Figure 13-19: Dreamweaver's Reports dialog

The results listed in site reports are not quite as interactive as those that appear in the Link Checker panel. However, you can still choose Open from the right-click menu and Dreamweaver will open the file in split screen view with the problem tag highlighted, ready to be corrected.

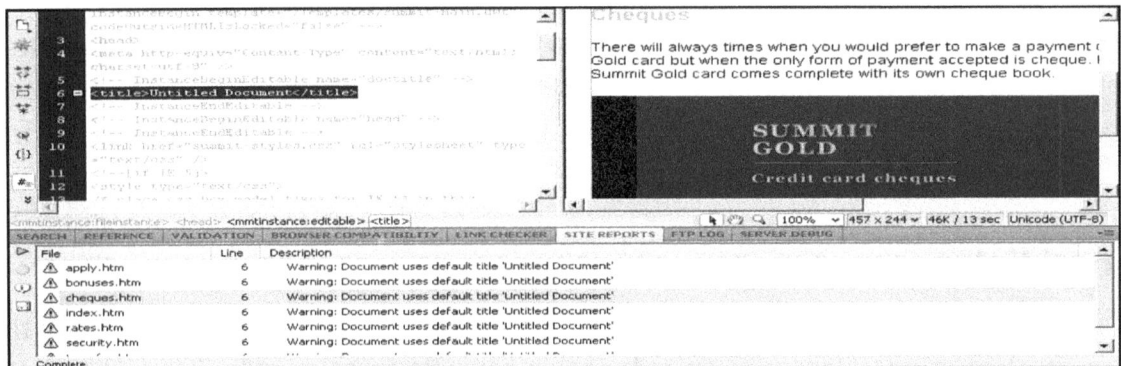

Figure 13-20: Double-click a file in the results displayed in the Site Reports panel and Dreamweaver opens it in split-screen view with the problem tag highlighted.

Uploading files to a server

Using Dreamweaver, you can make a website live simply by copying files from your local machine to the server. However, before you can do this, you need to add a remote server to your Site Setup. This can be done when you first define your site or, if the information is not available at that time, you can supply the necessary details later—which usually means when you sign up with a hosting company.

Adding a server

To add a server to your current Site Setup, begin by editing your current site. To do this, choose **Site > Manage Site** then click on the **Edit** button to invoke the Site Setup dialog window.

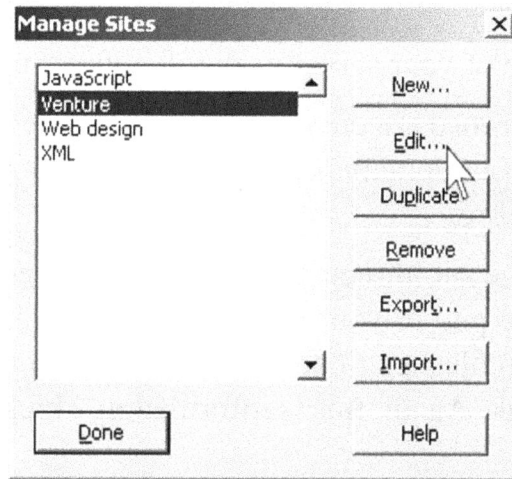

Figure 13-21: Editing a Dreamweaver site

Next, click on the **Servers** category on the left of the Site Setup dialog and click on the **Add Server** button (the + sign). Enter the server details in the pop-up window then click the **Save** button.

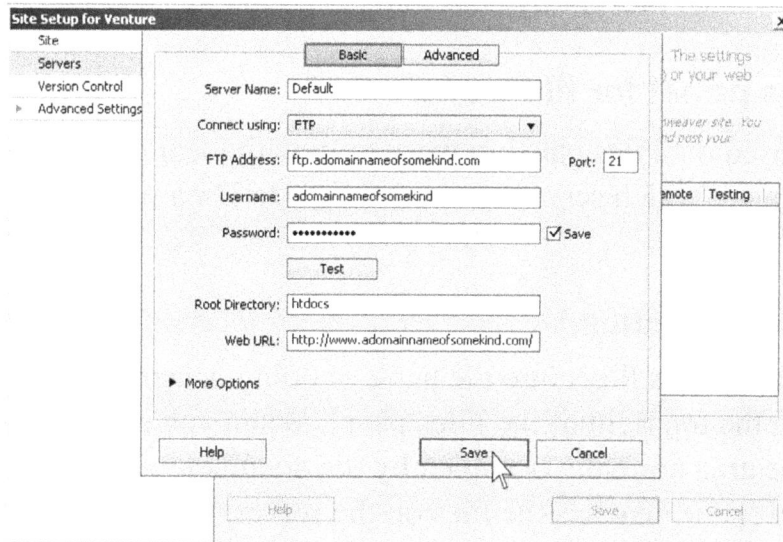

Figure 13-22: The Add Server pop-up window displaying options for FTP access

- **Server name** is a name of your choosing which distinguishes the server from any others you may add later.

- **Connect Using** will normally be **FTP** for a public website and **Local/Network** for a company intranet or any other local server.

If you choose FTP, then you will be asked for the information shown in figure 13-22, on page 239. All of this information is normally supplied via email when you sign up with a hosting company. If you take over the management of an existing website, contact the technical support department and ask them for the necessary information.

- **FTP host** is a name of your server or the IP address underlying the name.

- **Username** and **password** are created by the hosting company. The username is often based on your domain name and you are normally given the ability to change your password.

- **Root directory** is the sub-directory in which files need to be uploaded in order for them to become part of your website. Commonly used names are "htdocs" and "www". If web files are to be placed on the root of the server, simply leave this box blank. Again, this is information which your hosting company will supply.

- **Web URL** is the web address which will be used to access your website in a browser; for example, "http://www.adomainnameofsomekind.com/".

Dreamweaver CS5 is the first version of the program which allows you to define multiple servers—a very handy new feature. For example, you could define a main connection to the live server via FTP and a second, local network server to be used for testing. You could then switch between the two servers, depending on whether you were ready to make files live or just want to test them.

Using the Files panel for file transfer

So far, we have used the Files panel to work only with local files. In fact, it is a very versatile environment which serves as the interface to Dreamweaver's built-in FTP client software.

The Collapse/Expand button

One of the first things you'll get into the habit of doing is using the Collapse/Expand button located on the top right of the Files panel. When you click it, the Files panel expands to fill the area normally occupied by the document window and splits into two panes: the left pane displays the files on the server; the right panel displays your local version of the site.

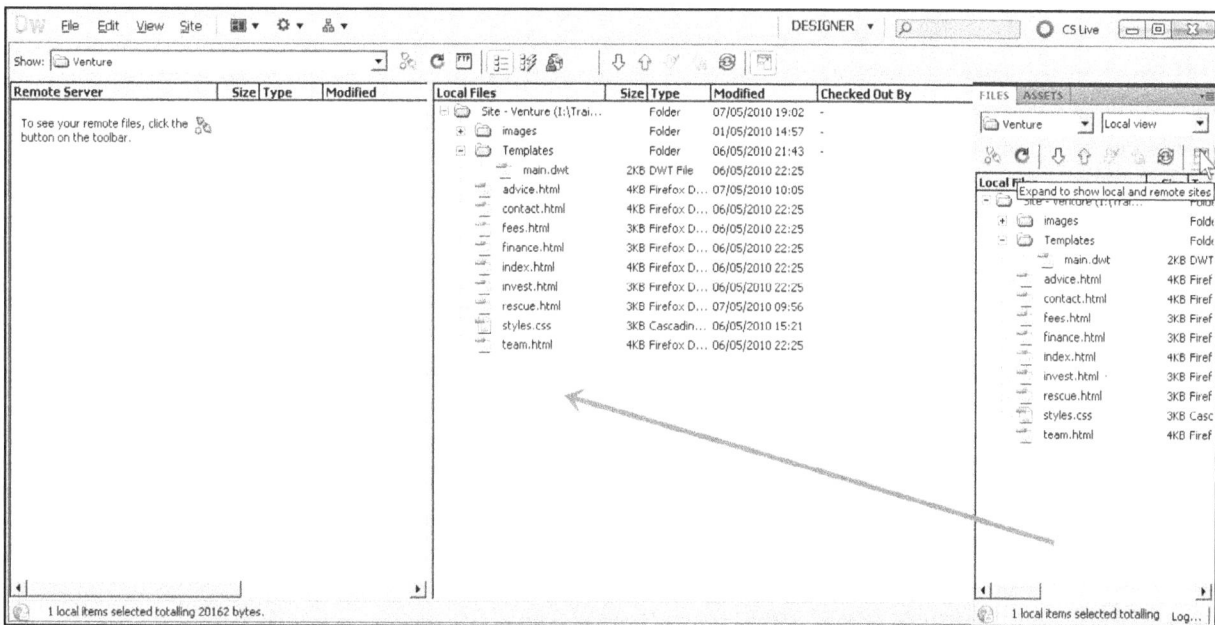

Figure 13-23: Using the Expand/Collapse button in the Files panel

Generally speaking, you will want your local version to be a mirror image of the remote version on the server. The five file transfer operations performed in the Files panel can be done in both collapsed and expanded modes.

Connect/Disconnect

If you want to view the files currently live on your server, you need to connect. If you have finished interacting with the server and wish to clear the list of remote files, you can click on the same button to disconnect from the server.

Refresh

The Refresh button is used to refresh both the local and remote list of files.

Get and Put

While it is possible to copy files from the local site to the remote, and vice versa, by simply dragging them from one location to the other, it is preferable to use the **Put** and **Get** buttons in the Files panel. To **Get** files means to download them from the server onto your local version of the site overwriting any files of the same name. To **Put** a file is to upload it to the server to make it live.

When you use **Get** and **Put**, Dreamweaver ensures that files copied are placed in the same relative location as the original file. If you rely on dragging files across, it's very easy to end up moving an item to the wrong location.

Synchronize

The Synchronize Files button allows you to maintain parity between local and remote versions of your site. (The same facility can be accessed by choosing **Site > Synchronize Sitewide**.) Both commands brings up the Synchronize Files dialog.

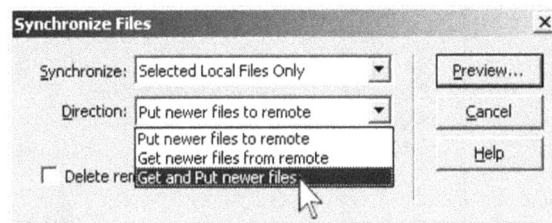

Figure 13-24: The Synchronize Files dialog

- From the **Synchronize** drop-down menu, at the top of the dialog, you can choose which files you wish to synchronize.

  - **Selected Local Files Only**—Only include those files you currently have selected in the local pane of the Files panel.

  - **Entire Site**—Examine and synchronize all files in the site.

- The **Direction** drop-down menu allows you to specify which version of the site (if any) should be regarded as definitive.

  - **Put newer files to remote**—Will cause Dreamweaver to upload files to the server whenever the date modified is later than that of the version of the same file on the server or where the file does not exist on the server.

  - **Get newer files from remote**—Will cause Dreamweaver to download files from the server whenever the date modified is later than that of the local version of the same file or where the file does not exist in the local site.

  - **Get and Put newer Files**—Dreamweaver will **Get** or **Put** whichever version of the file has the later modification date.

Before actually performing the specified **Put** and **Get** operations, it is always a good idea to click on the **Preview** button to get a listing of which files will be affected. (See figure 13-25, on page 243.)

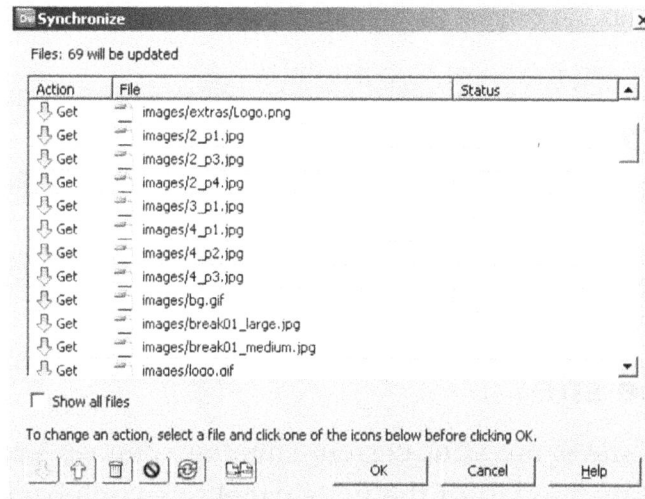

Figure 13-25: The Synchronize Preview report lists all files that will be affected by the Synchronize operation. The buttons at the bottom of the dialogue allow you to change the Put and Get settings for selected files, mark files for deletion and exclude files from the Synchronize operation.

Try it for yourself!

Completing the website creation cycle

Having discussed techniques for testing a site and making a site live, we can now look at completing the website creation cycle that we started back in chapter 11. Just to remind you of the key steps in the cycle; these are the steps we completed in chapter 11.

1. Plan and design

2. Create Local Site Folder

3. Create Default Images Folder

4. Define Dreamweaver site

    a. Local information

    b. Server information (when available)

5. Create all files and folders

6. Create template

7. Create CSS file

8. Link CSS file to template

9. Add content to template

    a. Create locked content

    b. Define editable region(s)

    c. Create CSS rules

    10. Apply template and add content to individual pages

And these are the steps we have yet to complete.

    11. Test site

    12.   Upload site to server and go live

Let's go ahead and complete these last two steps—or two and a half steps, to be more accurate; since we also need to go back and complete step 4b: server information.

Step 11: Test the site

1. If the **Venture** site is not your current site, then choose **Venture** from drop-down menu in the top left of the Files panel to switch back to that site.

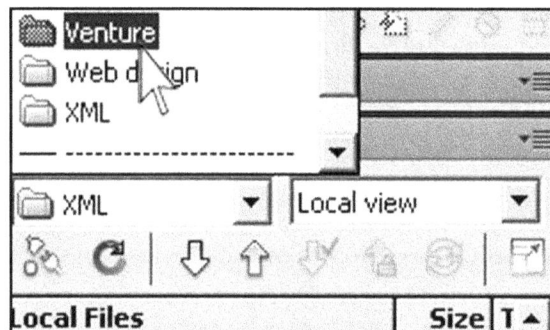

Link Checker

2.   Choose **Window > Results > Link Checker**.

3.   Click on the green **Check Links** button in the top left of the **Link Checker** window and choose **Check Links for Entire Current Local Site**, from the pop-up menu.

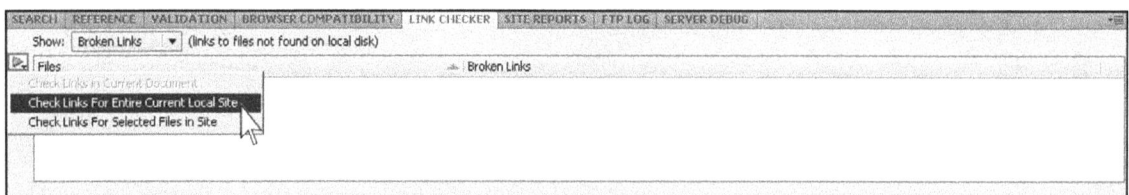

When the Link Checker finishes, there should be no files listed, because there are no broken links.

4.   Choose **External Links** from the drop-down menu at the top of the Link Checker panel.

The Link Checker panel should now list all pages containing email links, since the email addresses all contain the fictitious domain Rechelofventurecapital.com.

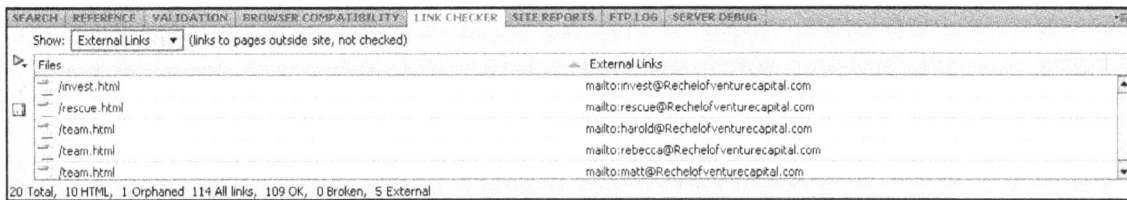

SEARCH | REFERENCE | VALIDATION | BROWSER COMPATIBILITY | LINK CHECKER | SITE REPORTS | FTP LOG | SERVER DEBUG

Show: External Links ▼ (links to pages outside site, not checked)

Files	External Links
/invest.html	mailto:invest@Rechelofventurecapital.com
/rescue.html	mailto:rescue@Rechelofventurecapital.com
/team.html	mailto:harold@Rechelofventurecapital.com
/team.html	mailto:rebecca@Rechelofventurecapital.com
/team.html	mailto:matt@Rechelofventurecapital.com

20 Total, 10 HTML, 1 Orphaned 114 All links, 109 OK, 0 Broken, 5 External

5. Choose **Orphaned Files** from the drop-down menu at the top of the Link Checker panel.

Dreamweaver displays just one file: "images/banner2.jpg". This is an alternative version of the banner we used as the background to the header. Since we will not need it, we can simply delete the file.

6. In the Files panel, open the "images" folder then click once on the file "banner2.jpg" to highlight it.

7. Press the Delete key on your keyboard to delete the file.

8. When Dreamweaver displays the following message, click the **Yes** button.

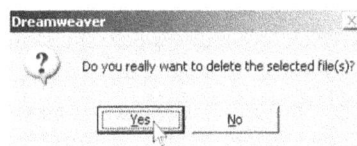

Site Reports

9. Click on the **Site Reports** tab of the Results panel.

10. Click on the green **Check Reports** button in the top left of the panel.

11. When the Reports dialog window appears, choose **Entire Current Local Site** from the **Report on** drop-down menu at the top of the dialog.

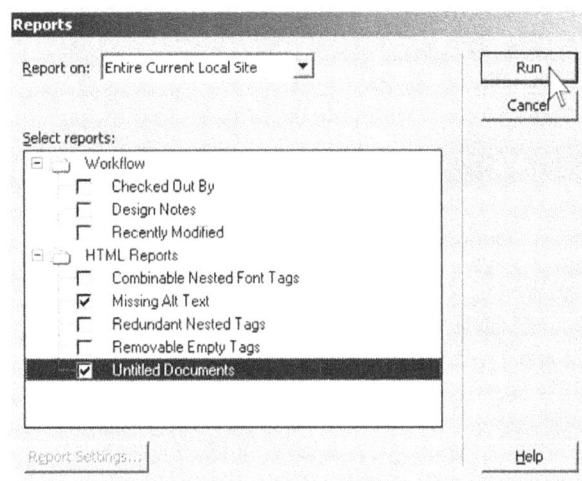

12. Activate the options **Missing Alt Tags** and **Untitled documents**.

13. Click the **Run** button.

There should be no missing **Alt** tags. However, since we did not enter any titles when we created our pages, a long list of errors is displayed in the Site Reports window. Failure to add a title to a web page is a serious omission and needs to be corrected. (If you spotted this and have already added a title to each page, pat yourself on the back and move on to step 12.)

14. Double-click on each file in the list to open it.

15. Copy and Paste the heading of the page directly into the **Title** box in the Document toolbar, as shown below.

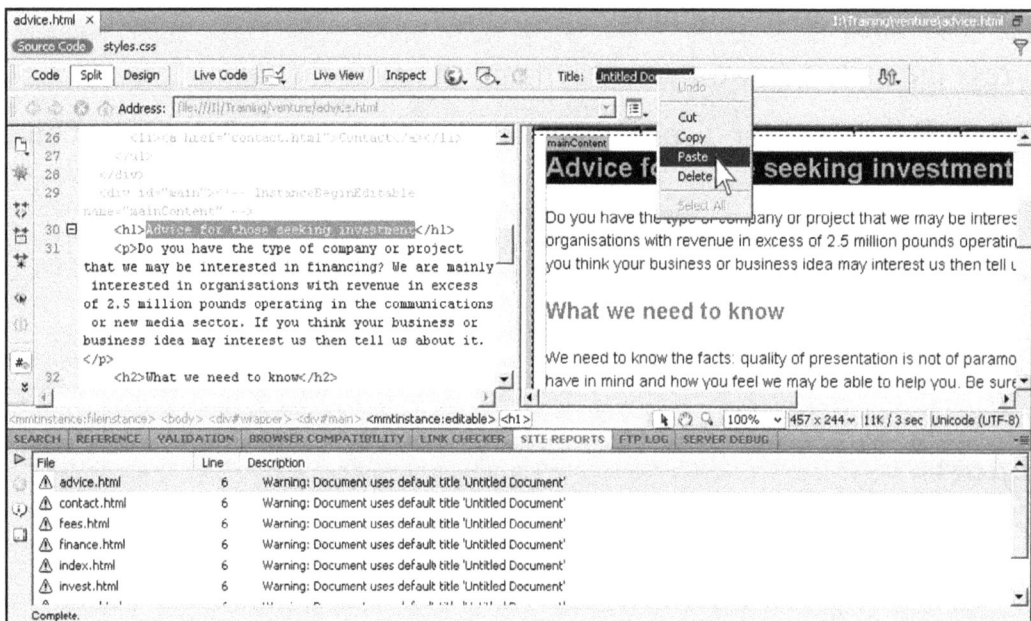

16. When you have added a title to each page, choose **File > Save All** then **File > Close All**.

Step 12: Upload site to server and go live

Finding a free web hosting account

In order to get some practice on interacting with a live server, you can sign up for a free website hosting account. If you already an account with a hosting company, you can skip this step and go straight to the section on adding a server to the Site Setup, on page 249.

Many web hosting companies will offer to host your website free of charge, with the proviso that advertising banners will automatically be displayed on your pages.

Naturally, they can safely anticipate that a certain percentage of their free hosting clients will upgrade to a paid account, without the advertising.

In this example, we will be using a hosting company called x10Hosting. Unlike most free hosting companies, they offer an ads-free package and they also allow server-side scripts written in PHP, Perl or ASP.Net. This means that we will finally be able to see a form-handling script in action. (See page 252.)

Additionally, a list of hosting companies offering free space can be found at:

www.thefreesite.com/Free_Web_Space

Feel free to visit a few of these sites and choose any one that takes your fancy; but I'd recommend that you stick with those that allow server side scripts.

Creating a free web hosting account with x10hosting.com

1. Open your web browser.

2. Navigate to the URL "http://x10hosting.com/".

3. Click on the **Apply Now** button in the **Free Web Hosting Package** section.

4. When a second screen appears summarizing the features of their free account, click on the **Get Started Now!** button.

5. Complete the sign up form.

6. Shortly after signing up, you will receive an email with the subject line: "10Hosting New Account Confirmation", containing a URL which will enable you to confirm your email address. Click the URL.

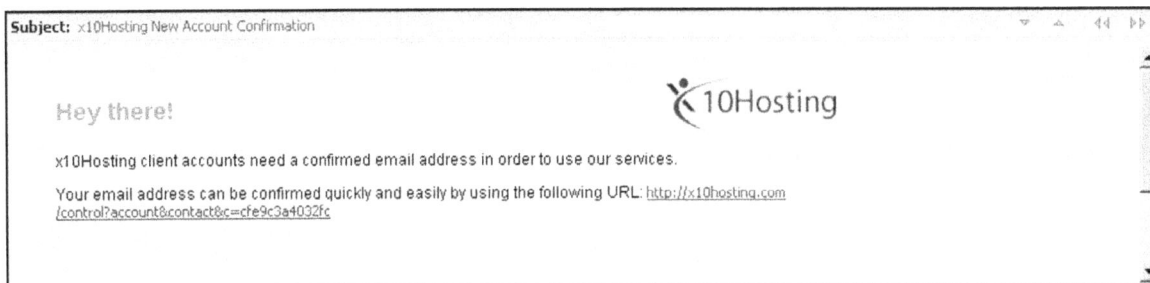

After your email has been verified and your account has been created, you will receive a second email with the subject line: "10Hosting New Account Confirmation".

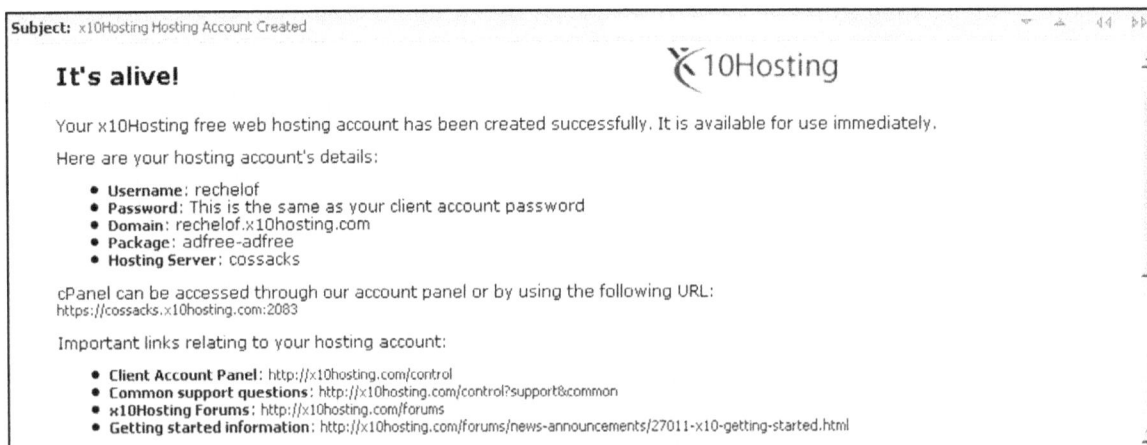

This email contains details of how to log into your control panel. The user name and password you chose when you signed up are used both for control panel and FTP login.

And that's it! You have some free web space which will enable you to make your web pages live.

The key points to note are as follows:

- The user name you chose will determine the URL of your website. For example if you chose "JillTestSite", the URL of your site will be:

  http://jilltestsite.x10hosting.com.

- Your FTP details will also be derived from your user name. For example if you chose "JillTestSite", your FTP server name will be:

  ftp.jilltestsite.x10hosting.com.

- Your FTP login name will be:

  jilltestsite@jilltestsite.x10hosting.com.

- Your FTP password will be the password you chose when you signed up.

Adding a server to the Site Setup

Now that we have space on a web server, we can edit our Site Setup and use the **Add Server** feature.

1. Choose **Site > Manage Sites** then click on the **Edit** button.
2. Click on the **Servers** category on the left of the dialog.
3. Click on the **Add Server** button (the plus sign).
4. Complete the dialog then click the **Save** button.

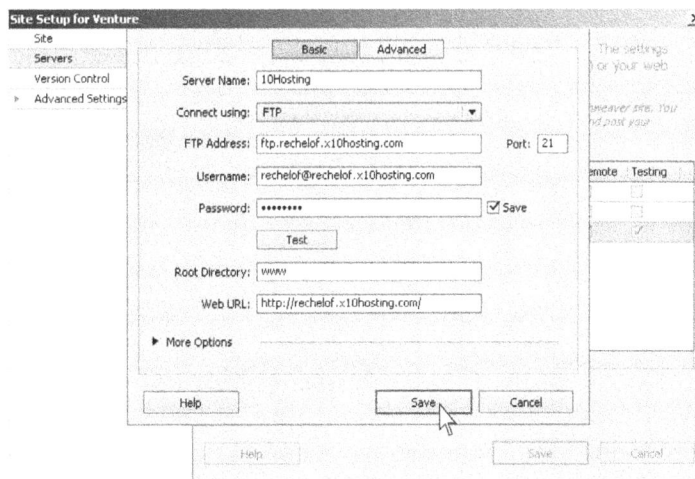

- **Server Name**—Enter any name you like, such as "x10Hosting".

- **Connect Using**—Choose **FTP** from the drop-down menu.

- **FTP Address**—Enter "ftp.YourUserName.x10hosting.com", substituting "YourUserName" with the user name you chose when you signed up.

- **Username**—Enter "YourUserName@YourUserName.x10hosting.com".

- **Password**—Enter the password you chose when you signed up.

- **Root Directory**—Enter "www", which is the sub-directory on their servers which is reserved for web files.

- **Web URL**—Enter "http://YourUserName.x10hosting.com.

5. Click on the Test button. With any luck, Dreamweaver should display the following confirmation.

6. Click **OK**, then **Save**, then **Save**, then **Done** to exit site management.

Uploading the files to the server

1. Click on the **Collapse/Expand** button in the top right of the Files panel.

2. Click on the **Connect** button to connect to the server.

3. Highlight the Local Site Folder (the first folder listed in the Files panel) and click on the **Put** button.

4. Click **OK** when Dreamweaver displays the following warning message.

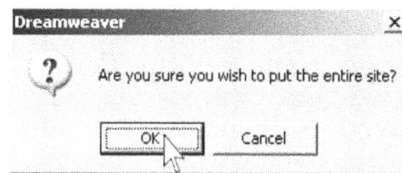

As it copies each file from your local machine up to the server, Dreamweaver displays a progress report in the Background File Activity dialog.

If this was a large site which would take several minutes to upload, you could carry on working on pages and doing other stuff while the process of uploading goes on in the background.

When the **Put** operation is complete, your remote site should contain all of the files in the local site plus some additional items which are standard on Apache servers.   .

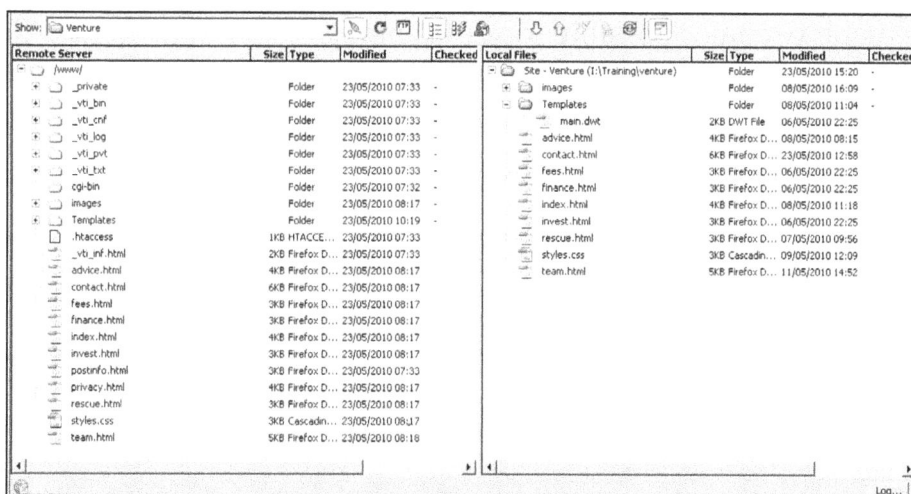

However, we don't really need to have the **Templates** folder on the live version of the site; so let's delete it.

5. Click on the Yellow **Templates** folder in the left pane of the Files panel.

6. Press Delete.

7. Click **Yes** when Dreamweaver displays the "Are you sure..." warning dialog.

Previewing the live site

1. Open your browser.

2. Navigate to the URL of your site—"http://YourUserName.x10hosting.com".

The Rechelof website is displayed in the browser window, free of any adverts.

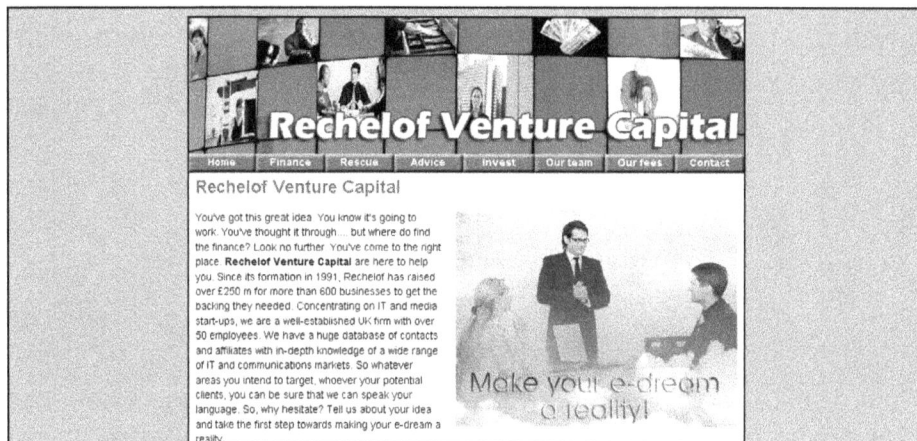

3. Close the browser window and return to Dreamweaver.

Installing a form-handler script

One of the main benefits of signing up with a web hosting company—free or otherwise, is that it becomes possible to start running server-side scripts. For example, our contact form is currently just a front-end: we can now add a back-end script which will email information submitted via the form to a staff member of Rechelof Venture Capital and redirect the user to a "Thank you" page.

Adding the script to the Venture site

1. Choose **File > Open**.

2. Navigate to the root of the training folder and open the file "contact.php".

3. Click on the **Code** button in the top left of the document window.

The script is pretty basic and is specifically designed to handle the form we created earlier—sending an email to the address specified on the first line of the script.

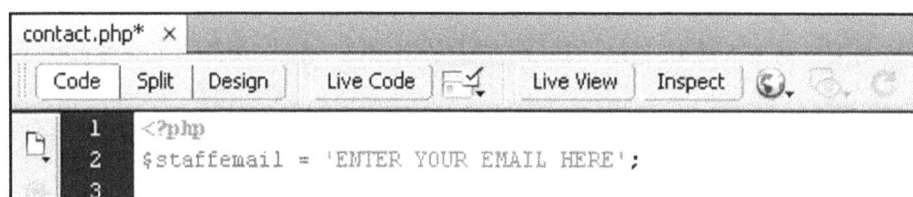

4. Replace the text "ENTER YOUR EMAIL HERE" with your email address.

5. Choose **File > Save As** and save a copy of the file in the **Venture** folder.

Pointing the contact form to the PHP script

To specify that our script will process the information submitted via **contact.html**, we need to set the **action** property of the **Enquiry** form.

6. In the Files panel, double-click on **contact.html** to open it.

7. Click anywhere within the form.

8. In the Tag Selector, click on **<form#Enquiry>** to select the form.

9. In the Properties panel, click on the **Browse for file** button—the folder icon, on the right of the **Action** field.

10. Locate and double-click on **contact.php** to set its file name as the value of the **action** property.

Creating a thank you page

The last line of the script:

> **header('Location: thankyou.html');**

redirects the user's browser to a page called "thankyou.html". To avoid getting a script error, we will need to create this page.

11. In the Files panel, right-click on any HTML page and choose **New** from the context menu to create a new page at the same level.

12. Name the new page "thankyou.html".

13. Double-click on "thankyou.html" to open it.

14. Choose **Modify > Templates > Apply Template to page**.

15. Highlight the template named **main** (the only one listed) and click the **Apply** button.

16. Enter a brief thank you message—e.g. "Thank you very much for your enquiry. A member of our team will contact you shortly."

17. Save and close the page.

Testing the form-handler script

To test the script, we first need to upload it to the server as well as the thank you page and the modified **contact.html**.

1. Click on the **Collapse/Expand** button in the top right of the Files panel.

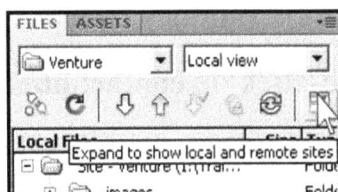

2. Hold down the Control key (Command on Mac) and click on "contact.html", "contact.php" and "thankyou.html" to select them.

3. Click on the **Put** button ⇧ at the top of the Files panel to upload the selected files to server.

4. Open your web browser.

5. Navigate to the URL of your site—"http://YourUserName.x10hosting.com".

6. Click on the **Contact** button to go to the contact page.

7. Complete the form and click the **Submit** button.

8. You should automatically be taken to the thank you page.

9. Check the inbox of the email address that you entered on the first line of the script and you should have an email confirming the details of the enquiry that you just submitted via the contact form.

Subject: Enquiry for Rechelof Venture Capital - from Martin Brewer

The following message was received on Mon 24th May 2010, 15:36 pm:

Client Name: Martin Brewer
Email Address: martinbrewer2132@smallfoot.com
Gender: Male

SUBSCRIPTIONS
Newsletter: Yes
Bulletin: No
Opportunities: Yes

ENQUIRY:
Interested in discussing ways of raising finance for an online startup. Is it possible to meet face-to-face?

If the thank you page is displayed after you submit the form but no email is received, carefully check the email address that you entered in the script—or try a different email address.

If an email is being received but some of the information entered in the form is not present, check the names of the fields. They should precisely match the field names referred to in the script.

If the email received always shows "No" for all subscriptions, regardless of which checkboxes you activate, click on each checkbox and, in the Properties panel, ensure that the value property is set to "yes" (in lowercase letters).

---

14. Introduction to JavaScript and Spry

Using Dreamweaver's JavaScript Behaviors

JavaScript is a well-established scripting language used to create code that can execute both when an HTML page loads and as a result of subsequent user activity. It is very efficient, since it can run independently on the computers of the visitors to your website—thus freeing up your server to do other things. It is so widely used on websites that, though it is possible for a user to disable JavaScript within their browser settings, most people will need to leave it active if they are to interact with the majority of the sites they visit. Adobe Dreamweaver allows web developers to add JavaScript to their pages by using what it refers to as behaviors.

A Dreamweaver behavior is an automatically generated script written in the JavaScript programming language and triggered by a given user or browser action. To use behaviors, choose **Window > Behaviors**. Before attaching a behavior, you must highlight one of the elements on your page such as a hyperlink, image or form field. Next, you need to choose a behavior by clicking on the plus sign in the top left of the Behaviors window.

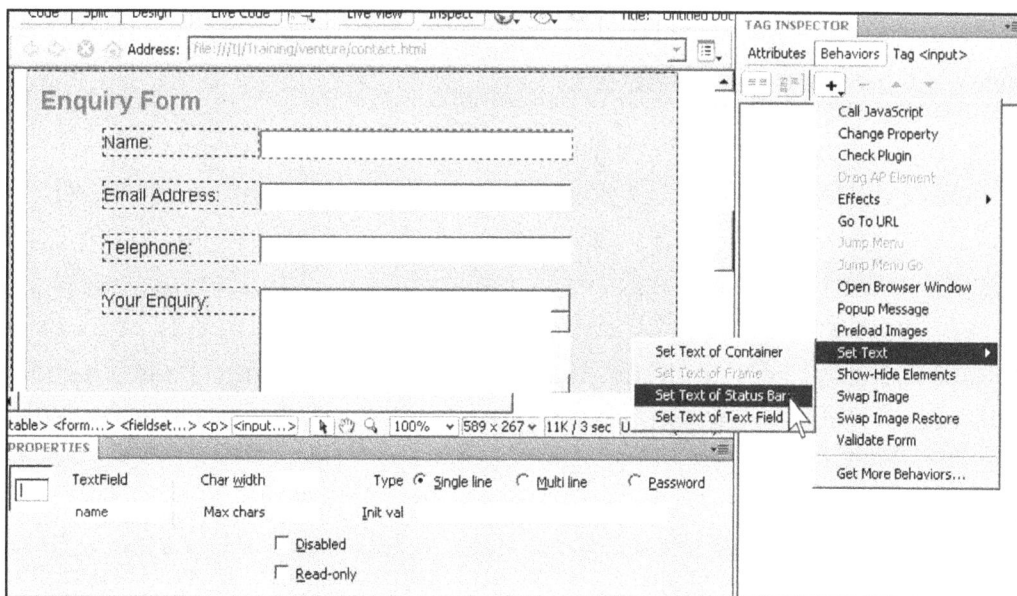

Figure 14-1: Attaching a Dreamweaver behavior to a form field

Dreamweaver then attempts to guess the event that you would like to trigger the behavior such as an **onmouseover**, **onclick** or **ondoubleclick**. If it guesses wrong, simply choose the correct event from the drop-down menu next to the name of the event.

Figure 14-2: Setting the event which will trigger a Dreamweaver behavior

To get a feel for how behaviors work, we will look at examples of two behaviors: **Swap Image** and **Open Browser Window**.

Try it for yourself!

Using the Swap Image Behavior

There was a time when almost every website featured a JavaScript rollover effect on its navigation buttons. Since it is possible to achieve the same effect using CSS alone, this is no longer the case. However, the facility of having an image change appearance when the mouse passes over it can still be useful. Dreamweaver achieves this effect with the "Swap Image" Behavior, which can either be added to an image or can be created automatically by inserting a rollover image using the command **Insert > Image Objects > Rollover Image**. (See page 72 for a description of using rollover images.)

The **Swap Image** behavior can be used to change the appearance of any image on the page not just the one the mouse passes over. So, in this example, we will be changing three black and white images to their colour versions when the mouse passes over any of the three images.

1. If the **Venture** site is not your current site, then choose **Venture** from drop-down menu in the top left of the Files panel to switch back to that site.

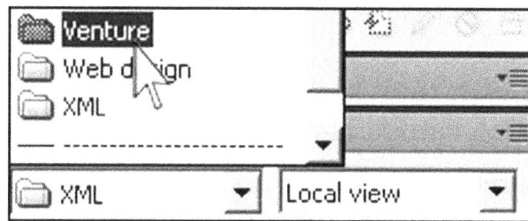

2. In the Files panel, double-click on the file "team.html" to open it.

Naming the images

Whenever you plan to attach a behavior to an image, it is very important to give the image a name which can then be used by the JavaScript to target that particular element.

3. Click on the photograph of Harold Johnson to select it.

4. Enter the name "harold" in the ID field of the Properties panel.

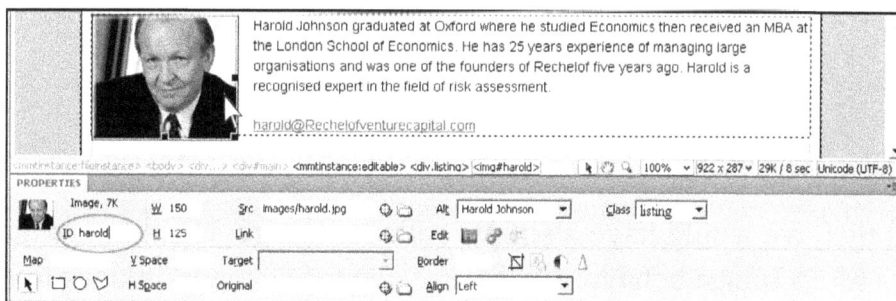

5. Enter the names "rebecca" and "matt" for the other two images.

Attaching the Swap Image behavior

6. Highlight the photo of Harold once more.

7. Click on the plus sign in the Behaviors window and choose **Swap Image** from the pop-up menu.

8. When the Swap Image dialog appears, click on the image named "harold".

(You can now see why it is essential to name each image that you want to swap: the images that have not been named are simply listed as unnamed **<img>** and are impossible to distinguish.)

9. Click on the **Browse** button.

10. Open the **images** folder.

11. Double-click on the file named "harold-col.jpg" to select it.

The path to the colour version of Harold's image is now displayed in the box marked **Set source to** and an asterisk is displayed next to the image named "harold", indicating that it is now set to be swapped.

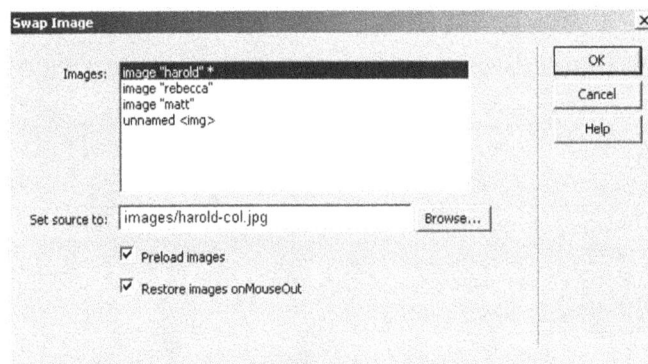

If we left it at that, we would have a simple rollover image. However, what's really cool about the **Swap Image** behavior is that we can set as many images to be swapped on a single behavior as we want. This means that we can now repeat the same process to swap the images of Rebecca and Matt for their colour equivalents too.

12. Click on the image named "rebecca".

13. Click on the Browse button and find "rebecca-col.jpg".

14. Repeat the same process to swap the image named "matt" for "matt-col.jpg".

All three named images should now be followed by an asterisk.

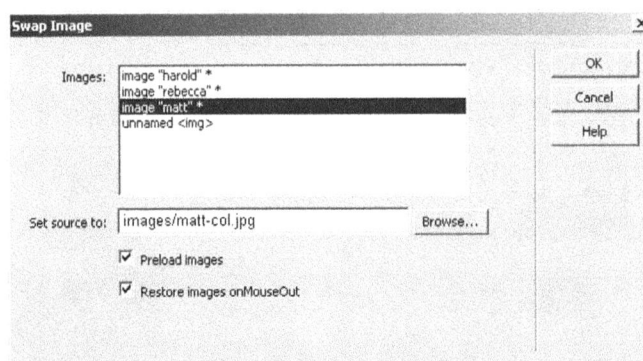

That completes the attachment of the **Swap Image** behavior to Harold's photo. Now, we simply need to repeat the same process for Rebecca's and Matt's.

Before clicking **OK**, take note of the two checkboxes at the bottom of the dialog. They represent two useful additional behaviors which Dreamweaver creates at the same time and which will help the **Swap Image** work more smoothly.

- **Preload Images** is a behavior which downloads the images which will be used during the swap to the user's cache, ready to be displayed as soon as the mouse moves over the image.

- **Restore Image on mouseout** leads Dreamweaver to create a **Swap Image Restore** behavior which will cause the original image to reappear when the mouse leaves the image.

15. Click **OK** to close the **Swap Image** dialog.

16. The Behaviors panel should be displaying two behaviors: **Swap Image Restore** and **Swap Image**; to be triggered by the **OnMouseOut** and **OnMouseOver** events, respectively.

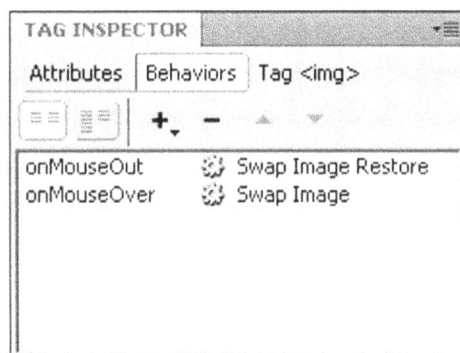

17. Click on Rebecca's photo to highlight it.

18. Repeat steps 7 to 14 above.

19. Repeat the same process to add the behaviors to Matt's photo.

20. Save your changes then press F12 (Mac: Option F12) to preview the page.

When you mouse over any of the images, the colour versions of all three images should appear. When you the mouse leaves an image all three should revert to black and white.

Using the Open Browser Window Behavior

As well as the simple **Pop-up Message** Behavior, which just causes a system alert box to appear, Dreamweaver also offers the more sophisticated **Open Browser Window**. This behavior allows you to create a pop-up window with the attributes that you specify. You get to choose the HTML file displayed in the window, the width and height—as well as the presence or absence of the title bar, scroll bars, etc.

Let's take an example of the legitimate use of this technique. (We've all encountered examples of the illegitimate use of pop-up windows.) Let's create a link that displays the company's privacy policy statement in a pop-up window while the user is filling out a form. The benefit of using JavaScript to create a new window is that we will be able to make the window small, so that the form remains visible in the background.

Creating the privacy policy page

A browser window is simply a container for displaying a web page; so we first need to create the HTML page which will be displayed in our pop-up window.

1. Right-click on any of the pages listed in the Files panel and choose **New File** from the context menu. (The new file will be added at the same level as the one you right-click on.)

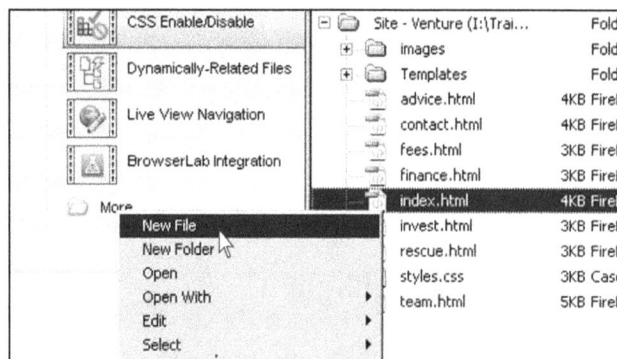

2. Enter the name "privacy.html" and press Enter.

3. Double-click on the new file to open it.

Adding CSS styles to the page

First of all, let's attach our existing CSS style sheet to the page so it blends in with the other pages in the site.

4. Choose **Attach Style Sheet** from the CSS Styles panel menu.

5. Click on the **Browse** button then locate and double-click "styles.css".

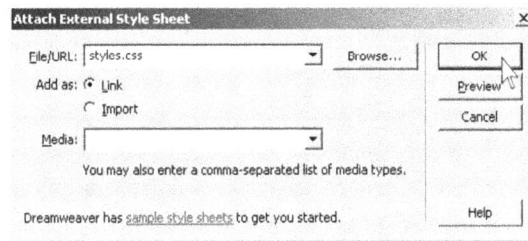

6. Click **OK**.

Now let us create a single DIV which will act as a container for the text.

7. Choose **Insert > Layout Objects > DIV Tag**.

8. In the **ID** field, enter the name "privacy".

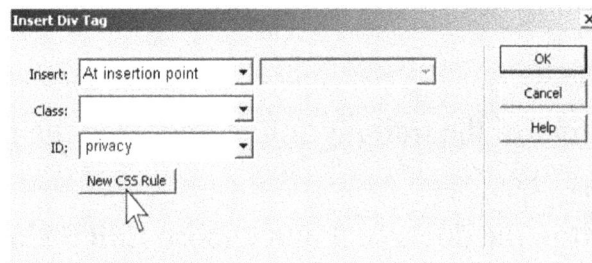

9. Click the **New CSS Rule** button.

The New CSS Rule dialog window appears with the **Selector Name** property automatically set to **#privacy**.

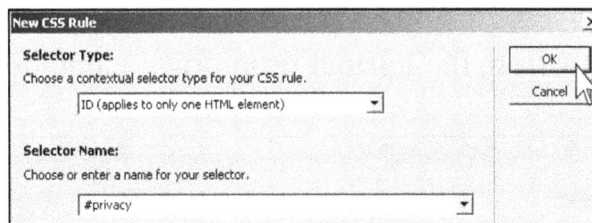

10. Click **OK** then select the **Background** category on the left of the CSS Rule Definition dialog.

11. Set the **Background-color** property to "#FFF" (white).

12. Click on the **Block** category and set the **Align-text** property to **Left**.

13. Click on the **Box** category and set the **Left** and **Right** padding to "10 px", unchecking the **Same for all** box.

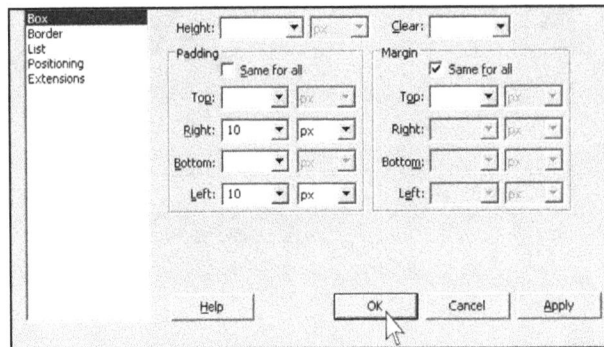

14. Click **OK** twice to close both dialogs.

Adding and styling the text

Now let's copy some dummy text to act as our privacy policy statement.

15. Choose **File > Open**.

16. Navigate to the root of the training folder and open the file called "privacy. txt".

17. Select all the text in the document and choose **Edit > Copy** (**Control/ Command-c**).

18. Close "privacy.txt" and return to "privacy.html".

19. Delete the placeholder text ('Content for id "privacy" Goes Here') then choose **Edit > Paste** (**Control/Command-v**).

20. Highlight the heading "Privacy Policy".

21. Choose **Heading 1** from the **Format** drop-down menu in the Properties panel.

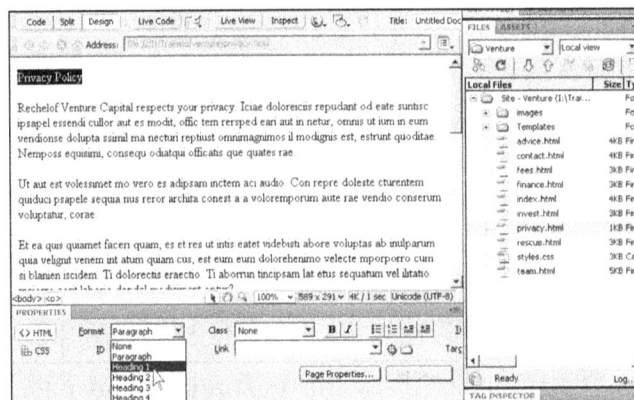

We want our headings to look like the headings and the paragraphs to look like the paragraphs on our other pages. We can achieve this by editing the names of the appropriate selectors so that they also target headings and paragraphs inside our privacy DIV.

22. In the CSS Styles panel, right-click on the style called **#main h1** and choose **Edit Selector** from the context menu.

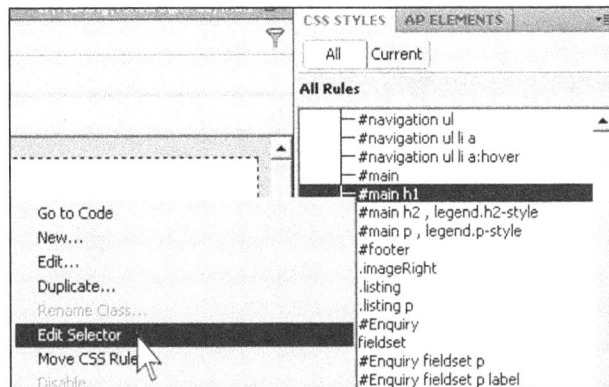

23. Change the selector name to **#main h1, #privacy h1** and press Enter.

24. Right-click on the style called **#main p, legend.p-style** and choose **Edit Selector** from the context menu.

25. Change the selector name to **#main p, legend.p-style, #privacy p** and press Enter.

26. To complete the page, click in the **Title** box, enter the title "Rechelof Venture Capital Privacy Policy" then press Enter.

27. Save your changes then close the page.

Creating a null link

28. In the Files panel double-click on "contact.html" to open it.

We now need to create a text link which will open the "privacy.html" page in a JavaScript controlled window. However, although we want the text to be a hyperlink, we will not be linking to a URL in the normal way. Instead, we need to create what's called a null link.

Let's place the link in a paragraph just above the Submit button.

29. Click on the **Submit** button to highlight it.

30. In the Tag Selector, click on the **<p>** tag to select the paragraph containing the **Submit** button.

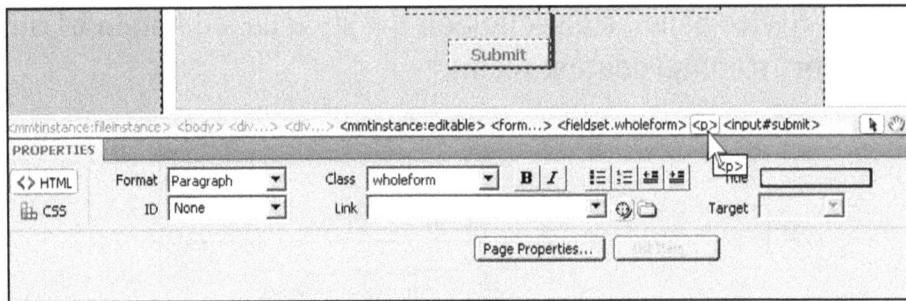

31. Press the Left arrow to move the cursor to a position just in front of the paragraph.

32. Press Enter to insert a new paragraph.

33. Enter the text "Privacy Policy".

34. Select the text you have just typed.

35. In the Link box in the Properties panel, enter the word "JavaScript" followed by a colon then a semi-colon ("JavaScript:;").

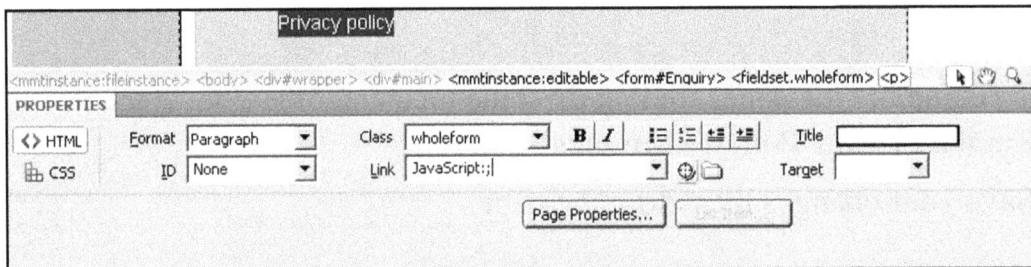

Attaching the behavior

36. With the text "Privacy policy" still highlighted, click on the plus sign in the Behaviors panel and choose **Open Browser window** from the pop-up menu.

37. Click on the **Browse** button, locate "privacy.html" in the "venture" folder then double-click on it to select it.

38. Set the **Window width** property to "400" and **Window height** to "200".

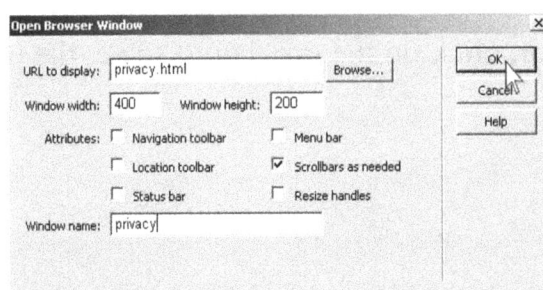

39. Activate the option **Scrollbars as needed**.

40. In the **Window name** box, enter "privacy".

41. Click **OK**.

42. Press F12 (Mac: Option F12) to preview the page.

43. Click on the "Privacy policy" link.

If your browser settings permit it, a pop-up window will appear containing the "privacy.html" page.

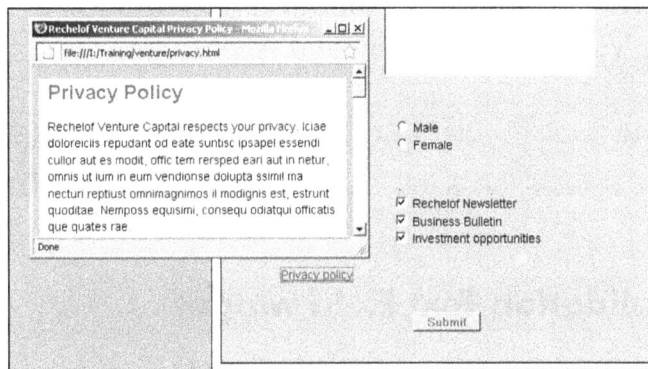

Using Spry widgets

Adobe Spry widgets are sophisticated interface elements which add complex interactivity to your pages. They are part of the Adobe Spry framework for Ajax, a library of JavaScript programs which developers can use to rapidly construct interactive web components. The Spry widgets in Dreamweaver use the same "black box" philosophy as behaviors; you simply add a widget to a page then customize it to suit your needs.

To give you some practice in working with Spry, we will look at using three widgets: Validation Text Field, Validation Confirm and Accordion.

Try it for yourself!

Using the Spry Validation Text Field widget

Dreamweaver's form validation widgets allow you add sophisticated validation and checking to your web forms. The Spry validation Text Field widget allows you to create a text input form field which will automatically be verified using the parameters that you specify. In this example, we will be using it to verify that an email address is valid.

Adding the Spry text field

1. If it is not already open, in the Files panel, double-click on "contact.html" to open it.

Spry validation requires the use of Spry form fields; so we will need to delete our original email field and insert the Spry version.

2. Click on the email field to highlight it.

3. In the Tag Selector, click on the **\<p>** tag to select the paragraph that contains the text field.

4. Press the Delete key on your keyboard to delete the paragraph.

5. Press Enter to create a new blank paragraph.

6. Choose **Insert > Form > Spry Validation Text Field** or **Insert > Spry > Spry Validation Text Field**.

7. Enter "email" in the ID box.

8. Enter "Email Address:" in the Label box.

9. Activate the option **Attach label using 'for' attribute**.

10. Leave the **Position** set to **Before form item**.

11. Enter "e" in the **Access key** box.

12. Enter "10" in the **Tab Index** box.

13. Click OK to create the field.

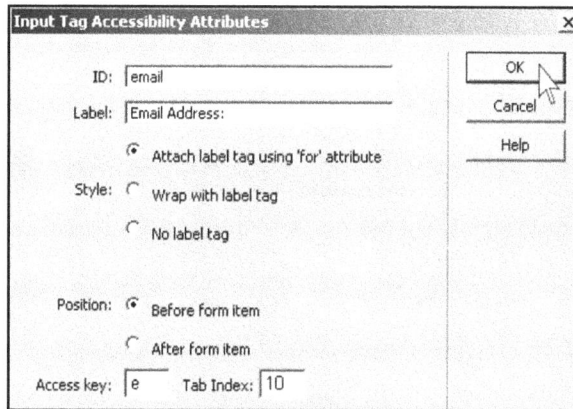

14. Click on the text field to select it.

15. In the Properties panel, set the class to **textfields**.

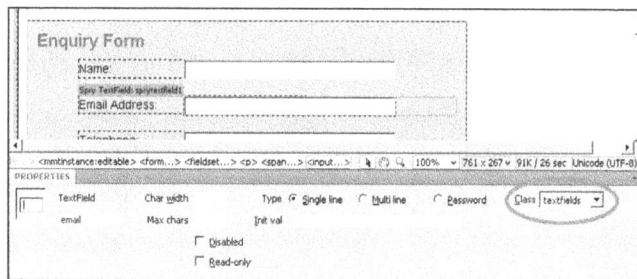

Naming the Spry text field

16. Select the Spry text field by clicking on the blue label which reads "Spry Text Field: sprytextfield1".

17. In the Properties panel, change the name to "spryEmail" then press Enter.

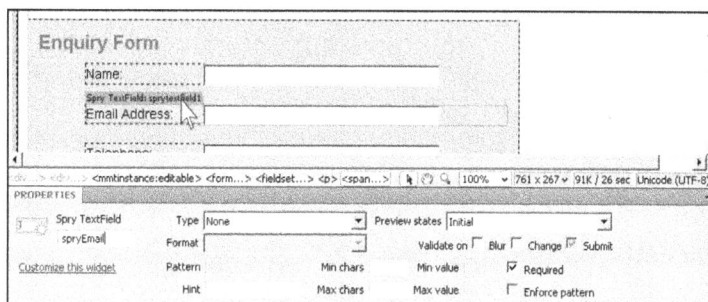

Setting the Type property

The **Type** drop-down menu contains options that allow you to specify the type of data which the field is meant to contain. The available types are integer, email address, date, time, credit card, zip code, phone number, social security number, currency, real numbers, IP address and custom.

> 18. Choose **Email** from the **Type** drop-down menu to invoke the email validation built-in to the widget.

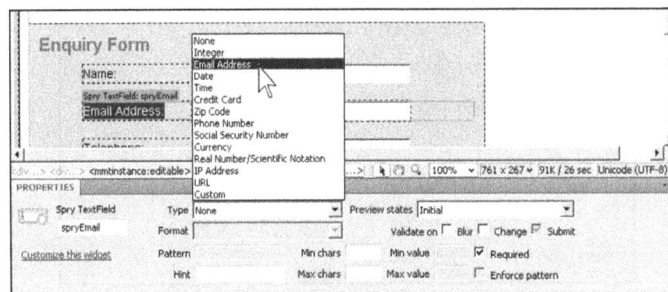

Preview states

One of the main tools for customization of the Validation Text Field widget is the ability to specify the messages which will be displayed to the user in different circumstances. This is done with the aid of the options in the Preview States drop-down menu.

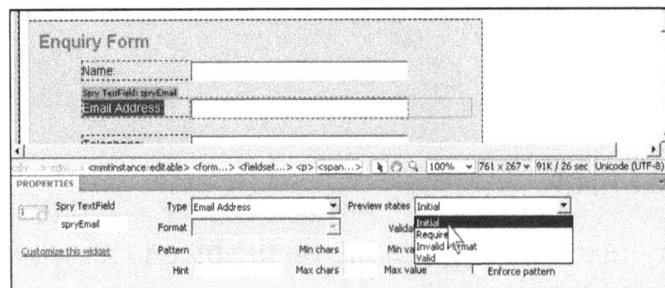

The options available depend on the **Type** setting: for example, when the **Type** property is set to **Email**, four states are shown:

- **Initial**—This state controls the field's appearance when the form first loads.

- **Required**—Use this state to specify the error message which will be displayed when a required field is left blank.

- **Invalid Format**—Is used to set the error to be displayed when inappropriate data is entered into the field.

- **Valid**—Can be used to show a "thumbs up" message when valid data has been entered into the field.

When changing the default messages associated with the various states, it is possible to delete the HTML **<span>** tags which Dreamweaver relies on to make this widget work. It is therefore best to be slightly over cautious: click after or before the text and delete it letter by letter.

If you are comfortable working with HTML code, click on the Split button in the top left of the document window and keep an eye on the code, making sure that the **<span>** tags don't get accidentally deleted.

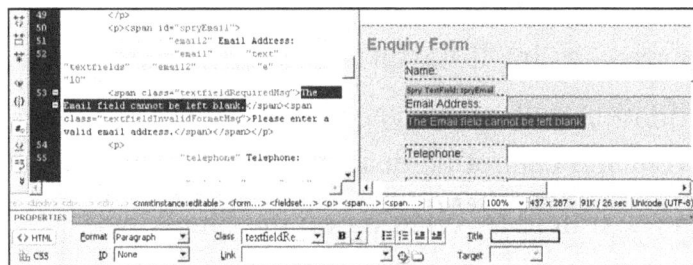

19. If necessary, select the Spry text field by clicking on the blue label in the top left of the field (which now should read "Spry Text Field: spryEmail").

20. Choose **Required** from the **Preview States** drop-down menu. The default error message ("A value is required") appears below the field.

21. Replace the message with the text "The Email field cannot be left blank.".

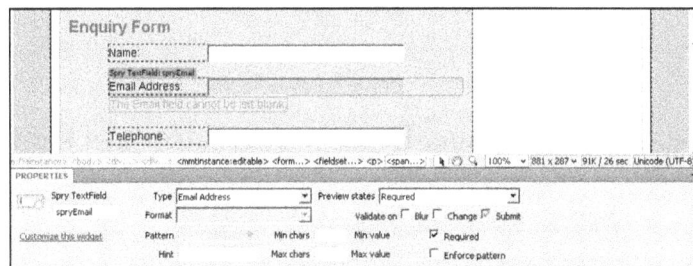

22. Select the Spry text field by clicking on the blue label.

23. Choose **Invalid Format** from the **Preview States** drop-down menu. The default error message "Invalid format" appears below the field.

24. Replace the message with the text "Please enter a valid email address.".

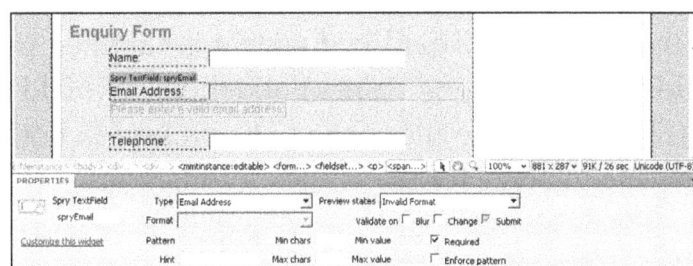

Setting the event that triggers validation

We also need to consider at what point the validation will take place. This is done by activating one or more checkboxes in the **Validate on** section, on the right of the Properties panel.

- **Blur**—Validation will take place when the user exits the field, either by pressing Tab or by clicking in another field. (Blur is the opposite of **Focus**.)

- **Change**—Validation will occur whenever the user changes the text in the field. This event offers the most immediate response and may be considered intrusive by users—as in: "I haven't finished typing yet. Give me a chance!".

- **Submit**—Validation will occur when the user clicks the submit button. This is the default event and cannot be deactivated.

25. Select the Spry text field by clicking on the blue label.

26. Activate the **Blur** checkbox in the **Validate on** section of the Properties panel.

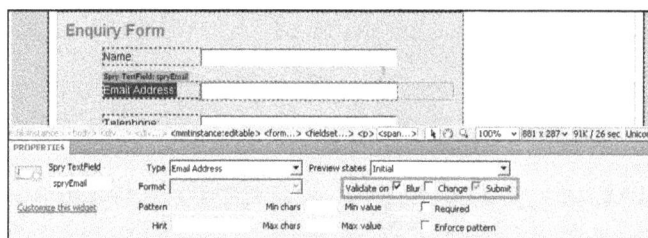

Spry Assets folder

27. Save your changes to the page. Dreamweaver displays the following message.

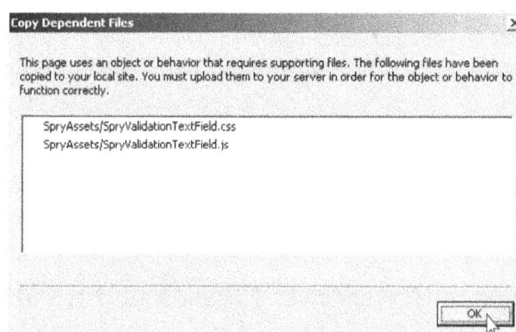

The functionality of the Validation Text Field widget is supplied by the code in the two files mentioned in the dialog: "SpryValidationTextField.css" and "SpryValidationTextField.js". These files need to be present in both the local and remote versions of the site in order for the widget to function.

28. Click **OK**.

Dreamweaver creates a folder in the root of the current site called "Spry Assets" and places the two files inside it.

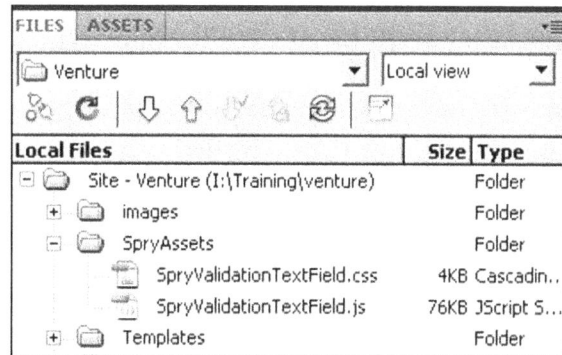

Testing the page

29. Press F12 (Mac: Option F12) to test the page in your primary browser.

30. Press the Submit button without entering an email address.

31. The message we entered in the **Required** state is displayed.

32. Now try entering an invalid email address and pressing the Tab key.

33. The message we entered in the **Invalid** state is displayed.

Using the Validation Confirm Widget

The Validation Confirm Widget is used to verify that the contents of one field are identical to those of another field. The most common use is to ensure that users enter a password or email address correctly by asking them to enter it in two separate fields. If the two entries do not match then an error has been made.

In this example, we will use the Validation Confirm widget to add a second email field and verify that the contents match those of the original email field when the form is submitted.

Inserting the Validation Confirm field

Let's add a new paragraph after the original email address and then insert the Validation Confirm field inside it.

1. Click on the email field to highlight it.

2. In the Tag Selector, click on the **<p>** tag to select the paragraph that contains the text field.

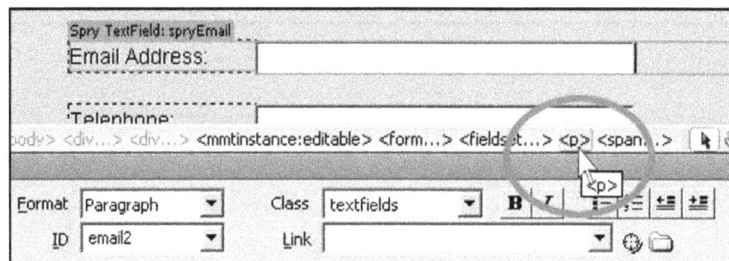

3. Press the Right cursor key on your keyboard (-->) to move the cursor one place beyond the paragraph.

4. Press Enter to create a new paragraph.

5. Choose **Insert > Form > Spry Validation Confirm** or **Insert > Spry > Spry Validation Confirm**.

6. Enter "emailConfirm" in the ID box.

7. Enter "Re-enter Email:" in the Label box.

8. Activate the option **Attach label using 'for' attribute**.

9. Leave the **Position** set to **Before form item**.

10. Enter "c" in the **Access key** box.

11. Enter "12" in the **Tab Index** box.

12. Click **OK** to create the field.

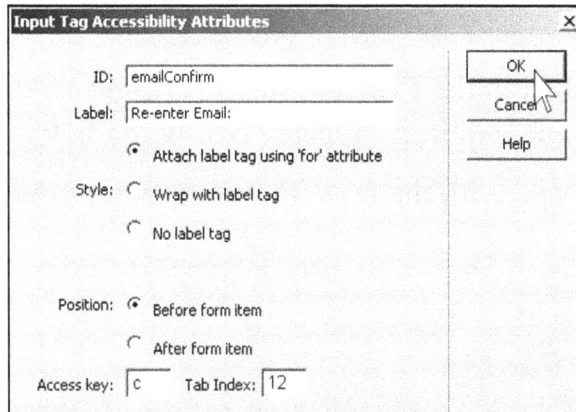

13. Click on the text field to select it.

14. In the Properties panel, set the class to **textfields**.

15. Select the Spry text field by clicking on the blue label in the top left of the widget which reads "Spry Text Field: spryconfirm1".

16. On the left of the Properties panel, change the name to "spryEmailConfirm" then press Enter.

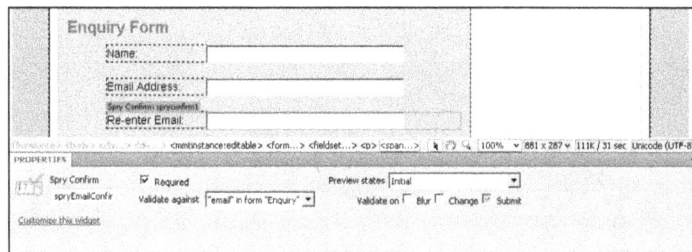

Validate against

The **Validate against** drop-down menu allows you to specify the field whose contents the confirm field must mimic.

17. Choose **"email" in form Enquiry** from the **Validate against** drop-down menu.

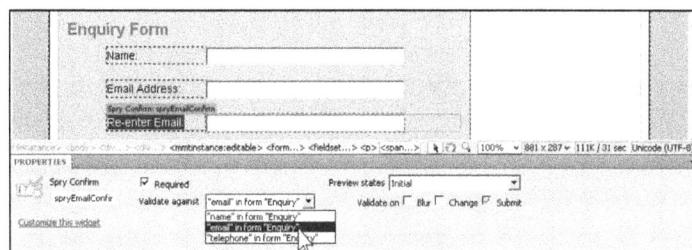

Customizing the states

18. Choose **Required** from the **Preview States** drop-down menu. The default error message "A value is required" appears below the field.

19. Replace the message with the text "Please re-enter your email address.".

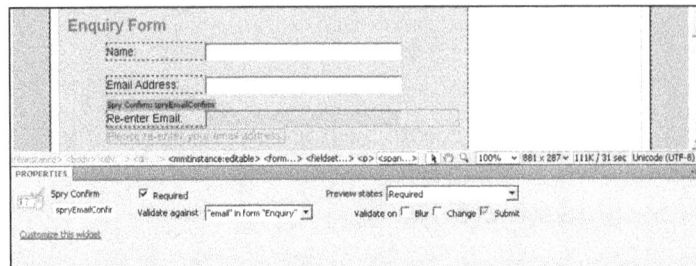

20. Select the Spry text field once more, by clicking on the blue label.

21. Choose **Invalid** from the **Preview States** drop-down menu. The default error message "The values don't match." appears below the field.

22. Replace the message with the text "The two email addresses are not the same.".

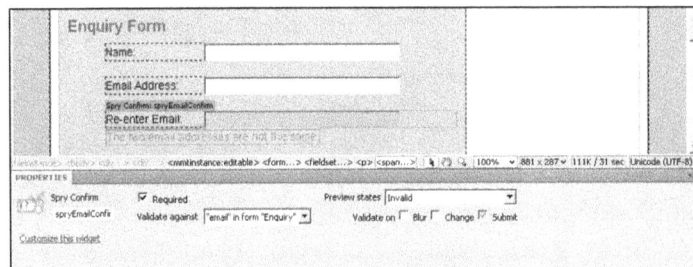

Setting the event that triggers validation

23. Select the Spry text field by clicking on the blue label.

24. Switch on the **Blur** checkbox in the **Validate on** section of the Properties panel.

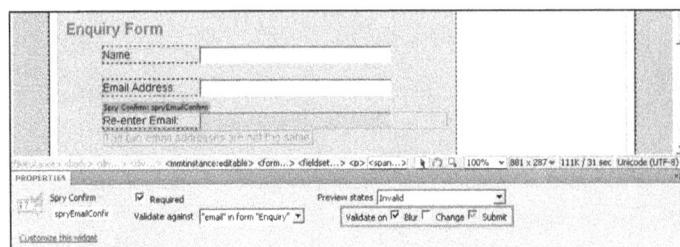

25. Save your changes to the page and click **OK** when Dreamweaver displays the **Copy Dependent Files** dialog.

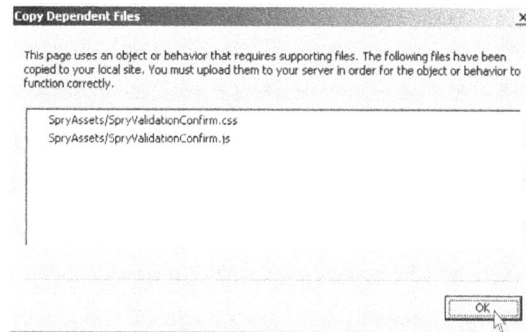

Dreamweaver adds two file to the **Spry Assets** folder: "SpryValidationConfirm.css" and "SpryValidationConfirm.js".

Testing the page

26. Press F12 (Mac: Option F12) to test the page in your primary browser.

27. Enter an email address.

28. Now try entering a slightly different address in the **Re-enter Email** field and pressing the Tab key or clicking in another field.

29. The message specified for the **Invalid** state is displayed.

Using the Accordion widget

The Accordion widget is a group of collapsible DIV panels which afford an efficient and visually appealing way of revealing and hiding web page content. When the user clicks on a panel label, the contents of that panel become visible and the contents of all other panels in the accordion are hidden. The visual appeal of the widget comes from the way in which panels smoothly slide to open and close.

Try it for yourself!

In this work-through example, we will be modifying the "team.html" page in the Venture site, so that the profiles of the senior partners are displayed in an accordion.

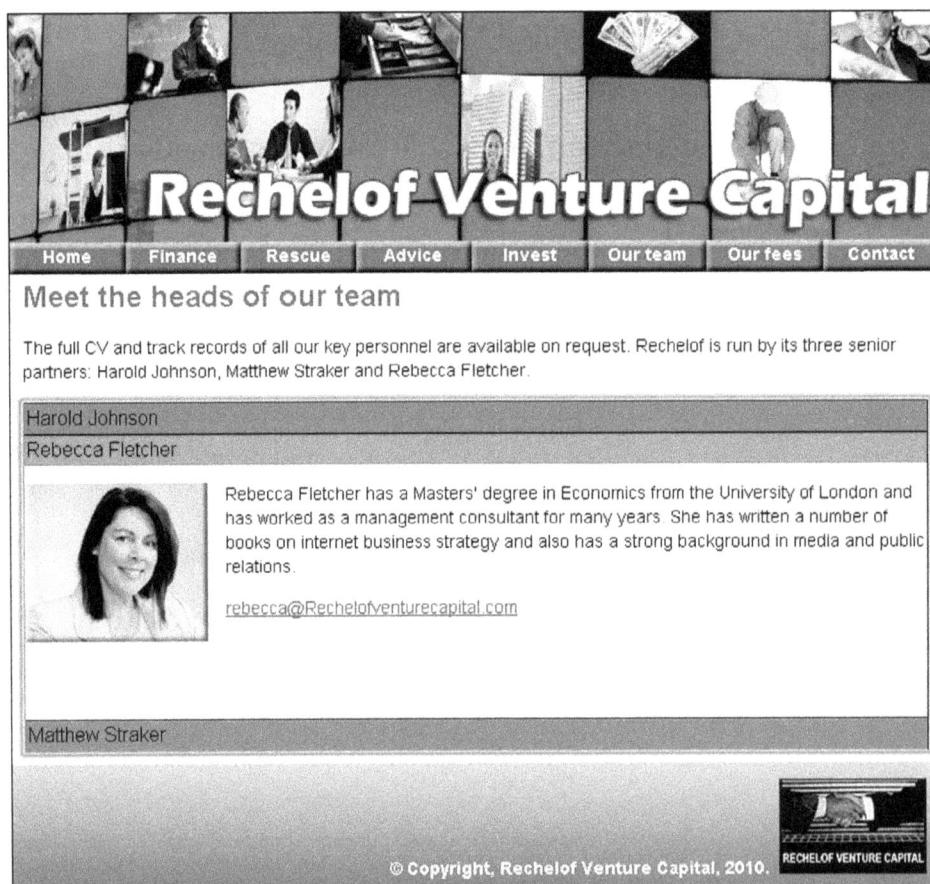

Removing the Swap Image behaviors

Since each image will now be placed inside a panel of the accordion, our Swap Image behaviors can no longer function as designed. So we may as well remove them.

1. Close "contact.html" if you still have it open and, in the Files panel, double-click on "team.html" to open it.

2. If the Behaviors panel is not open, choose **Window > Behaviors**.

3. Click on the picture of Harold Johnson to highlight it.

4. In the Behaviors panel, highlight the **Swap Image** behavior.

5. Click on the **Remove Event** button (the minus sign) to delete the behavior.

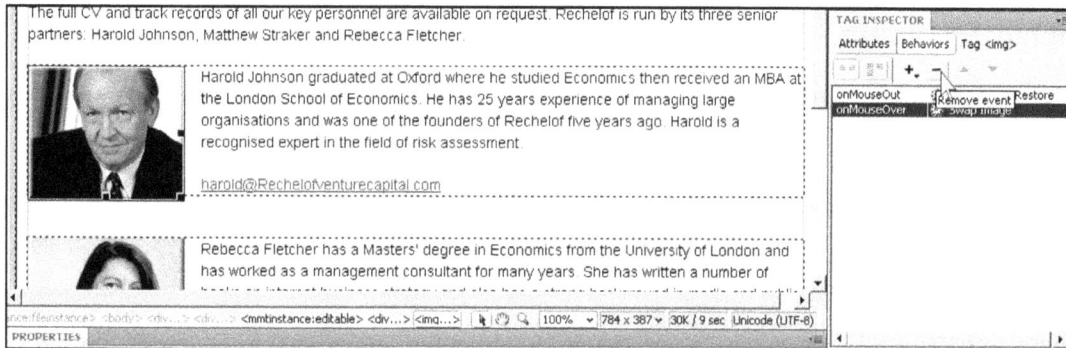

6. Do the same for the **Swap Image Restor**e behavior.

7. Repeat steps 3 to 6 (above) to remove the behaviors from the photos of Rebecca Fletcher and Matthew Straker.

Inserting the Accordion widget

8. Position the cursor after the first paragraph (ending "Harold Johnson, Matthew Straker and Rebecca Fletcher.").

9. Choose **Insert > Spry > Spry Accordion**.

Dreamweaver inserts the **Accordion** widget at the cursor position. The default Accordion contains two panels headed "Label 1" and "Label 2". The panel headed "Label 1" is open and contains the placeholder text "Content 1 "; the other panel is closed.

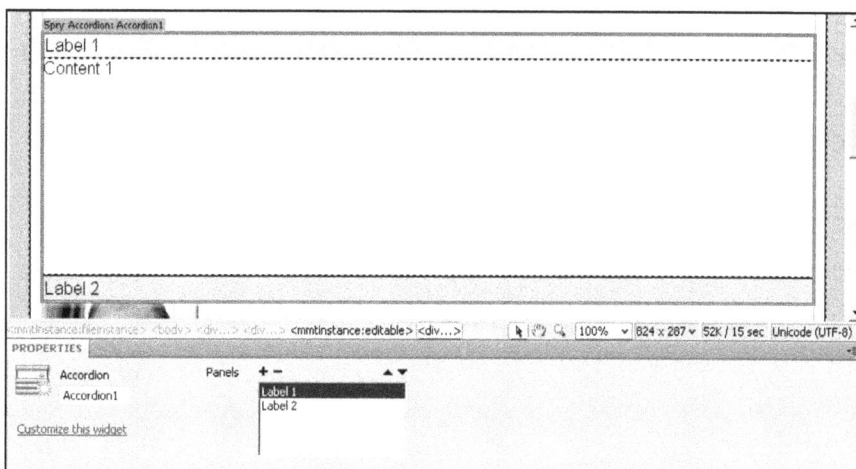

10. With the widget still highlighted, enter the name "AccordionTeam" on the left of the Properties panel then press Enter.

Adding a panel

We have three profiles to accommodate and we will therefore need an additional panel in our accordion.

11. If necessary, click on the blue label in the top left of the accordion widget to select it.

12. Click on the **Add Panel** button in the **Panels** section of the Properties panel (the **+** sign) to add a new panel to the accordion.

The **Panels** section of the Properties panel also allows you to reorder the panels.

13. If necessary, click on the **Move panel down/up in list** buttons to change the order of the panels to 1, 2, 3.

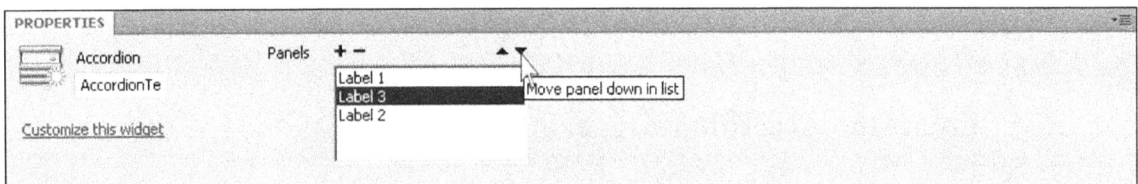

Changing the panel labels

When editing accordions, the Properties panel is only used for setting the name of the widget, adding and deleting panels, and reordering panels. To change the panel labels and content, we need to edit the accordion directly on the page.

14. Replace the default "Label 1" with "Harold Johnson".

15. Replace "Label 2" with "Rebecca Fletcher".

16. Replace "Label 3" with "Matthew Straker".

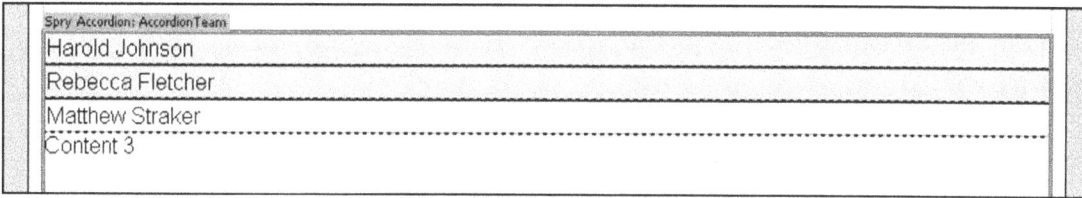

Changing the panel content

Now we just need to transfer each of the partners' profiles into the panels of our accordion. Each profile is inside a DIV tag; so we can simply cut and paste each of the DIVs into the appropriate panel.

Harold Johnson

17. Click on Harold Johnson's photo below the accordion.

18. In the Tag Selector click on the tag **<div.listing>** to highlight the DIV containing Harold's photo and profile.

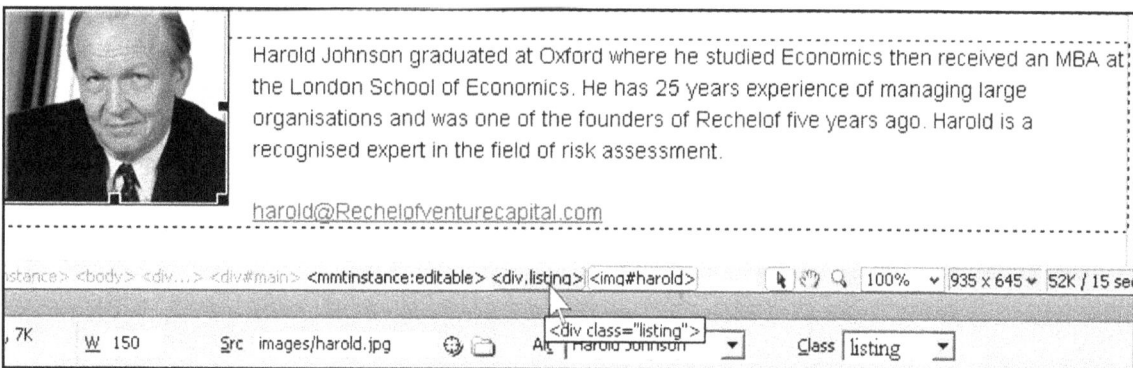

19. Choose **Edit > Cut**.

There are two ways of making the contents of an accordion panel visible. Let's look at the first method.

20. Click on the blue label in the top left of the accordion to highlight it.

21. In the **Panels** section of the Properties panel, click on the panel name **Harold Johnson**. (Selecting a panel name simultaneously reveals the content of that panel and hides the content of all other panels.)

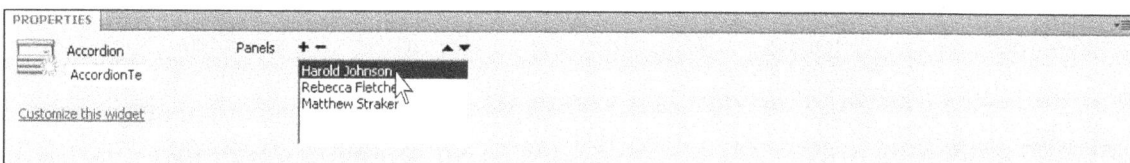

22. Delete the placeholder text "Content 1" and choose **Edit > Paste**.

Rebecca Fletcher

23. Click on Rebecca Fletcher's photo below the accordion.

24. In the Tag Selector click on the tag **<div.listing>** to highlight the DIV containing her photo and profile.

25. Choose **Edit > Cut**.

Now let's use a second method to make the contents of the **Rebecca Fletcher** panel visible.

26. Move the cursor over the label of the **Rebecca Fletcher** panel.

27. Click on the eye symbol which appears on the right of the panel to reveal the panel content.

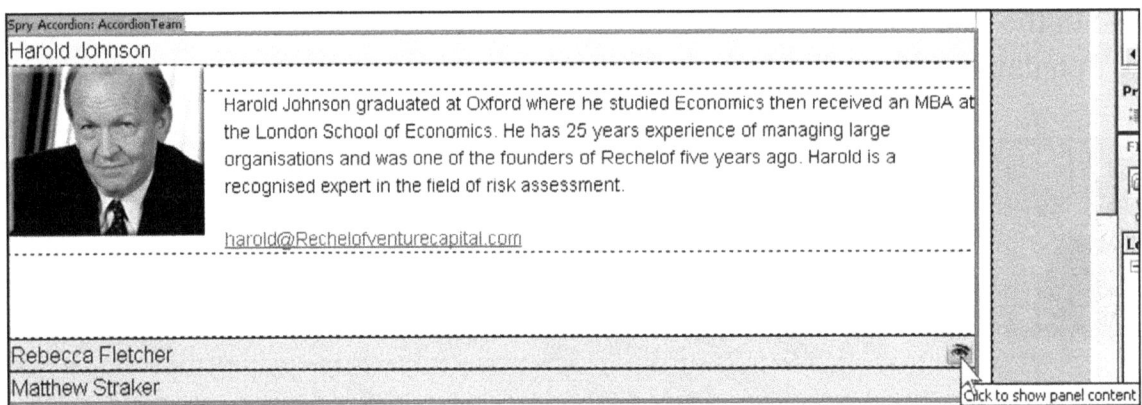

28. Delete the placeholder text "Content 2" and choose **Edit > Paste**.

Matthew Straker

29. Click on Matthew Straker's photo.

30. In the Tag Selector click on the tag **<div.listing>** to highlight the DIV containing his photo and profile.

31. Choose **Edit > Cut**.

32. Move the cursor over the label of the **Matthew Straker** panel.

33. Click on the eye symbol which appears on the right of the panel to reveal the panel content.

34. Delete the placeholder text "Content 3" and choose **Edit > Paste**.

Since we have been using **Cut** and **Paste** rather than **Copy** and **Paste**, all of the profile information should now be in the accordion panels and there should be no remnants of the original content below the accordion.

35. Save your changes to the page.

36. Click **OK** when Dreamweaver displays the Copy Dependent File dialog.

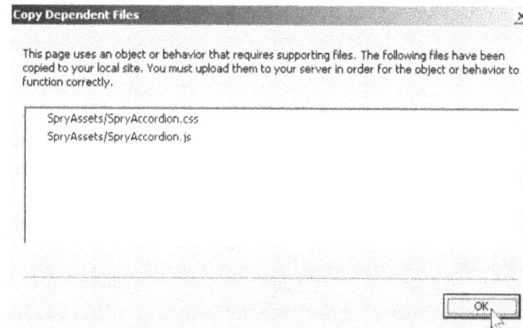

Testing the page

37. Press F12 (Mac: Option F12) to test the page in your primary browser.

When the page loads, the content of Harold's panel will be visible and the content of the other two panels will be hidden.

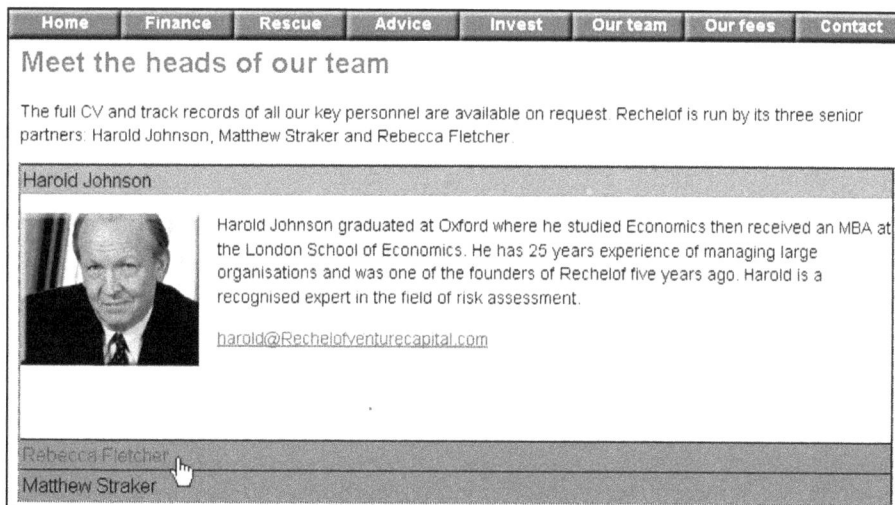

38. Click on the Rebecca Fletcher panel and the label should slide up, revealing the content of Rebecca's panel while hiding the content of Harold's.

Index

A

Accessibility

Accessibility preferences 42, 70

Alternate text 21, 43, 69, 70, 72, 80, 82, 161, 177, 179

Image accessibility preferences 70

Long description 70, 71

Making hotspots accessible 81

Access key 77, 190, 207, 208, 209, 269, 274

Accordion

Adding a panel 280

Changing panel content 281

Changing panel labels 280

Alternate text 21, 43, 69, 70, 72, 80, 82, 161, 177, 179

Assets panel

Applying a template to a page 122

Importing images using the Assets panel 67

Using Library Items 124–126

Attach Style Sheet command (CSS Styles panel)

Use of 58, 59, 60, 107, 136, 262

Media attribute 59

B

Behaviors

Open Browser Window behavior 262

Swap Image Behavior 258–261, 278–279

broken links 15, 131, 235, 236, 237, 244

20% Discount off
Dreamweaver Training

Do you live within easy reach of central London?
Looking for live, tutor-led training on Dreamweaver CS5?
Get 20% discount off any Dreamweaver course.
To register, just fill in the form below and mail this page (not a copy) to:

TrainingCompany.Com
3rd Floor, United House
North Road
Islington
London N7 9DP

Name: ....

Company: ....

Address: ....

....

....

Email: ....

Telephone: ....

I may be interested in attending:

❑ Dreamweaver Introduction

❑ Dreamweaver Intermediate

❑ Dreamweaver Advanced

❑ Dreamweaver 1 Week Intensive

(Visit www.trainingcompany.com for course details.)

To qualify for the 20% discount, you must book a Dreamweaver course within a year of registering.

www.ingramcontent.com/pod-product-compliance
Lightning Source LLC
Chambersburg PA
CBHW082309210326
41599CB00029B/5741